Mathematica: A Practical Approach

Nancy Blachman

Variable Symbols, Inc.
Stanford University

Prentice Hall, Englewood Cliffs, New Jersey 07632

Library of Congress Cataloging-in-Publication Data

BLACHMAN, NANCY R.
    Mathematica: A Practical Approach

    Includes index.
    1. Mathematica (computer program) 2. Scientific computing 3. Title
ISBN 0-13-563826-7

Editorial production supervision: *Barbara Marttine*
Cover and Graphic Design: *Peter Altenberg*
Prepress buyer: *Mary McCartney*
Manufacturing buyer: *Susan Brunke*
Acquisitions editor: *Paul Becker*

The publisher offers discounts on this book when ordered
in bulk quantities. For more information, write:

> Special Sales / Professional Marketing
> Prentice-Hall, Inc.
> Professional & Technical Reference Division
> Englewood Cliffs, New Jersey 07632

Mathematica is a registered trademark of Wolfram Research, Inc. Macintosh and the Finder Macintosh icon are registered trademarks of Apple Computer, Inc. Windows is a trademark and Microsoft and MS-DOS are registered trademarks of Micorsoft Corporation. NeXT and the NeXT logo are trademarks of NeXT Computer, Inc. PostScript is a trademark of Adobe Systems, Incorporated. T$_E$X is a trademark of the American Mathematical Society. T$_E$Xtures is a trademark of Blue Sky Research. UNIX is a registered trademark of AT&T. All other product names are trademarks of their producers. *Mathematica* is not associated with Mathematica, Inc., Mathematica Policy Research, Inc., or Math Tech, Inc.

Prentice Hall, Variable Symbols, Inc., and Nancy Blachman have used their best efforts in preparing this book. These efforts include the development and testing of the code which appears in this book. We make no warranty of any kind, expressed or implied, with regard to the code or the documentation contained in this book. The author and publisher shall not be liable in any event for incidental or consequential damages in connection with, or arising out of, the furnishing, performance, or use of information appearing in this book.

Printed in the United States of America

10 9 8 7 6 5 4 3 2 1

ISBN 0-13-563826-7

Prentice-Hall International (UK) Limited, *London*
Prentice-Hall of Australia Pty. Limited, *Sydney*
Prentice-Hall Canada Inc., *Toronto*
Prentice-Hall Hispanoamericana, S.A., *Mexico*
Prentice-Hall of India Private Limited, *New Delhi*
Prentice-Hall of Japan, Inc., *Tokyo*
Simon & Schuster Asia Pte. Ltd., *Singapore*
Editora Prentice-Hall do Brasil, Ltda., *Rio de Janeiro*

Contents

Part I: Introduction to *Mathematica*   1

Chapter 1: Getting Started with *Mathematica*   3

Chapter 2: Numerical Capabilities   23

Chapter 3:   Algebraic or Symbolic Capabilities

Chapter 4:   Graphics

Chapter 5: Getting Around with *Mathematica*   107

Part II: Programming   115

Chapter 6: List Manipulation   117

Chapter 14: Input and Output

Chapter 15: Packages

Part III: Appendices

Appendix A: Answers to the Exercises

Appendix B: Bibliography   309

Appendix C: Commands   313

Appendix D: Directories of the *Mathematica* Packages   323

Appendix E: Electronic Information   331

Appendix F: The Front End   335

Appendix G: Glossary   341

Appendix H: Help   345

Appendix I: Index   349

Appendix J: Just What More?   365

Foreword

I used to delight in saying that, unlike the experimental scientists, mathematicians could travel with very little baggage, set up shop in a new location, and prove theorems. All we needed, I said, was pencil and paper.

For me that isn't so any more. I need also to be able to work out cases, see examples, try scenarios, etc., using the fastest computer that I can get my hands on, with the most capable, highest level, plushest symbol–manipulating computer mathematics package that I can find. Now that these tools are available to me, I don't know how I ever got along without them.

I hope and expect that this lovely book by Nancy Blachman will help its readers to become as spoiled as I am by the luxuries of high-tech mathematical computing.

Herbert S. Wilf
Philadelphia, PA

Preface

As scientists, engineers, and mathematicians, you spend a great deal of time performing mathematical calculations and manipulations by hand. Many of these calculations can be handled by a software program called *Mathematica*. This book offers a tutorial introduction to *Mathematica*.

Mathematica performs three basic types of computation: numerical, symbolic, and graphical. It works with numbers of arbitrary magnitude and precision, as well as with polynomials, power series expansions, matrices, and graphs. *Mathematica* provides standard symbolic operations of algebra and calculus, including integration and differentiation. It can also plot functions and data in two or three dimensions.

Even though they included hundreds of functions, the developers of *Mathematica* were aware that they could not anticipate the needs of all users. Therefore, *Mathematica* was designed to be extensible by including its own programming language. It is flexible and extremely useful software for anyone who regularly performs complicated mathematical computations.

Although I wrote this book for people new to *Mathematica*, it contains information of interest to those who have experience with the program. For those who do not have *Mathematica*, this text describes the capabilities of the software in sufficient detail to enable you to decide whether it suits your needs.

My book does not teach mathematics. It assumes you understand the theory behind what you want to do and just need to be told what *Mathematica* commands to use to make it happen. It teaches *Mathematica* by showing some common patterns of usage. It also shows you how to find commands you need to solve your problems, use *Mathematica* interactively, manipulate expressions, visualize functions and data, write functions and packages, and import and export data. At the end of each chapter is a set of exercises designed to give you practice with the material presented.

Why did I write this book? Because there wasn't such a book when I was learning *Mathematica*.

Can't you learn *Mathematica* from Stephen Wolfram's book *Mathematica: A System for Doing Mathematics by Computer*? Yes, but it's a bit like learning English from a dictionary. As the definitive reference for *Mathematica*, Wolfram's book describes all the functions built into the program. On the other hand, my book focuses on how to use *Mathematica*. It provides examples of useful constructs and functions, problem sets as well as their solutions. It also describes features available on specific versions of *Mathematica*. It mentions differences between version 1.2 and version 2.0 of the software. In my book, I strive to show the versatility of the program as well as its limitations. This book is intended to get you up to speed quickly.

Mathematica: A Practical Approach primarily grew out of two undergraduate courses I taught at Stanford University in 1990 and 1991. Though it was originally designed to be used for teaching courses or workshops in *Mathematica*, I am sure that by reading my book and working the exercises you can learn to use, and program in *Mathematica*.

Organization of this Book

This book is divided into three parts. The first discusses how to use *Mathematica* interactively, the second focuses on programming, and the third provides information and references on *Mathematica*. The following is a brief sketch of the contents of this book:

Part I: Introduction to *Mathematica* explains how to use *Mathematica* interactively, and is intended for those who have little or no experience with the program. It starts by describing how to access on-line help and how to give an instruction to *Mathematica* and then discusses the numerical, symbolic, and graphical capabilities. The final chapter mentions utilities for referring to previous results, editing expressions, and timing calculations.

Part II: Programming is intended for those who have used *Mathematica* interactively and who are interested in learning to write functions and packages. First it describes the constructs frequently used when writing functions. Then it shows how to write your own functions, and discusses both procedural and rule-based techniques for programming. It describes mechanisms for importing, exporting, and formatting data and expressions. It devotes a chapter to common traps and pitfalls and debugging techniques. The final chapter in this section focuses on techniques for writing a *Mathematica* package.

Part III: Appendix offers additional information on *Mathematica*. It contains answers to many of the odd-numbered exercises, a listing of all commands built into *Mathematica*, packages distributed with *Mathematica*, information about the Notebook Front End, a glossary, and a list of other references on *Mathematica*.

At the end of each chapter is a problem set to give you practice with the material presented. I strongly urge you to work through the examples in the chapter and the exercises at the end of each chapter. Only through practice will you become proficient at *Mathematica*.

Though it was developed using the versions 1.2 and 2.0 of *Mathematica* (on a Macintosh, a Hewlett-Packard 9000/375, an IBM PS/2 with a 287 math co-processor, a NeXT computer with a 68030, and a Sun 3/50) this book illustrates general techniques that can be used with other versions of the software. Earlier versions of *Mathematica* do not have some of the capabilities described and later versions have capabilities that are not addressed. When certain functions are only available on a particular version of *Mathematica*, it is so noted. This book focuses on general techniques and thus should be of interest to most *Mathematica* users regardless of the version of the software they are using.

About the Author

I heard about *Mathematica* in the summer of 1988 when numerous articles started appearing in the press. I first saw *Mathematica* in action in August of 1988 at SIG-GRAPH, a computer graphics conference. I was pleased to see that the program lived up to much of the hype that it had received. In the fall of 1988, I joined Wolfram Research, where I gave talks, seminars, and workshops on *Mathematica*.

Before getting involved with *Mathematica* I was at Stanford University, where I was the instructor for a course on computer graphics and a teaching assistant for a course in concrete mathematics. In addition to teaching, I have developed software at Bell Laboratories, Resonex, and the Research Institute for Advanced Computer Science at NASA Ames. I hold a B.S. in mathematics from the University of Birmingham in the United Kingdom, an M.S. in operations research from the University of California at Berkeley, and an M.S. in computer science from Stanford University.

About Variable Symbols

Corporations, colleges, and universities are adopting *Mathematica* as a standard research and teaching tool, and typically need training for their staff in the use of the software. To serve that need, I founded Variable Symbols, Inc.

During the past two years, I have traveled around the country giving hands-on workshops on *Mathematica* at industrial institutions including: Argonne National Laboratory, Boeing, Chevron, Lawrence Livermore National Laboratory, MITRE, Naval Research Laboratory, Shell, Xerox, and Wolfram Research, Inc., the developer of *Mathematica*. I have also given workshops at academic institutions including: Boston University, Northwestern University, Stanford University, the University of California Berkeley Extension, and the University of California Santa Cruz Extension. Winter quarter of 1990 I gave a course at Stanford University entitled *Problem Solving with Mathematica*. Because of its popularity, the Stanford Instructional Television Network (SITN) produced an 8-part video series of this course. Spring quarter of 1991, I gave another 10-week course in *Mathematica* at Stanford University. I have also given workshops at the 1990 and 1991 *Mathematica* Conferences. This book is based on material used in courses and workshops given by Variable Symbols.

How this Book was Produced

This book began as a *Mathematica* Notebook. I converted the Notebook to TEX with the aid of a preliminary version of Art Ogawa's Notebook-to-TEX converter. Peter Altenberg produced the illustrations with *Mathematica* and Adobe Illustrator. Some of the illustrations were first generated in *Mathematica* and then converted to Adobe Illustrator. The book was typeset using TEXtures on a Macintosh IIfx and printed using a Linotronic 300 at Canterbury Press in Berkeley, California.

Acknowledgments

First, I offer thanks to Herb Wilf, Henry Cejtin, and my mother and father, Nelson and Anne Blachman for their support, encouragement, and suggestions. This book is based on notes that were initially prepared for the first workshop I gave on *Mathematica*. It has been revised for subsequent courses by incorporating the valuable comments and suggestions from many people to whom I am grateful. They include: Paul Abbott, Arnold O. Allen, Peter Altenberg, Eric Apgar, Sheldon Axler, Rick Beldin, Susan Blachman, Robert Campbell, Rolan Christofferson, Anne Coleman, Shawn Ewing, Richard Fateman, Yossi Friedman, Richard Gaylord, Bruce Herman, Thomas Highes, David Jacobson, Pat Lampert, Matthew Lutzker, Rafael O. Marrero, Wanda Martinez, Julia Olkin, Larry Seiford, Sha Xin Wei, Malcolm Slaney, Cameron Smith, Anton, Tran, Ilan Vardi, Roger W. Vidal, Jim Wendel, Stephen Wolfram, and Eran Yehudai.

I used an early draft of this book to teach an undergraduate course in *Mathematica* at Stanford University. I am grateful to the following CS 50 students for their ideas for improving the text: Greg Baker, Ed DeGrange, Derek Fong, Bonnie

Gorsic, Steve Greidinger, Jeff Gruda, Jim Hwang, Blair Ireland, Stan Isaacs, Phil Isubaki, Richard O. Kahn, Karen Kraemer, Bing Kongmebhol, Eric Lim, David G. Lowell, Paul R. McGill, Motegi Tsuyoshi, Wentao Pan, Chris Phoenix, Dave Raisin, Kevin W. Rudd, Haydee Saffari, Phil Tsubaki, and Qinping Yang. I would also like to extend thanks to Ken Yue, the teaching assistant for the course.

I wish to thank Peter Altenberg for the overall design, illustrations, and TEX tweaking, Amy Hendrickson for developing LATEX macros, Art Ogawa for letting me use a preliminary version of his Notebook-to-TEX conversion program, and Cameron Smith for advice on TEX.

I would also like to thank Dennis Allison, Paul Becker, and Ray Henderson of Prentice–Hall for taking an interest in this book.

Last, but definitely not least, I would like to thank Barbara Kramer for editorial assistance with this book and Bernice Chin, Joyce VanGinkel, and Gabe Webster for handling Variable Symbols business while I was working on the book.

Nancy R. Blachman
Berkeley, California
July 1991

Part I:

Introduction to *Mathematica*

As computer power and memory have increased, so has the capacity of software developers to write programs that assist people with time-consuming tasks. *Mathematica* is such a program. It works problems that are impractical to do by hand, freeing your time for your own work. *Mathematica* is a useful tool for those who do quantitative analysis, symbolic calculations and manipulations, as well as for those who want to visualize functions or data. With it you can calculate, model, prototype, and analyze results.

Mathematica is an interpreted language. In other words, it reads an expression, evaluates the result, and then prints it out. Being interactive makes it easier to use than compiled languages such as C, FORTRAN, or Pascal.

Mathematica is programmable. Any function not available, you can write yourself. *Mathematica* offers many of the primitives and constructs found in C, FORTRAN, and Pascal. In addition to procedural programming, *Mathematica* supports rule-based programming using pattern matching.

Mathematica runs on a wide range of computers from hardware vendors including Apple, Convex, Data General, Digital Equipment, Hewlett-Packard/Apollo, IBM, MIPS, NeXT, Silicon Graphics, Sony, and Sun. Functions written in *Mathematica* are portable; you can run the same program on a personal computer as on a workstation.

Mathematica was developed by Wolfram Research, Inc., an Illinois-based company, which currently has about 120 employees. For more information or to order *Mathematica*, visit your local software dealer or contact:

Wolfram Research, Inc.
100 Trade Center Drive
Champaign, IL 61820-7237
Fax: 217-398-0747
Telephone: 217-398-0700

Wolfram Research (UK) Ltd.
P.O. Box 114
Abington, Oxon OX13 6TG
U.K.
Fax: +44 (235) 550 445
Telephone: +44 (235) 550 440

Getting Started with Mathematica

This chapter gets you started with *Mathematica*. It discusses the structure of *Mathematica*. Then it describes some of the conventions used in *Mathematica*. It shows how to use *Mathematica* interactively, i.e., how to call built-in functions to manipulate and evaluate expressions. It discusses how to access on-line help. The chapter ends by describing how to load and call functions defined in packages or files containing *Mathematica* definitions.

1.1 Machine-Specific Notes

When I discuss machine-specific capabilities, I indicate so with an icon in the margin and the notation: **Macintosh** for the Macintosh version of *Mathematica*, **Notebook Front End** for the Notebook Front End version that is currently available on the NeXT and Macintosh, **Unix** and a shell icon for the Unix-based workstation versions, **MS-DOS** for the MS-DOS version of *Mathematica*, and **NeXT** for the version that runs on NeXT workstations.

Machine-specific documentation, distributed with most versions of *Mathematica*, contains more detailed information on using *Mathematica* on a particular computer.

1.2 Version-Specific Documentation

This book shows examples based on version 1.2 and version 2.0 of *Mathematica*.

The icon shown in the left margin and the notation **Version 1.2** indicates that the example runs on version 1.2 of *Mathematica* but not on version 2.0.

The icon shown in the left margin and the notation **Version 2.0** indicates that the example works on version 2.0 of the software but not on version 1.2.

1.3 The Front End Versus the Kernel

Mathematica consists of two parts: the Kernel and the Front End. The Kernel is the computational engine. It calculates and computes results. The *Mathematica* Kernel is essentially identical on the various computers. The Front End is the user interface to the *Mathematica* Kernel.

This book concentrates on the *Mathematica* Kernel. Most of the material should be of interest to all *Mathematica* users, whether they are using a personal computer, such as a 386-based MS-DOS computer or a Macintosh, or a workstation.

1.3.1 Notebook Front Ends

Any document that you create while using the Notebook Front End is called a *Notebook*. Notebooks are documents that can contain a mixture of text, graphics and *Mathematica* definitions. Because Notebooks are a convenient tool for documenting computations, many instructors are using them for their course materials. Notebook Front Ends to *Mathematica* are currently found on the Macintosh and NeXT computers. Wolfram Research, Inc. is planning to release a Notebook Front End for Microsoft (MS) Windows for MS DOS-based computers.

The Front End and the Kernel are separate. The Front End sends a calculation to the Kernel only when instructed to do so. Requests for calculations to be performed are sent to the Kernel when the user either:

1. Uses the *<enter>* key or

2. Depresses the *<return>* while the *<shift>* key is held down.

Start *Mathematica* by double clicking on the *Mathematica* icon. With Notebook Front Ends, exit from or quit out of *Mathematica* by using the *Exit* command listed in the *File* menu.

Depressing a "." while the *<command>* key is held down, interrupts a calculation. On the Macintosh, the *<command>* key has a bitten apple on it. It is usually located near the space bar.

1.3.2 Macintosh

The Kernel needs to be loaded into memory before *Mathematica* will perform any computations. By selecting the option *Automatically start local kernel* in the *Startup Settings* template, in the *Setting* submenu of the *Edit* menu, the Kernel is automatically loaded when you start *Mathematica*. Otherwise it is loaded before *Mathematica* computes the first result. Loading the Kernel takes around a minute on a Macintosh II.

Be aware that it is advisable to run *Mathematica* with at least four megabytes of RAM with version 1.2 and five megabytes with version 2.0.

1.3.3 MS-DOS

Mathematica runs on 386-based MS-DOS computers. It will run on 286-based MS-DOS machines.

The MS-DOS version of *Mathematica* provides a command-line interface. The current user input is displayed on the last line of the screen. You can edit the current input line by using the arrow keys, the insert key, the delete key, the home key (to go to the beginning of the line), the end key (which moves the cursor to the end of what is so far typed in), and the up arrow key (to recall earlier commands).

MS-DOS supports virtual memory. With version 1.2, a user can get away with 640K of memory and one megabyte of extended memory. With version 2.0, you need at least 4 megabytes of extended memory. With more memory, *Mathematica* runs faster.

Start *Mathematica* by typing `math`. It is nice to invoke *Mathematica* when in the directory where you plan to store *Mathematica* input and output; you need not be in the directory where *Mathematica* is stored if it is in your PATH. To exit from *Mathematica*, type `Quit`.

1.3.4 Unix-based Workstations

The workstation version offers a command-line interface to *Mathematica*. Though *Mathematica* running under X windows or in a tty window does not offer the mouse-oriented editing capabilities found on the Notebook Front Ends, you can edit your input using your favorite editor by using one of the functions: `Edit`, `EditIn`, or `EditDefinition` (`EditDef` in version 1.2).

Start *Mathematica* by typing `math`, provided the directory containing *Mathematica* is in `$PATH`. Use the function `Quit[ ]` to end a *Mathematica* session.

1.3.5 Remote Kernel

Many people prefer the Notebook Front End to the user interface available on workstation versions of *Mathematica*, but prefer the power of the workstation. Because of the modular design of *Mathematica*, you can have the best of both worlds. Using a remote kernel, you can enter your commands using the Notebook Front End while having the computations performed on a workstation.

1.4 Notational Conventions

This book contains descriptions of functions and actual examples that demonstrate some of the capabilities of *Mathematica*. The descriptions sometimes include a function template. In a template, words and symbols in a `typewriter` font are to be typed exactly as shown, but words and symbols in *italics* must be replaced by actual *Mathematica* expressions. For example, the template for `Apply` shows that this function requires two arguments, the first of which is a function and the second, an expression.

Apply [*function*, *expr*]

The best way to learn about *Mathematica* is to use the program. Each example consists of the user input labeled with *In[n]* and *Mathematica*'s response labeled with *Out[n]*. Try typing in the examples in this book. If you do not get the same or similar results, try again by retyping the input exactly as it appears. Be careful to use the same:

- Capitalization (lower- and upper-case letters)
- Type of parentheses or brackets
- Number of spaces
- Punctuation (commas and semi-colons)

Like the C programming language, *Mathematica* is case sensitive, e.g., `Log[x]` is different from `log[x]`. The names of all built-in functions begin with an upper-case letter.

Each type of bracket has a different meaning as you will see later in this chapter.

Spaces must be put between symbols for variables that are to be multiplied together and there must not be spaces in names of commands, or multi-letter symbols or function names. Otherwise spaces are ignored. You may want to put some in to make your input easier to read.

When using *Mathematica*, use a fixed-width font, a font in which all characters are the same width. `Courier` is such a font. Notice how *Mathematica* represents the quantity $mammal^2 + mammal^3 + mammal^4$ with a fixed-width font and a variable-width font. Exponents and subscripts are correctly aligned when you use a fixed-width font.

```
         2         3         4
mammal   + mammal   + mammal    (fixed-width font)
```

$$mammal^2 + mammal^3 + mammal^4 \quad \text{(variable-width font)}$$

1.5 Using *Mathematica* Interactively

Using *Mathematica* is like having a conversation. Ask a question and *Mathematica* responds with a result. *Mathematica* assigns a number in sequence for each input output pair or exchange. The *n*th user input in a *Mathematica* session is labeled *In[n]* and the corresponding computer output is labeled *Out[n]*. You can refer to earlier inputs and output with these labels.

Notebook Front End: The Notebook Front End inserts *In[n]* after *Mathematica* computes the result. Send input to the Kernel by either hitting the *<enter>* key or by depressing the *<return>* while the *<shift>* key is held down.

Macintosh: The Kernel needs to be loaded into memory before *Mathematica* will perform any computations. The Kernel can be automatically loaded when you start up *Mathematica* (see section 1.3.2 on page 4). Otherwise it gets loaded before *Mathematica* computes the first result. Loading the Kernel into memory takes about a minute on a Macintosh II.

In the first exchange, which is labeled with *In[1]*, I ask *Mathematica* for 5^{10}.

```
·In[1] := 5^10
 Out[1] = 9765625
```

The number assigned to an exchange can be used to reference any previous result. You can check the result by taking the 10th root of the result, *Out[1]*, which is abbreviated %1.

```
In[2] := %1^(1/10)
 Out[2] = 5
```

A user most commonly wants to refer to her most recent result. The character % refers to the previous result. In the following example, % is replaced by the last result computed, i.e., 5.

```
In[3] := % + a
 Out[3] = 5 + a
```

You can refer to a previous result by using one or more percent signs; that is, % refers to the last result, %% refers to the second to last result, %%% reference the third to last result, and so forth. It is also possible to reference a particular result with %*n*, where *n* is the number of the output line. *Note*: If you restart *Mathematica*, you cannot refer to results with the numbers assigned during an earlier session.

If you assign a name to a result, you can later reference that result with the assigned name. The command boatLength = 3 causes the interpreter to associate the value 3 with the name boatLength.

In[4] := boatLength = 3
Out[4] = 3

Once the name boatLength has been defined to be the number 3, I can refer to the value 3 by name.

In[5] := boatLength
Out[5] = 3

You can also perform operations by using the name or variable.

In[6] := 20 boatLength
Out[6] = 60

You can tag values with units. Make sure to put a space between the value and the tag. *Mathematica* evaluates and combines terms whenever possible.

In[7] := 2 m + 3 m
Out[7] = 5 m

In this section, you have seen how to request *Mathematica* to perform a calculation, how to assign a name to a value, and how to refer to a previous result. Next you will learn how to find the names of functions that are built into *Mathematica*.

1.6 Built-In Names

The names of all functions, variables, options, and constants built into *Mathematica* start with capital letters, e.g., Integrate, Plot. If a name consists of two or more words, the first letter of each word is capitalized, e.g., ContourPlot, InterpolatingPolynomial, and MapAt.

Most names of objects built into *Mathematica* are complete words. Unlike Unix, MS-DOS, and other systems, *Mathematica* rarely uses abbreviations. Abbreviations are used only where they are extremely well-known. The following table contains examples of some of the abbreviations that are built into *Mathematica*.

Function	Description
Abs	gives the absolute value of a number
Cos	gives the trigonometric function cosine
D	computes the derivative
Det	calculates the determinant of a matrix
GCD	computes the greatest common divisor

1.7 Help

There are more than 700 functions built into *Mathematica*. The name of a *Mathematica* function in general indicates the function's purpose.

Function	Description
Binomial	gives the binomial coefficient
Eigenvalues	gives a list of the eigenvalues
FindRoot	searches for a numerical solution to an equation
Integrate	evaluates the integral
Timing	returns the time used in evaluating an expression

If the name isn't enough of a clue, you can use the *Mathematica* Quick Reference Guide [MmaQuickRef], the *Mathematica* Help Stack [MmaHelpStack], or *Mathematica*'s built-in on-line help.

1.7.1 Built-In Help

On-line help can be used to access information, including names of commands. The ? operator is for obtaining information. The question mark must be in the first position in the line. The symbol * used with the ? operator acts as a wild card character, i.e., it can match any alphanumeric character or sequence of characters. If more than one command matches the request, *Mathematica* lists the names of all the commands.

  Macintosh, version 1.2: Make sure to load the package Info.m before requesting on-line help; otherwise *Mathematica* does not provide explanations of how the command should be called and what it returns. You can load Info.m with the command << Info.m. The file Info.m is quite large. If you have less than five megabytes of memory on your Macintosh or you want to conserve memory for calculations, instead of loading the file Info.m, you can use the *Mathematica* Quick Reference Guide [MmaQuickRef].

Given ?Factor* as input, *Mathematica* lists the commands that begin with the word Factor.

```
In[8] := ?Factor*
        Factor            FactorInteger      FactorSquareFreeList
        FactorComplete    FactorList         FactorTerms
        Factorial         FactorSquareFree   FactorTermsList
        Factorial2
```

If only one command matches the request, *Mathematica* prints the usage statement associated with the command. The usage statement typically consists of a template showing how to call the command, i.e., what the command expects as an argument. Here is what I obtain when I ask for information on the command FactorInteger.

In[9] := ?FactorInteger
    FactorInteger[n] gives a list of the prime factors of the
        integer n, together with their exponents.

This usage statement indicates that this command expects an integer-valued argument. With FactorInteger, I find the prime factors of 75.

In[10] := FactorInteger[75]
Out[10] = {{3, 1}, {5, 2}}

This result indicates that 75 is equal to $3^1 \times 5^2$.

The wild card character is particularly useful for browsing the built-in commands. For example, to find the names of some of the graphics commands, ask for commands whose names contain the words Graphic or Plot.

In[11] := ?*Graphic*
    ContourGraphics   Graphics   Graphics3D
    DensityGraphics   GraphicsArray   SurfaceGraphics
    FullGraphics   GraphicsSpacing

In[12] := ?*Plot*
    ContourPlot   ParametricPlot3D   PlotPoints
    DensityPlot   Plot   PlotRange
    ListContourPlot   PlotColor   PlotRegion
    ListDensityPlot   PlotDivision   PlotStyle
    ListPlot   PlotJoined   Plot3D
    ListPlot3D   PlotLabel   Plot3Matrix
    ParametricPlot

1.7.2 Additional Information

Use ?? to see more information on a function, object, option, or variable. In addition to the usage statement, you obtain the default values of the options of Plot. These options specify the minimum number of points *Mathematica* samples in determining the shape of a graph, the location of the axes, the labels for the plot and the axes, the size of the graph, among other things.

In[13] := ??Plot

Plot[f, {x, xmin, xmax}] generates a plot of f as a
function of x from xmin to xmax. Plot[{f1, f2, ...},
{x, xmin, xmax}] plots several functions fi.

Attributes[Plot] = {HoldAll, Protected}

Options[Plot] =
  {AspectRatio -> GoldenRatio^(-1), Axes -> Automatic,
   AxesLabel -> None, AxesOrigin -> Automatic,
   AxesStyle -> Automatic, Background -> Automatic,
   ColorOutput -> Automatic, Compiled -> True,
   DefaultColor -> Automatic, Epilog -> {},
   Frame -> False, FrameLabel -> None,
   FrameStyle -> Automatic, FrameTicks -> Automatic,
   GridLines -> None, MaxBend -> 10.,
   PlotDivision -> 20., PlotLabel -> None,
   PlotPoints -> 25, PlotRange -> Automatic,
   PlotRegion -> Automatic, PlotStyle -> Automatic,
   Prolog -> {}, RotateLabel -> True,
   Ticks -> Automatic, DefaultFont :> $DefaultFont,
   DisplayFunction :> $DisplayFunction}

To be able to distinguish symbols you define from those built into *Mathematica*, you are advised to assign names that start with a lower-case letter. If you follow this convention, then the command ?@ lists all the objects you defined since you started up *Mathematica*.

In[14] := ?@
         a   m

Version 2.0: Besides matching any lower-case character or sequence of characters, @ matches the character $.

1.7.3 Command Completion (Notebook Front End and MS-DOS)

Command completion is a useful capability for new users and poor typists. This capability is currently available on the Notebook Front End, MS-DOS based computers, and with David Jacobson's Math-Mode package for emacs users (see appendix H.2 on page 346). Type the beginning of the name of a symbol (built-in or user-defined). Then press the <*command*> key with the letter K (on the Notebook Front End) or F2 key (on MS-DOS) and *Mathematica* displays all possible completions in a pop-up menu if there is more than one, (see figure 1.1). Move the mouse or use the arrow keys to select the desired item, then click the mouse or hit the <*return*> key. Typing additional letters narrows the choices.

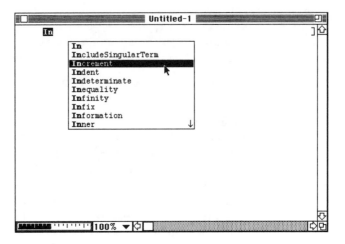

Figure 1.1: *Mathematica* can display all possible completions in a pop-up menu.

Notebook Front End: Choosing the *Action* menu, selecting the *Prepare Input* submenu and then the item *Complete Selection* is equivalent to *<command>*-K.

1.7.4 Function Templates (Notebook Front End and MS-DOS)

A template for a command indicates the number and type of arguments with which to call the function. For instance, the template for Sort

```
Sort[list]
```

indicates that the Sort function takes a list as an argument. A list is several expressions separated by commas and enclosed in curly braces, e.g., {2, 4, 3}. Notice Sort returns a list whose elements are in increasing order.

```
In[15] := Sort[{2, 4, 3}]
Out[15] = {2, 3, 4}
```

Notebook Front End and MS-DOS users can instruct *Mathematica* to provide a template listing the arguments of the function. For example, *Mathematica* indicates that the Table command takes two arguments: an expression and an iterator, Table[expr, imax]. To get the arguments for a function, type the name of the function, such as ContourPlot, and then press the *<command>* key together with the letter I (on the Notebook Front End) or the F3 key (on MS-DOS).

```
ContourPlot[f, {x, xmin, xmax}, {y, ymin, ymax}]
```

Notebook Front End: Selecting the *Action* menu, choosing the *Prepare Input* submenu, and then selecting the item *Make Template* is equivalent to *<command>*-I.

Macintosh, version 1.2: Make sure you have loaded `Info.m`, the file containing the usage statements for all functions built into *Mathematica*.

1.8 Mathematical Notation

Typically *Mathematica* uses English words. Most people are used to referring to standard mathematical functions with symbols rather than words, i.e., symbols such as +, -, *, /, <, and > rather than the words `Plus`, `Minus`, `Times`, `Divide`, `Less`, and `Greater`.

Mathematical Symbol	Function Call
+	Plus
-	Minus, Subtract
*	Times
/	Divide
^	Power
!	Factorial
<	Less
<=	LessEqual
>	Greater
>=	GreaterEqual

Mathematica translates an expression into function calls; so you can use many of the mathematical symbols to which you have grown accustomed as well as many others. Here are examples that use some of the built-in mathematical symbols.

```
In[16] := 4 + 7
Out[16] = 11
```

```
In[17] := 4/2
Out[17] = 2
```

```
In[18] := 3 < 6
Out[18] = True
```

Just as you can ask *Mathematica* about functions, you can ask about mathematical symbols or other special forms.

```
In[19] := ?<
          x < y yields True if x is determined to be less
             than y. x1 < x2 < x3 yields True if the xi form
             a strictly increasing sequence.
```

Version 1.2: Though @@ is an alias for the function Apply, I cannot obtain a usage statement because ?@@ has another meaning. It lists any sequence of zero or more lower-case characters.

> *In[20]* := ?@@
>
>   a m

   Mathematical symbols and other special forms are aliases for functions built into *Mathematica*. The function Alias returns the function that corresponds to a special form.

> *In[21]* := Alias["<"]
> *Out[21]* = Less

> *In[22]* := Alias["="]
> *Out[22]* = Set

   The inside back cover of this book lists of many of the mathematical symbols that can be used in your *Mathematica* input.

1.9 Brackets, Parentheses, and Braces

Brackets, parentheses, and braces are intended for different purposes. Each has a different meaning.

1.9.1 Parentheses: Groupint

Parentheses are used for grouping. Without parentheses, multiplication and division have a higher precedence than addition and subtraction.

> *In[23]* := 1 + 2 * 3
> *Out[23]* = 7

> *In[24]* := 1 / 2 - 5
>
>   9
> *Out[24]* = -(-)
>   2

   Notice that by using parentheses, I change the grouping of arguments.

In[25] := (1 + 2) * 3
Out[25] = 9

In[26] := 1 / (2 - 5)

$$Out[26] = -\left(\frac{1}{3}\right)$$

Parentheses can be used to make your code more understandable to those who look at it.

1.9.2 Square Brackets

Square brackets are used for specifying arguments of functions. For example, the function `Divisors`, takes a single argument, an integer, as you can see from the built-in on-line help message.

In[27] := ?Divisors
        Divisors[n] gives a list of the integers that divide n.

When I call `Divisors` with a number, *Mathematica* returns a list of integers that divide the number.

In[28] := Divisors[100]
Out[28] = {1, 2, 4, 5, 10, 20, 25, 50, 100}

This result indicates that the integers 1, 2, 4, 5, 10, 20, 25, 50, and 100 divide 100 evenly.

Some functions, such as `Random`, do not require an argument. Even though I do not pass an argument to the function, I still call the function with square brackets, [ ]. If no argument is specified, `Random` returns a real number in the range 0 to 1.

In[29] := ?Random
        Random[ ] gives a uniformly distributed pseudorandom
            Real in the range 0 to 1. Random[type, range] gives
            a pseudorandom number of the specified type, lying
            in the specified range. Possible types are: Integer,
            Real and Complex. The default range is 0 to 1. You
            can give the range {min, max} explicitly; a range
            specification of max is equivalent to {0, max}.

In[30] := Random[ ]
Out[30] = 0.846026

Notice Random can be called with a single argument (a type) or two arguments (a type and a range that is a pair containing a minimum value and a maximum value).

In[31] := Random[Integer]
Out[31] = 0

In[32] := Random[Integer, {50, 60}]
Out[32] = 56

Some functions take a fixed number of arguments while others can be called with zero or more arguments.

1.9.3 Braces

Braces are used for specifying lists, vectors, and matrices. A list or vector is several expressions separated by commas and enclosed in braces.

In[33] := {x, x^2, x^3}

$$
Out[33] = \{x, x^2, x^3\}
$$

In *Mathematica*, a matrix is represented as a list of lists. With *Mathematica*, you can construct a matrix of any dimension. Below is a 2 by 2 matrix, whose elements are a[i, j], where i specifies the row of the matrix element and j the column.

In[34] := {{a[1,1], a[1,2]}, {a[2,1], a[2,2]}}
Out[34] = {{a[1, 1], a[1, 2]}, {a[2, 1], a[2, 2]}}

The function MatrixForm displays a matrix in a more conventional form.

In[35] := MatrixForm[{{a[1, 1], a[1, 2]}, {a[2, 1], a[2, 2]}}]
Out[35] = a[1, 1]   a[1, 2]

      a[2, 1]   a[2, 2]

Because *Mathematica* makes extensive use of lists, both in terms of input and output, I devote a chapter to the topic.

1.9.4 Double Square Brackets

Double square brackets are used for indexing, i.e., for denoting an object or set of objects in a list. Suppose I have a vector v as shown below.

In[36] := v = {a, b, c}
Out[36] = {a, b, c}

The notation v[[*i*]] returns the *i*th element in the vector or list called v if *i* is an appropriate integer. Be aware that in *Mathematica*, numbering starts with 1, unlike the C programming language, which starts with 0.

In[37] := v[[2]]
Out[37] = b

As was mentioned before, in *Mathematica* a matrix is represented as a list of lists. I assign the name m to a 2-by-3 matrix.

In[38] := m = {{1, 2, 3}, {4, 5, 6}}
Out[38] = {{1, 2, 3}, {4, 5, 6}}

In[39] := MatrixForm[m]
Out[39] = 1   2   3

         4   5   6

Notice that I can get the *i*th row of the matrix m by using m[[*i*]] if *i* is an appropriate integer.

In[40] := m[[2]]
Out[40] = {4, 5, 6}

The notation m[[*i*, *j*]] returns the *j*th element in the *i*th row.

In[41] := m[[2, 1]]
Out[41] = 4

With double square brackets, you can select specific elements from a list.

1.9.5 Comments

Text enclosed between (* and *) is not evaluated. It is taken to be a comment.

In[42] := 2 + 7 (* This is a Mathematica comment. *)
Out[42] = 9

1.10 Packages

Most of *Mathematica* is written in the C programming language. Some of *Mathematica* is written in *Mathematica*'s own programming language. Definitions specified in files are called packages. Appendix D contains a list of the names of packages that are distributed with version 1.2 and version 2.0. For more information on the packages distributed with *Mathematica*, see Wolfram Research, Inc. Technical Report 10, *Guide to Standard Mathematica Packages*, or the *Mathematica* Quick Reference Guide [MmaQuickRef]. To access the functions defined in a package, you must load the package.

1.10.1 Loading Packages

There are several mechanisms for loading a package:

Mechanism for Loading Packages	Versions Supporting the Mechanism
<< *PackageName*	Macintosh
<< *Directory/PackageName*	MS-DOS and Unix
Needs ["*context*'"]	All systems
<< *context*'	Version 2.0

The command << works slightly differently on different machines. On the other hand, the Needs command is portable across machines.

The function Mean is defined in a package called DescriptiveStatistics.m in the subdirectory or folder DataAnalysis (in version 1.2) and in the subdirectory Statistics (in version 2.0) in the Package directory. The argument of Needs is the name of a context or list of contexts. A context name is a string that ends with a back quote or grave accent, '. By convention, the context name consists of the name of the directories or folders containing the package concatenated with the name of the package, excluding the suffix .m. See section 15.2 on page 247 for a description of contexts.

Version 1.2: Load the Mean function by calling Needs as follows:

    In[43] := Needs ["DataAnalysis'DescriptiveStatistics'"]

MS-DOS: The names of directories and files (excluding the suffix .m) are at most eight characters long. See appendix D (page 323) for the names of the packages included with MS-DOS *Mathematica*.

Version 2.0: There is a new mechanism for loading packages:

    << *context*'

With version 2.0, load the Mean function, as follows:

    In[43] := << Statistics'DescriptiveStatistics'

After loading the package DescriptiveStatitistics.m, *Mathematica* can tell us about the Mean function that is defined in the package.

    In[44] := ?Mean
        Mean[list] gives the mean of the entries in list.
           Mean[distribution] gives the mean of the specified
           statistical distribution.

The function Mean computes the mean or average of a list of numbers.

In[45] := Mean[{1, 2, 3, 4, 5, 6}]

$$Out[45] = \frac{7}{2}$$

Warning: If you call a function, such as Mean, before loading the package in which it is defined and then you load the package, you cannot use the function unless you first invoke the command Remove[Mean]. (See section 15.6 on page 256.)

The package named Graphics.m contains routines for producing graphics, including log plots, bar charts, pie charts, and error bars. After loading this package, you can display a pie chart of *Mathematica* users classified by field (see figure 1.2).

```
In[46] := Needs["Graphics`Graphics`"]
In[47] := PieChart[{
            {28, "Engineering"},
            {21, "CS"},
            {20, "Science"},
            {12, "Math"},
            {6, "Bus."},
            {13, "Other"}
          }];
```

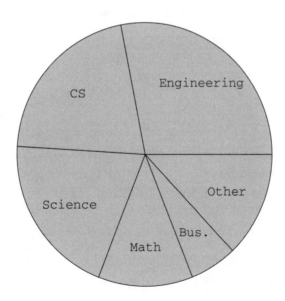

Figure 1.2: A pie chart of *Mathematica* users classified by field.

1.11 Summary

This chapter should get you started with *Mathematica*. You have seen how to give an instruction to *Mathematica*, reference previous results, assign a name to a value, access the built-in on-line help, and how to load and use functions that are defined in packages. Here is a summary of some of the information presented.

1.11.1 On-Line Help

You can obtain more information on a *Mathematica* function or object by using the on-line help. The question mark (?) must be the first position of the line.

Command	Description
?var	Show information on var.
??var	Show extra information on var.
?xyz*	List objects whose names begin with xyz.
?*xyz*	List objects whose names contain xyz.
?@	List objects whose names begin with a lower-case letter.

1.11.2 Bracket Summary

Each type of bracket has a different meaning and is reserved for a specific purpose. Be aware that *Mathematica* has adopted slightly different conventions from C, Pascal, and FORTRAN. Here is a summary of the different types of brackets.

Bracket	Purpose	Examples
(*term*)	Grouping	(a + b)/(c + d)
f[*expr*]	Arguments of function	Sin[2 Pi x]
{*a*, *b*, *c*}	Vectors, matrices, & lists	{x, 2 x, 3 x}
v[[*i*]]	Indexing	m[[3]], m[[1, 2]]
(* *Comment* *)	Commenting	(* watch out *)

1.11.3 Packages

Packages are files containing definitions of functions and objects. To access such functions, you must load the package.

Packages can be loaded on all systems by using the Needs command.

Needs["*Context*‘"]

 Version 2.0: Load a package with << followed by the context for the package.

<< *Context*‘

1.12 Exercises

This problem set is designed to give you experience in using *Mathematica*.

1.1 Use the built-in on-line help to:

(a) Find all the commands whose names begin with the letter O.

(b) Find all commands that have the word List in their names.

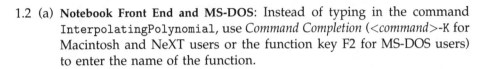

1.2 (a) **Notebook Front End and MS-DOS**: Instead of typing in the command InterpolatingPolynomial, use *Command Completion* (*<command>*-K for Macintosh and NeXT users or the function key F2 for MS-DOS users) to enter the name of the function.

(b) **MS-DOS and Notebook Front End**: Find out the arguments for the command If by using the *Make Template* capability (*<command>*-I for Macintosh and NeXT users or the function key F3 for MS-DOS users).

Macintosh, version 1.2: If *Make Template* does not work, load Info.m using the command Needs["Info`"] or << Info.m.

1.3 Use Alias[ ] to generate a list of the aliases built into *Mathematica*.

1.4 Evaluate the expressions by using *Mathematica*.

(a) 3 x + 7 x

(b) 2 meters + 13 meters

(c) 120 lbs (1 kg/(2.2 lbs))

1.5 After loading the package Graphics.m, make a bar chart showing the percentage of *Mathematica* users by job title.

Version 1.2: On some versions of *Mathematica* the titles are clipped.

```
BarChart[{
        {31, "Research"},
        {26, "Prof"},
        {15, "Eng"},
        {8, "Student"},
        {13, "CS"},
        {7, "Other"}
}];
```

2

1.41421356237309504880168872420969807856967187537694807317667973799073247846210\
70388503875343276415727350138462309122970249248360558507372126441214970999358\
31413222665927505592755799950501152782060571470109559971605970274534596862014\
72851741864088919860955232923048430871432145083976260362799525140798968725339\
654633180882964062061525835239505474575028775996172983557522

Numerical Capabilities

Like a calculator, *Mathematica* can perform arithmetic operations. *Mathematica* handles integers, floating-point numbers[1] (numbers with a decimal point), rationals, and complex numbers. *Mathematica* represents quantities as exactly as possible and tries to return a result in the same form as the input or in a similar form. In addition to single numbers, *Mathematica* works with vectors and matrices. Like a scientific calculator, *Mathematica* has built-in functions and constants. *Mathematica* offers considerably more functions than even the most sophisticated calculators on the market today. This chapter shows some of the numerical capabilities of *Mathematica*, including how to find roots and how to compute the value of a definite integral.

2.1 Arithmetic Operations

Like a calculator, *Mathematica* supports arithmetic operations such as: addition, subtraction, multiplication, division, and exponentiation. To add two numbers, just type the first number, a plus sign (+), and the second number. Feel free to put spaces before and after the plus sign to make the input easier to read.

> *In[1]* := 53 + 78
> *Out[1]* = 131

In many computer languages, the product of a times c (a × c) is written as a * c. *Mathematica* understands this notation.

> *In[2]* := 127*9721
> *Out[2]* = 1234567

---

[1]The number on the left-hand page was generated with the command N[Sqrt[2], 370].

In mathematical notation, the product of a and c is commonly written as a c. *Mathematica* also understands this notation. The asterisk ∗ denoting multiplication is optional. A blank character or space also denotes multiplication. So 127 times 9721 can be expressed as:

In[3] := 127 9721
Out[3] = 1234567

Unlike a calculator, when working with integers, *Mathematica* displays the exact result even if it has more digits than will fit across the screen. *Mathematica* returns the exact value of 34^{56}.

In[4] := 34^56
Out[4] = 579187732052871278420442541261795998528409684920561 6\
          40628436923601663717797466902364 16

This section has shown you how *Mathematica* works with integers. The next section describes how *Mathematica* handles rationals.

2.2 Rationals

Rationals are numbers that can be represented as the quotient of one integer divided by another integer. The way *Mathematica* deals with rational numbers is different from the way most calculators do. If you ask a calculator to compute the sum 2/4 + 24/144, most return something like 0.6666667, which is only an approximation to the result.

As long as *Mathematica* is dealing with rationals as quotients of integers, it keeps them in this form. Notice that, when I ask *Mathematica* for the sum of two rationals, *Mathematica* returns a rational.

In[5] := 2/4 + 24/144

             2
Out[5] = -
             3

For calculations involving only rational numbers, *Mathematica* returns a rational or an integer.

In[6] := 2 + 2/5

            12
Out[6] = -
            5

Though the number 12/5 is equivalent in value to 2.4, *Mathematica* represents these two quantities differently.

2.3 Irrationals

Mathematica represents results as precisely as it can or to the precision requested by the user. Irrationals cannot be represented exactly as a ratio of two integers. If you ask for the $\sqrt{17}$, *Mathematica* returns the exact value, i.e., Sqrt[17], an expression that represents $\sqrt{17}$.

> *In[7]* := Sqrt[17]
> *Out[7]* = Sqrt[17]

Notice that, if you ask for the square root of a floating-point number, i.e., $\sqrt{17.0}$, *Mathematica* approximates its value.

> *In[8]* := Sqrt[17.0]
> *Out[8]* = 4.12311

Mathematica does not substitute an inexact numerical value for an exact value, whether it be an integer, a rational number, or a symbol. Given an approximate number as input, *Mathematica* returns an approximation to the result.

2.4 Decimal Approximations

A floating-point number, a number with a decimal point, is interpreted as an approximation. If there is a floating-point number in the expression, *Mathematica* treats the entire expression as an approximation and tends to represent the result in terms of floating-point numbers.

> *In[9]* := 1/2 + 2.4/144
> *Out[9]* = 0.516667

Not all approximate results are expressed entirely in terms of floating-point numbers. Though $.5/7 + \pi$ contains a floating-point number, *Mathematica* does not approximate π.

> *In[10]* := .5/7 + Pi
> *Out[10]* = 0.0714286 + Pi

2.5 Complex Numbers

In addition to working with floating-point numbers, *Mathematica* also knows about complex values. Following the convention that all built-in *Mathematica* function names begin with a capital letter, a capital I represents the imaginary number $\sqrt{-1}$. When working with complex rationals, *Mathematica* makes the denominator integer-valued.

In[11] := (3 + 4I)/(5 + 2I)

          23   14 I
Out[11] = -- + ----
          29   29

There are several built-in functions for working with complex numbers. The function Re returns the real part of its argument.

In[12] := Re[3 + 4I]
Out[12] = 3

The function Im gives the imaginary part of its argument.

In[13] := Im[3 + 4I]
Out[13] = 4

The function Conjugate returns the conjugate of its argument.

In[14] := Conjugate[3 + 4I]
Out[14] = 3 - 4 I

The function Abs gives the absolute value of its argument.

In[15] := Abs[3 + 4I]
Out[15] = 5

Version 1.2: Some functions, such as Round, ignore the imaginary part of their arguments.

In[16] := Round[2.7 - 8.5 I]
Out[16] = 3

Version 2.0: Round rounds both the real and imaginary parts of its argument.

In[17] := Round[2.7 - 8.5 I]
Out[17] = 3 - 8 I

There are many more functions in *Mathematica* that work with complex numbers, including Sin, Cos, Exp, and Log.

2.6 Symbols versus Numbers

Mathematica considers a letter or sequence of letters a symbol. Variable names must start with a letter (or $) and cannot contain spaces. For example, a and a7 are valid variable names since each start with a letter. Because variable names never start with a number, 7a is interpreted as 7 times a, even though there is no space between the 7 and the a. Notice that when given 7a as input, *Mathematica* returns a result that has a space between the 7 and the a.

> *In[18]* := 7a
> *Out[18]* = 7 a

The package `Miscellaneous/Units.m` contains a list of units as well as functions for converting units.

> *In[19]* := Needs["Miscellaneous`Units`"]

A symbol can be used to specify units.

> *In[20]* := 120 Pound

The function `Convert` converts units. I convert 120 pounds to kilograms.

> *In[21]* := Convert[120 Pound, Kilogram]
> *Out[21]* = 54.4311 Kilogram

2.7 Approximations

Mathematica represents integers and rational numbers exactly but the function N gives a numerical approximation. Using N, I obtain a numerical approximation for $\sqrt{17}$.

> *In[22]* := N[Sqrt[17]]
> *Out[22]* = 4.12311

Mathematica typically displays six significant figures, though it computes more decimal digits of precision. The function `Precision` gives the number of decimal digits of precision for a particular result.

> *In[23]* := Precision[%]
> *Out[23]* = 19

The default precision of a calculation depends on the floating-point hardware of the computer being used. On a Macintosh, the default precision is 19 while on a Hewlett-Packard 9000/375 workstation the default is 16.

With the function N, it is possible to request more precision. Be aware that the more precision you ask for, the longer it takes for *Mathematica* to compute the result. Here I ask for $\sqrt{17}$ to 100 decimal digits of precision.

> *In[24]* := N[Sqrt[17], 100]
> *Out[24]* = 4.1231056256176605498214098559740770251471992253736 2\
>   0434398633573094954346337621593587863650810684297

Mathematica can compute results to more than the floating-point precision of the computer on which it is running.

2.7.1 Exact versus Approximate

Mathematica distinguishes between exact and approximate values. Exact values may contain integers, rationals, symbols, and functions, or a combination thereof.

> *In[25]* := 3/10 + 1/2
>
> $$Out[25] = \frac{4}{5}$$

When a value is exact, its precision is infinite.

> *In[26]* := Precision[%]
> *Out[26]* = Infinity

Any expression containing a number with a decimal point is recognized as an approximate expression, even if it also contains integers, rationals, or symbols.

> *In[27]* := .37 + 1/2
> *Out[27]* = 0.87

> *In[28]* := Precision[%]
> *Out[28]* = 19

The precision indicates whether a result is considered to be an approximation or an exact value.

2.7.2 Converting Approximate Values to Exact Values

There are several functions that convert an approximate number into an exact value: Rationalize, Round, Chop, Floor, and Ceiling. The function Rationalize converts a floating-point number to a rational.

> *In[29]* := Rationalize[3.1416]
>
> $$Out[29] = \frac{3927}{1250}$$

Notice *Mathematica* does not always rationalize a number.

> *In[30]* := Rationalize[3.1415926536]
> *Out[30]* = 3.14159

The second argument to Rationalize specifies a threshold, *dx*. Rationalize converts a number to a rational whenever the error is smaller in magnitude than the threshold.

> Rationalize[*x*, *dx*]

Mathematica will always rationalize a number if the second argument to Rationalize is 0. If the threshold is 0, then Rationalize converts numbers that it otherwise would not.

> *In[31]* := Rationalize[3.1415926536, 0]
>
> *Out[31]* = $\dfrac{3926990817}{1250000000}$

Round gives the closest integer when given a floating-point number.

> *In[32]* := Round[2.574]
> *Out[32]* = 3

As with several other functions in *Mathematica*, the argument to Round must be a number. Round returns unevaluated when given a symbolic expression, such as Sqrt[17], as an argument.

> *In[33]* := Round[Sqrt[17]]
> *Out[33]* = Round[Sqrt[17]]

Use N to obtain the numerical value of an expression.

> *In[34]* := Round[N[Sqrt[17]]]
> *Out[34]* = 4

The function Chop converts an approximate value near zero to exactly zero.

> *In[35]* := Chop[0.00000000002]
> *Out[35]* = 0

2.7.3 Working with a Fixed Level of Precision

The precision to which *Mathematica* calculates a result depends on the floating-point hardware of your computer. On a Macintosh, by default, *Mathematica* calculates the result to 19 decimal digits of precision. On many Unix workstations, *Mathematica* calculates results to 16 decimal digits of precision. As was explained in section 2.7 on page 27, you can instruct *Mathematica* to compute a result to more places of precision by using N. The function nThirty, defined below, gives a decimal approximation with 30 places of precision.

> *In[36]* := nThirty[x_] := N[x, 30]

The notation x_ instructs *Mathematica* to assign the name x to the argument of nThirty. When I call nThirty[5/7], the name x is assigned the value 5/7 and *Mathematica* returns the result of N[5/7, 30].

In[37] := nThirty[5/7]
Out[37] = 0.714285714285714285714285714286

$Post is a global variable whose value, if set, is applied to every output expression. $Post can be set to a function that takes one argument. The function nThirty takes a single argument. Notice if you set $Post to be equal to nThirty, this function is applied to every subsequent output expression in that session.

In[38] := $Post = nThirty
Out[38] = nThirty

Now *Mathematica* prints all numbers to 30 places of precision, even if the number is irrational, as you can see.

In[39] := Sqrt[3]
Out[39] = 1.73205080756887729352744634151

In[40] := Precision[%]
Out[40] = 30.

Note: $Post was applied to the result returned by Precision. So instead of the integer value 30, *Mathematica* returned a floating-point number.

Remove the definition by setting $Post equal to ".". Do not put a space between the equal sign and the period.

In[41] := $Post =.

Be aware that if you ask for N of a floating-point number, *Mathematica* can return no more precision than the number already had.

In[42] := N[Pi, 25]
Out[42] = 3.141592653589793238462643

In[43] := N[%, 200]
Out[43] = 3.141592653589793238462643

2.8 Formatting Numbers

What if you don't like the way that *Mathematica* represents a number? There are several functions built into *Mathematica* intended for formatting expressions. Many of these functions have the word Form in their name. Notice all the options for the function NumberForm.

In[44] := Options[NumberForm]
Out[44] ={DigitBlock -> DirectedInfinity[1], NumberPoint -> ".",
        SignPadding -> False, NumberSigns -> {"-", ""},
        ExponentStep -> 1, NumberFormat -> Automatic,
        NumberPadding -> {"", ""}, NumberSeparator -> ",",
        ExponentFunction -> Automatic}

Version 2.0: Setting the option ExponentStep appropriately large, NumberForm prints a large number without the exponential term. With the option NumberSigns, I instruct *Mathematica* to put a plus sign in front of a positive number.

In[45] := NumberForm[123456789 10^20,
        ExponentStep->1000,
        NumberSigns -> {"-", "+"}
    ]
Out[45] =+12345678900000000000000000000

2.9 Commonly Used Constants

Mathematica knows about common mathematical constants. The symbol Pi represents π. E represents e, which is approximately equal to 2.71828. Degree has the value $\pi/180$, i.e., the degree-to-radian conversion factor. GoldenRatio represents the golden ratio $(1 + \sqrt{5})/2$.

Constant	Symbol	Description	Value
$\sum_{k=0}^{\infty}(-1)^k/(2k+1)^2$	Catalan	Catalan's constant	≈ 0.915966
$\pi/180$	Degree	Degree to radian conversion	≈ 0.017453
e	E	Exponential constant	≈ 2.71828
γ	EulerGamma	Euler's constant gamma	≈ 0.577216
$(1 + \sqrt{5})/2$	GoldenRatio	The golden ratio	≈ 1.61803
i or j	I	The imaginary unit	$\sqrt{-1}$
π	Pi	Circumference of a circle divided by its diameter	≈ 3.14159

These symbols are taken to represent exact mathematical quantities. *Mathematica* does not calculate their approximate values unless you instruct it to do so.

In[46] := Pi
*Out[46] =*Pi

If you request a decimal approximation to these constants and many others, *Mathematica* computes the value to the desired level of accuracy.

With NumberForm, I separate the digits in the decimal expansion of π into blocks of five digits.

```
In[47] := NumberForm[
             N[Pi, 45],
             NumberSeparator -> " ",
             DigitBlock -> 5
          ]
Out[47] = 3.14159 26535 89793 23846 26433 83279 50288 41971 6939
```

In addition to being able to compute a decimal approximation to various constants, *Mathematica* knows certain relationships among various constants. For instance, there are rules built into *Mathematica* specifying the relationship between Log and E and between the trigonometric functions and Pi.

```
In[48] := Log[E]
Out[48] = 1
```

```
In[49] := Cos[Pi/3]

                1
Out[49] = -
                2
```

The argument of Sin or Cos is assumed to be in radians. However, you can specify the argument in degrees.

```
In[50] := N[Sin[45 Degree]]
Out[50] = 0.707107
```

Those constants not built in can be easily added. I define avogadro to be Avogadro's number.

```
In[51] := avogadro = 6.02250 10^23

                23
Out[51] = 6.0225 10
```

Many commonly used constants are built into *Mathematica*. With an assignment statement, you can easily define other constants.

2.10 Random Numbers

Sometimes you may not want a specific number, but you may want a random number that has certain properties. *Mathematica* provides the function Random for generating a uniformly distributed pseudorandom number. If no arguments are specified, Random generates a floating-point number uniformly distributed in the range [0, 1].

> *In[52]* := Random[ ]
> *Out[52]* = 0.662388

Random[Integer] returns a random integer uniformly-distributed in the range [0,1], i.e., either 0 or 1, with the two being equally likely.

> *In[53]* := Random[Integer]
> *Out[53]* = 1

Random can return a number in a specified range. Here I ask for a random integer uniformly distributed in the range [0, 100] inclusive.

> *In[54]* := Random[Integer, {0, 100}]
> *Out[54]* = 22

If you want a complex random number, define a complex range. Specifying the range as {1 + 3 I, 4 + 7 I}, *Mathematica* generates a random number where the real part lies between 1 and 4 and the imaginary part lies between $3i$ and $7i$.

> *In[55]* := Random[Complex, {1 + 3 I, 4 + 7 I}]
> *Out[55]* = 2.436528 + 5.379642 I

The packages ContinuousDistributions.m and DiscreteDistributions.m contain definitions for generating random numbers based on other distributions. In version 1.2 these packages can be found in the directory DataAnalysis. In version 2.0, the directory has been renamed Statistics.

> *In[56]* := Needs["Statistics`ContinuousDistributions`"]
> *In[57]* := Random[NormalDistribution[5]]
> *Out[57]* = 4.78541

By default, Random uses the time of day as its seed. The function SeedRandom resets the pseudorandom number generator. Using SeedRandom, you can regenerate a sequence of random numbers.

> *In[58]* := SeedRandom[2]
> *In[59]* := {Random[ ], Random[ ]}
> *Out[59]* = {0.410746, 0.731996}

> *In[60]* := SeedRandom[2]
> *In[61]* := {Random[ ], Random[ ]}
> *Out[61]* = {0.410746, 0.731996}

Random number generators are useful for generating test data.

2.11 Iterators

Iterators indicate the number of times a calculation is to be performed. Several *Mathematica* functions use iterators, e.g., Do, Product, Sum, and Table. The following table describes these four functions and contains an example of the four different types of iterators.

Function	Description
Do[*expr*, {*max*}]	Evaluates *expr max* times
Product[*expr*, {*i*, *max*}]	Evaluates the product of *expr* with *i* running from 1 to *max*
Sum[*expr*, {*i*, *min*, *max*}]	Evaluates the sum of *expr* with *i* running from *min* to *max*
Table[*expr*, {*i*, *min*, *max*, *step*}]	Generates a list of *expr* with *i* running from *min* to *max* incrementing i by *step*

The second argument of these functions is an iterator. An iterator is a list containing at least one and at most four elements.

The simplest iterator, $\{n\}$, executes the function n times. I use Table to generate a list of 2 x's.

```
In[62] := Table[x, {2}]
Out[62] = {x, x}
```

Iterators of the form {*var*, *vmax*} execute a function for *var* = 1 to *var* = *vmax*, incrementing *var* by one each iteration. Here I compute a product of $x + ky$, where k assumes the integer values from 1 to 3.

```
In[63] := Product[x + k y, {k, 3}]
Out[63] = (x + y) (x + 2 y) (x + 3 y)
```

An iterator of the form {*var*, *vmin*, *vmax*} executes the function for *var* = *vmin* to *var* = *vmax*, incrementing *var* by one at each iteration. I instruct *Mathematica* to print "*k*: " followed by the current value of k, for k taking on integer values from 7 to 9.

```
In[64] := Do[Print["k: ", k], {k, 7, 9}]
           k:  7
           k:  8
           k:  9
```

Using such an iterator, I can find the threshold for Chop. For various values of k, using Table I print k, 10^{-k} and Chop[N[10^{-k}]]. I display the results using TableForm so that *Mathematica* prints a result for each value of k on a separate line.

```
In[65] := TableForm[
           Table[
                {k, 10^(-k), Chop[N[10^(-k)]]},
                {k, 9, 11}
           ]
       ]
```

$$
\begin{array}{ccc}
                            & \dfrac{1}{1000000000} & 1. \; 10^{-9} \\
Out[65] = 9 & & \\[1em]
10 & \dfrac{1}{10000000000} & 1. \; 10^{-10} \\[1em]
11 & \dfrac{1}{100000000000} & 0
\end{array}
$$

On this computer, the threshold for Chop is 10^{-10}. Chop approximates numbers less than 10^{-10} by the exact value 0 (an integer). Numbers larger than the threshold are left unchanged.

The last type of iterator, which has four elements, {*var*, *vmin*, *vmax*, *vstep*}. It is for executing an expression with *var* = *vmin* to *var* = *vmax*, incrementing *var* by *vstep* units in each iteration. Here I ask *Mathematica* to compute the sum of ix^i with i taking on values from 3 to 18 in steps of 5.

```
In[66] := Sum[i x^i, {i, 3, 18, 5}]
```

$$
Out[66] = 3 \; x^3 + 8 \; x^8 + 13 \; x^{13} + 18 \; x^{18}
$$

2.12 Matrix Calculations

Functions for performing matrix calculations and manipulations are built into *Mathematica*, including matrix multiplication (or Dot as it is referred to in *Mathematica*), Inverse, Det (determinant), Eigenvalues, Eigenvectors, LinearSolve, NullSpace, and RowReduce. This section shows how to compute the inverse of a matrix and how to multiply two matrices.

I use Random to generate a floating-point number in the range [0,1] and Table to produce a list of lists (*Mathematica*'s representation of a matrix) of random floating-point numbers. I assign the name m to this matrix so that I can easily refer to it later.

In[67] := m = Table[Random[ ], {3}, {3}]
Out[67] = {{0.91255, 0.613129, 0.759439},
        {0.762714, 0.54405, 0.43345},
        {0.520752, 0.0855305, 0.11192}}

The function Inverse computes the inverse of a matrix. I assign the name mInv to an approximation of the inverse of the matrix m.

In[68] := mInv = Inverse[m]
Out[68] = {{-0.411866, 0.0634034, 2.54918},
        {-2.42715, 5.07278, -3.17653},
        {3.77121, -4.17166, -0.498567}}

I verify that mInv is the right inverse of m by multiplying m times mInv using the function Dot (.) to multiply m and mInv.

In[69] := m . mInv

Out[69] = {{1., -2.1684 10^{-19}, 1.35525 10^{-19}},

      {-1.0842 10^{-19}, 1., 2.71051 10^{-20}},

      {-8.13152 10^{-20}, 1.0842 10^{-19}, 1.}}

Applying the Chop function replaces values that are approximately equal to zero, with exactly zero.

In[70] := Chop[%]
Out[70] = {{1., 0, 0}, {0, 1., 0}, {0, 0, 1.}}

The function MatrixForm prints the elements of a matrix in rows and columns that are aligned. (Note that this form is only for display purposes. The output of MatrixForm cannot be used for calculations. Since the output does not have braces, *Mathematica* cannot compute the inverse of MatrixForm[m].)

In[71] := MatrixForm[%]
Out[71] = 1.   0   0

       0   1.   0

       0   0   1.

In this section, you have seen *Mathematica* works not only with single values but also works with matrices of floating-point numbers. For matrices of exact values, i.e., integers or rationals, the exact inverse is calculated. *Mathematica* can also work with matrices of complex numbers. Though not shown in this section,

Mathematica includes matrix functions for computing eigenvalues, eigenvectors, and a row-reduced form of a matrix.

2.13 Finding Roots

Mathematica includes functions for numerically finding roots of equations: NRoots and FindRoot. The notation == is for denoting equality and for specifying an equation in *Mathematica*.

The function NRoots returns the numerical approximations to the roots of a polynomial equation. I ask NRoots for numerical approximations to the roots of the equation $x^4 + 3x^2 + 5x = 7$ for the variable x.

> *In[72]* := NRoots[x^4 + 3x^2 + 5x == 7, x]
> *Out[72]* = x == -1.63541 || x == 0.390304 - 2.2034 I ||
>   x == 0.390304 + 2.2034 I || x == 0.854804

The symbol || is the logical *or* function. This result states that, if x is equal to -1.63541 or $x = 0.390304 \pm 2.2034i$ or $x = 0.854804$, the equation $x^4 + 3x^2 + 5x = 7$ is satisfied.

The function FindRoot searches for a numerical solution to the equation *lhs* = *rhs*, starting with the approximation $x = x_0$.

> FindRoot[*lhs* == *rhs*, $\{x, \ x_0\}$]

I ask FindRoot to find a root of the equation $\sin x / x = 0$, starting at $x = 2$.

> *In[73]* := FindRoot[Sin[x]/x == 0, {x, 2}]
> *Out[73]* = {x -> 3.14159}

The function FindRoot uses Newton's method. This method uses the derivative of a function. If your starting value is near a section of the function where the absolute value of the slope is large, Newton's method finds a root near the starting value. On the other hand, if the starting value is in a flat section of the curve, the root might be quite far from the starting value.

The Bessel function J_0 has roots near 2.5, 5.5, 9, 12, 15, and 18, as you can see in figure 2.1.

The derivative of the Bessel function[2] $J_0(x)$ is shown in figure 2.2. Notice the derivative of the curve is relatively large at $x = 12$. So Newton's method finds a root near 12. If the first argument to FindRoot is not an equation, *Mathematica* assumes that your input is the left hand side of the equation *lhs* = 0.

---

[2] This plot was generated using Plot[Release[D[BesselJ[0, x], x]], {x, 0, 20}] (in version 1.2). Release is used to force *Mathematica* to evaluate the derivative before calling Plot. In version 2.0 of *Mathematica*, the function Release has been superseded by two functions ReleaseHold and Evaluate. In version 2.0, generate this plot by using the command Plot[Evaluate[D[BesselJ[0, x], x]], {x, 0, 20}].

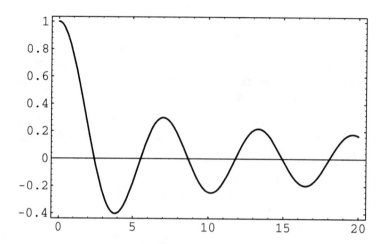

Figure 2.1: A plot of the Bessel function, J_0.

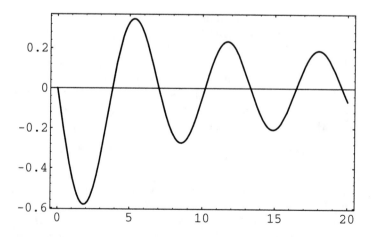

Figure 2.2: A plot of $-J_1(x)$, the derivative of the Bessel function $J_0(x)$.

In[74] := `FindRoot[BesselJ[0, x], {x, 12}]`
Out[74] = `{x -> 11.7915}`

The derivative of $J_0(x)$ is small at x = 7. Notice that `FindRoot` finds a root, but not the closest one to 7.

In[75] := `FindRoot[BesselJ[0,x], {x, 7}]`
Out[75] = `{x -> -52.6241}`

With `FindRoot`, if you pick a starting value that is close to a root, Newton's method most likely finds the nearest root.

`NRoots` and `FindRoot` are for obtaining numerical approximations to the roots of an equation. Be aware that, because `FindRoot` uses Newton's method, it does not always find the nearest root to the starting value.

2.14 Numerical Integration

Mathematica can numerically integrate and numerically solve differential equations. The function `NIntegrate` gives a numerical approximation to the integral of an expression *expr* with respect to *x* from *min* to *max*, i.e., $\int_{min}^{max} expr\ dx$.

`NIntegrate[`*expr*`, {`*x*`, `*min*`, `*max*`}]`

Here I integrate $\sin x^2 / x^2$ from $x = 0$ to $x = 1$.

In[76] := `NIntegrate[Sin[x^2]/x^2, {x, 0, 1}]`
Out[76] = `0.967577`

2.15 Solving Differential Equations Numerically

Using *Mathematica*, you can obtain the numerical solution to a differential equation by using `NDSolve` in version 2.0 or functions in the package `RungeKutta.m`.

 Version 2.0: The function `NDSolve` was added to version 2.0 to find numerical solutions to differential equations. `NDSolve` finds the numerical solution to the differential equations, eqn_i, for the dependent variable, *y[x]*, for the independent variable *x* in the range x_{min} to x_{max}.

`NDSolve[{`*eqn₁*`, `*eqn₂* `...}, `*y[x]*`, {`*x*`, `x_{min}`, `x_{max}`}]`

Mathematica returns an interpolating function.

In[77] := `NDSolve[{`
        `y''[x] - y'[x] + x y[x] == 0, y'[0] == -1, y[0] == 1},`
        `y, {x, 0, 5}]`
Out[77] = `{{y -> InterpolatingFunction[{0., 5.}, <>]}}`

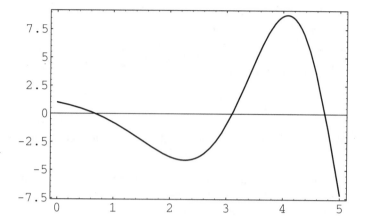

Figure 2.3: The solution to the differential equation $y''(x) - y'(x) + xy(x) = 0$ with the boundary conditions $y'(0) = -1$ and $y(0) = 1$.

You can plot this solution with the `Plot` command.

In[78] := `Plot[y[x] /. %, {x, 0, 5}];`

The notation `y[x] /. %` instructs *Mathematica* to replace y with the value given in the previous result. The result, `InterpolatingFunction[0., 5., <>]`, represents the solution to the differential equation $y''(x) - y'(x) + xy(x) = 0$ in the range [0, 5] with the boundary conditions $y'(0) = -1$ and $y(0) = 1$. Figure 2.3 shows this solution.

2.16 Summary

Like a calculator, *Mathematica* can perform numerical computations. Unlike a calculator, *Mathematica* is not limited by the size of a fixed screen width nor by a fixed word size of the computer you are using. When working with integer or rational numbers, *Mathematica* gives exact results. The following table lists the types of expressions which *Mathematica* supports.

Type	Description	Example
`Integer`	An integer number	3
`Real`	A floating-point (real) number of the form nn.mm	3.4
`Rational`	A rational number a/b, for integers a and b	3/4
`Complex`	A complex number of the form r + I c	3 + 4.2I
`Symbol`	A variable or value represented by a symbol	E
`List`	Used for representing vectors and matrices	{1, 2, 3}

Mathematica provides several functions for converting a real to an integer or a rational number and vice versa.

Function	Description	Example
Ceiling[x]	The smallest integer $\geq x$	Ceiling[3.4] $\Rightarrow$ 4
Floor[x]	The largest integer $\leq x$	Floor[3.4] $\Rightarrow$ 3
Round[x]	The integer closest to x	Round[5.6] $\Rightarrow$ 6
Chop[x]	Replaces reals close to zero with 0	Chop[0.00000000001] $\Rightarrow$ 0
N[x]	The approximate numerical value of x	N[Pi] $\Rightarrow$ 3.14159
Rationalize[x]	Converts a floating-point number to a rational	Rationalize[3.14] $\Rightarrow$ 157/50

Here is a summary of some conventions pertaining to numbers as well as to symbols.

Notation	Description
a * b	The product of a and b. (The * may be replaced by a space.)
a b	The product of a and b.
3a	The product of 3 and a. No space is needed if the multiplier (the first factor) is a numerical quantity.
a3	A symbol whose name consists of two characters.
a^b	a^b (a raised to the power b.)

In addition to being able to work with single values, *Mathematica* can work with complex numbers, vectors, and matrices. There are numerous functions for computing results numerically. This chapter described functions for computing numerical approximations to the roots of an equation, integrals, and the solutions differential equations. The functions presented in this chapter are shown in the following table.

Function	Description	Added to 2.0
Exp, Log	Exponential and log functions	
Cos, Sin, Tan, etc.	Trigonometric and functions	
FindRoot	Uses Newton's method to find a root of an equation	
NRoots	Gives a list of numerical approximations to the roots of a polynomial equation	
NDSolve	Finds a numerical solution to a set of differential equations	yes
NIntegrate	Gives a numerical approximation for an integral	
NSum, NProduct	Gives numerical approximations to a sum or product	

See appendix C on page 313 or the inside front cover for a complete list of the functions built into *Mathematica*.

2.17 Exercises

This problem set gives you the opportunity to use some of *Mathematica*'s numerical capabilities.

2.1 Compute the number of minutes in a 365-day year.

2.2 (a) Using N, compute π to 770 places. There should be six consecutive 9's somewhere in the result.

   (b) Use N to determine how close $e^{\pi\sqrt{163}}$ is to an integer.

2.3 Use NumberForm to separate the digits of the number 123456789 into blocks of 3 digits.

2.4 Generate two random numbers with Random. Add these numbers.

2.5 Enter the following expressions into *Mathematica* and see what *Mathematica* returns. Determine whether the last inequality is true or false.

   (a) $\sqrt{3} + 3$ (Notice *Mathematica* changes the order of the terms.)

   (b) Exp[2Pi I]

   (c) $5 > 3$

   (d) $\pi^e > e^\pi$

2.6 (a) Use on-line help to learn about the commands Table, Sum, and Product. If *Mathematica* does not show you a usage statement, make sure that you spell the command correctly, you capitalize the first letter of each word, and if you use version 1.2 on a Macintosh, that you load the file Info.m. **Macintosh, version 1.2:** To load the file, invoke the command Needs["Info'"] or << Info.m.

   (b) Use Table to make a list of five 9's.

   (c) Use Table to make a list of the squares of the first 10 positive integers.

   (d) Use Sum to verify that $100 * 101/2$ is the sum of the first 100 positive integers.

   (e) Use Sum to compute the sum of the series
   $$1 + 1/1! + 1/2! + 1/3! + \ldots + 1/10!$$

   (f) Use Product to compute 6!, i.e., $6 * 5 * 4 * 3 * 2 * 1$.

2.7 Compute the inverse of the 3-by-3 Hilbert matrix, the matrix whose i,jth element is $1/(i + j - 1)$ for $1 \le i,j \le 3$. You can generate the Hilbert matrix using Table.

2.8 Compute an approximation to π by using numerical integration, NIntegrate, to compute the area under the curve $4/(1 + x^2)$ in the range $[0, 1]$.

2.9 Find five roots of the equations:

(a) $x^5 + 5x^4 + 4x^3 + 3x^2 + 2x + 1 = 0$

(b) $\sin^2 \pi x - x^2 \cos \pi x = x$

   Hint: Try using Table and FindRoot. Look in the range $[-5, 5]$.

(c) $x \tan x = 1$

   Hint: Look in the range $[0, 13]$.

$\pi \quad \Sigma \quad \Delta \int \quad \rightarrow \quad j \quad \gamma$

Algebraic or Symbolic Capabilities

In the last chapter, you saw how *Mathematica* works with numerical expressions. This chapter discusses how *Mathematica* handles algebraic expressions-expressions that contain variables or symbols. You will see how *Mathematica* can find the exact roots of a polynomial equation, solve a set of simultaneous equations, manipulate or simplify an expression, integrate and differentiate, determine the power-series expansion of a function, and solve differential equations.

3.1 Algebra

In addition to being able to manipulate numbers, *Mathematica* can manipulate algebraic expressions. See how *Mathematica* expands $(x + 2y + z)^4$.

```
In[1] := Expand[(x + 2y + z)^4]

          4       3        2  2          3       4       3
Out[1] = x  + 8 x  y + 24 x  y  + 32 x y  + 16 y  + 4 x  z +

              2              2         3        2  2
          24 x  y z + 48 x y  z + 32 y  z + 6 x  z  +

                2       2  2        3       3    4
          24 x y z  + 24 y  z  + 4 x z  + 8 y z  + z
```

Though potentially time consuming, expansions can be performed by hand or with the aid of a calculator. Determining the factors of a fourth-degree polynomial is often difficult to do by hand. Notice that *Mathematica* can find the factors of the previous result, a fourth-degree polynomial.

In[2] := `Factor[%]`

$$Out[2] = (x + 2 y + z)^4$$

You might think that finding the factors was easy because they were all the same. Let's take an expression whose factors are all different.

In[3] := `Factor[6x^3 + 35 x^2 y + 58 x y^2 + 21 y^3]`
Out[3] = `(2 x + y) (x + 3 y) (3 x + 7 y)`

3.2 Solving Equations

You saw in the last chapter that `NRoots` and `FindRoot` compute numerical approximations to the roots of an equation. Using `NRoots` you obtain numerical approximations to the roots of $x^3 - 3x^2 - 17x + 51 = 0$.

In[4] := `NRoots[x^3 - 3 x^2 - 17 x + 51 == 0, x]`
Out[4] = `x == -4.12311 || x == 3. || x == 4.12311`

The symbol `||` is the logical *or* function. This result tells us that, if x is equivalent to -4.12311, to 3., or to 4.12311, then $x^3 - 3x^2 - 17x + 51$ is approximately equivalent to 0.

Mathematica can also find the exact solutions to a polynomial equation of degree four or less (as well as some polynomial equations of higher degree). `Solve` provides the exact roots of this third order polynomial equation.

In[5] := `Solve[x^3 - 3 x^2 - 17 x + 51 == 0, x]`
Out[5] = `{{x -> 3}, {x -> Sqrt[17]}, {x -> -Sqrt[17]}}`

This solution is stated in terms of a list of replacement rules. The equation $x^3 - 3x^2 - 17x + 51 = 0$ is satisfied if x is replaced by 3 (x -> 3), x is replaced by $\sqrt{17}$ (x -> Sqrt[17]), or x is replaced by $-\sqrt{17}$ (x -> -Sqrt[17]). Notice that the three values returned by `NRoots` (-4.12311, 3., and 4.12311) are numerical approximations to the values returned by `Solve` ($-\sqrt{17}$, 3, and $\sqrt{17}$).

Besides being able to find roots, *Mathematica* can solve simultaneous equations. The first argument to `Solve` can be a list of equations.

`Solve[{`*eqn₁*`, `*eqn₂*`, ..., `*eqnₙ*`}]`

Here I ask *Mathematica* to solve the set of simultaneous equations $xy + 5x + 6y = 7$ and $x^2 + 5x + 7y = 8$ and use `ColumnForm` to display each solution on a separate line.

```
In[6] := ColumnForm[
          Solve[{x y + 5x + 6y == 7,
                 x^2 + 5x + 7y == 8}]
       ]
```

$$Out[6] = \{x \rightarrow 1, \ y \rightarrow \frac{2}{7}\}$$

$$\{x \rightarrow \frac{-222 + 37 \ Sqrt[37]}{37}, \ y \rightarrow \frac{-10 + 2 \ Sqrt[37]}{2}\}$$

$$\{x \rightarrow \frac{-222 - 37 \ Sqrt[37]}{37}, \ y \rightarrow \frac{-10 - 2 \ Sqrt[37]}{2}\}$$

The three solutions to the given set of equations ($xy + 5x + 6y = 7$, $x^2 + 5x + 7y = 8$) are presented as a list of three lists of replacements for x and y. In other words, the equations are satisfied when x is replaced by 1 (x -> 1) and y is replaced by 2/7 (y -> 2/7). This solution corresponds to the first pair in the list.

3.2.1 Using the Solution

With the operator /. (no space between the / and the .) or ReplaceAll, one can apply a rule or list of rules to an expression. The input x + 5y /. {x -> 1, y -> 2/7} replaces x with the value 1 and y with the value 2/7 in the expression x + 5y.

```
In[7] := x + 5y /. {x -> 1, y -> 2/7}
```

$$Out[7] = \frac{17}{7}$$

Unlike Set (=), a rule does not make an assignment. (See chapter 7 on page 137 for more discussion on the difference between an assignment made with = and a rule specified with ->).

Solve is intended for solving systems of polynomial equations. Most equations of degree five or more are not solvable with radicals. Notice the result *Mathematica* returns when it cannot find a solution.

```
In[8] := Solve[2 x^5 + 12 x^2 + 18 x - 14 == 0]
```

$$Out[8] = \{ToRules[Roots[-7 + 9 x + 6 x^2 + x^5 == 0, x]]\}$$

This result says that the solution to $2x^5 + 12x^2 + 18x - 14 = 0$ can be found by solving the equation $-7 + 9x + 6x^2 + x^5 = 0$. Using N, you can obtain numerical values for the roots.

In[9] := N [%]
Out[9] = {{x -> -1.1265 - 0.733957 I}, {x -> -1.1265 + 0.733957 I},
        {x -> 0.554934}, {x -> 0.849033 - 1.26694 I},
        {x -> 0.849033 + 1.26694 I}}

Unlike NRoots, Solve returns exact values. Solve returns a list of replacement rules involving integers, rationals, and symbols.

3.3 Simplify

If you end up with a complicated result, you can ask *Mathematica* to simplify it. The function Simplify tries to apply rules to restate a result more simply.

When I ask *Mathematica* to solve the quadratic formula, I obtain a result in form different from what you may have learned in school.

In[10] := Solve[a x^2 + b x + c == 0, x]

$$Out[10] = \left\{\left\{x \to \frac{-\left(\dfrac{b}{a}\right) + \sqrt{\dfrac{b^2}{a^2} - \dfrac{4c}{a}}}{2}\right\},\right.$$

$$\left.\left\{x \to \frac{-\left(\dfrac{b}{a}\right) - \sqrt{\dfrac{b^2}{a^2} - \dfrac{4c}{a}}}{2}\right\}\right\}$$

This result can be stated more succinctly as Simplify tells us.

In[11] := Simplify[%]

$$Out[11] = \left\{\left\{x \to \frac{-b + \sqrt{b^2 - 4 a c}}{2 a}\right\},\right.$$

$$\left.\left\{x \to \frac{-b - \sqrt{b^2 - 4 a c}}{2 a}\right\}\right\}$$

Simplify uses a brute-force approach, and as a result can be slow. Simplify examines each part of an expression to see if it can be simplified by applying a rewrite rule. Every time an expression is transformed, *Mathematica* starts over, checking each part of the new expression, including those subexpressions that it was unable to simplify previously.

3.3.1 Alternatives to Simplify

There are other functions for manipulating algebraic quantities including: Apart, Cancel, Collect, Expand, ExpandAll, ExpandDenominator, ExpandNumerator, and Together.

Below are examples involving some of these functions.

```
In[12] := x /((x + 2)(x - 2))

                  x
Out[12] = ----------------
          (-2 + x) (2 + x)
```

The function Apart transforms a result to its partial fractions.

```
In[13] := Apart[%]

               1           1
Out[13] = ---------- + ---------
          2 (-2 + x)   2 (2 + x)
```

The function Together combines two or more fractions over a common denominator and cancels common factors in the result.

```
In[14] := Together[%]

                  x
Out[14] = ----------------
          (-2 + x) (2 + x)
```

Version 1.2: In version 1.2.1 and earlier versions of *Mathematica*, there was a bug in Together that would cause *Mathematica* to occasionally return the wrong answer when manipulating expressions involving nth roots.

There is a canonical order that *Mathematica* uses to display results. Constants are listed first and then symbols, listed in alphabetical order, with lower-order terms listed first. It is best to get used to this ordering as it is not possible to override it.

In[15] := Expand[(1 + 2y + 3z)^3]

$$Out[15] = 1 + 6\ y + 12\ y^2 + 8\ y^3 + 9\ z + 36\ y\ z +$$

$$36\ y^2\ z + 27\ z^2 + 54\ y\ z^2 + 27\ z^3$$

I collect terms involving the same powers of y by using the function Collect.

In[16] := Collect[%, y]

$$Out[16] = 1 + 8\ y^3 + 9\ z + 27\ z^2 + 27\ z^3 +$$

$$y^2\ (12 + 36\ z) + y\ (6 + 36\ z + 54\ z^2)$$

3.3.2 Trigonometric Expressions

By default, *Mathematica* does not factor or expans trigonometric expressions. For example, Factor does not replace the expression Sin[x]/Cos[x] with Tan[x]. Notice *Mathematica* leaves this expression unchanged.

In[17] := Expand[Sin[x]/Cos[x]]

$$Out[17] = \frac{Sin[x]}{Cos[x]}$$

Trigonometric simplifications are specified in a package called Trigonometry.m. The package includes the functions TrigReduce, TrigFactor, and TrigCanonical. After loading the package, *Mathematica* can simplify the expression.

In[18] := Needs["Algebra'Trigonometry'"]
In[19] := TrigReduce[Sin[x]/Cos[x]]
Out[19] = Tan[x]

Version 2.0 An option called Trig has been added to Expand, Factor, and Simplify. The default value of the option is False for Expand and Factor and True for Simplify.

In[19] := Expand[Sin[x]/Cos[x]', Trig ->True]
Out[19] = Tan[x]

The functions ComplexToTrig and TrigToComplex in the package Trigonometry.m, are for translating expressions between complex exponential form and trigonometric form.

In[20] := `TrigToComplex[Sin[x]]`

$$Out[20] = \frac{-I}{2} (-E^{-I x} + E^{I x})$$

3.3.3 Working with Results with Many Terms

If you are expecting a result involving many terms, you might want to use the Short command to display a shortened representation of a result.

In[21] := `Short[Expand[(x + 2y + 3z)^9]]`

$$Out[21] = x^9 + 18 x^8 y + <<52>> + 19683 z^9$$

The notation <<52>> indicates that there are 52 terms or expressions that are not displayed. This notation not only saves screen space but also time, since printing large expressions can be slow and is usually not especially useful.

Setting the global variable $PrePrint to Short instructs *Mathematica* to call Short before printing the result on the screen.

In[22] := `$PrePrint = Short`
In[23] := `Expand[(x + 2y + 3z)^9]`

$$Out[23] = x^9 + 18 x^8 y + <<52>> + 19683 z^9$$

To see the complete result, type:

In[24] := `Print[%]`

Clear the value of $PrePrint with the command:

In[25] := `$PrePrint =.`

3.4 Summation

In addition to being able to compute the numerical value of a sum, there are definitions in the packages GosperSum.m (version 1.2) and SymbolicSum.m (version 2.0) for computing sums of some algebraic expressions.

Version 1.2: The function GosperSum is named after Bill Gosper.

```
In[26] := Needs["Algebra'GosperSum'"];
In[27] := GosperSum[i^2, {i, n}]
```

$$Out[27] = \frac{n\ (1 + 3n + 2\ n^2)}{6}$$

Version 2.0: The package SymbolicSum adds additional rules to Sum.

```
In[26] := Needs["Algebra'SymbolicSum'"];
In[27] := Sum[i^2, {i, n}]
```

$$Out[27] = \frac{n\ (1 + n)\ (1 + 2\ n)}{6}$$

3.5 Calculus

In addition to being able to do algebra, *Mathematica* can help in doing calculus. There are functions built into *Mathematica* for doing integration and differentiation. The Integrate function takes two arguments: an expression and a variable, i.e.,

$$\text{Integrate}[\textit{expr}, \ x]$$

Macintosh, version 1.2: Make sure to load the package IntegralTables.m with the command Needs["IntegralTables'"] or << IntegralTables.m before attempting to do integration.

Here I ask *Mathematica* for the indefinite integral $\int x^4 \cos x \, dx$.

```
In[28] := Integrate[x^4 Cos[x], x]
```

$$Out[28] = -24\ x\ \text{Cos}[x] + 4\ x^3\ \text{Cos}[x] + 24\ \text{Sin}[x] -$$
$$12\ x^2\ \text{Sin}[x] + x^4\ \text{Sin}[x]$$

Let's integrate $\int (2 + 3x^2)^{-3} dx$.

```
In[29] := Integrate[1/(2 + 3x^2)^3, x]
```

$$Out[29] = \frac{x}{8\ (2 + 3\ x^2)^2} + \frac{3\ x}{32\ (2 + 3\ x^2)} + \frac{3\ \text{ArcTan}\left[\frac{3\ x}{\text{Sqrt}[6]}\right]}{32\ \text{Sqrt}[6]}$$

It is prudent to check the results you obtain. Differentiating this result should return the expression I integrated. Now I use the function D to differentiate the previous result.

In[30] := D[%, x]

$$
Out[30] = \frac{3}{64\left(1 + \dfrac{3x}{2}\right)^2} - \frac{3x^2}{2\,(2 + 3x^2)^3} + \frac{1}{8\,(2 + 3x^2)^2} -
$$

$$
\frac{9x^2}{16\,(2 + 3x^2)^2} + \frac{3}{32\,(2 + 3x^2)}
$$

This result does not look like what I asked *Mathematica* to integrate. With the aid of Simplify, you can see that the result above is equivalent to the expression I integrated.

In[31] := Simplify[%]

$$
Out[31] = (2 + 3x^2)^{-3}
$$

3.5.1 Definite Integrals

It is possible to integrate a function over an interval either symbolically or numerically. First I integrate symbolically and then compute a numerical approximation to the result.

In[32] := Integrate[Exp[x], {x, -1, 1}]

$$
Out[32] = -\left(\frac{1}{E}\right) + E
$$

In[33] := N[%]
Out[33] = 2.3504

Now let us integrate numerically, in other words, compute the area under the curve.

In[34] := NIntegrate[Exp[x], {x, -1, 1}]
Out[34] = 2.3504

In this particular case, I obtain the same result with numerical evaluation of symbolic integration and with numeric integration. Numerical integration can solve some of the problems that symbolic integration cannot. When *Mathematica* cannot solve a problem, it returns your input unevaluated. For example, it does not evaluate $\int_0^1 \sin(\sin x)dx$.

In[35] := Integrate[Sin[Sin[x]], {x, 0, 1}]
Out[35] = Integrate[Sin[Sin[x]], {x, 0, 1}]

NIntegrate returns the numerical value of this definite integral.

In[36] := NIntegrate[Sin[Sin[x]], {x, 0, 1}]
Out[36] = 0.430606

3.5.2 Singular Integrals

Mathematica has been known to make mistakes in evaluating definite integrals. The mistakes tend to arise in cases involving branch cuts or in regions with singularities. Certain measures can be taken to increase the chances of obtaining the correct result. Take, for instance, $\int_{-1}^1 x^{-2} \, dx$.

In[37] := Integrate[1/x^2, {x, -1, 1}]
Out[37] = -2

This negative-valued result should look suspicious since $1/x^2$ is never negative for real x. The problem lies in the fact that that there is a singularity at $x = 0$. Let us now try integrating $1/x^2$ numerically.

Version 1.2: Notice that NIntegrate gives warning messages if, when it subdivides the interval, the result does not converge.

In[38] := NIntegrate[1/x^2, {x, -1, 1}]
            NIntegrate::conv:
                Numerical integral failed to reach specified
                accuracy after 7 recursive subdivisions
                near -0.0164299 for variable number 1.

            NIntegrate::conv:
                Numerical integral failed to reach specified
                accuracy after 7 recursive subdivisions
                near 0.0148201 for variable number 1.
Out[38] = 7727.83

Version 2.0: Unlike version 1.2, in version 2.0 the function `NIntegrate` returns the expression unevaluated.

> *In[38]* := `NIntegrate[1/x^2, {x, -1, 1}]`
>
> $$\hspace{15em} 1$$
> `Power::infy: Infinite expression - encountered.`
> $$\hspace{13.5em} 0$$
> `NIntegrate::inum:`
> `    Integrand ComplexInfinity is not numerical at {x} = {0}.`
> *Out[38]* = `NIntegrate[1/x^2, {x, -1, 1}]`

With `NIntegrate`, you can tell *Mathematica* about singularities. Integrate the function f with singularities at x_{s1}, x_{s2}, ..., x_{sn}, using

> `NIntegrate[f, {x, x0, xs1, xs2, ..., xsn, x1}]`

Notice that *Mathematica* returns a result *closer* to the actual value of $\int_{-1}^{1} x^{-2}\, dx$ when I specify that there is a singularity at $x = 0$. In calculating the integral, `NIntegrate` subdivides the interval.

Version 1.2: *Mathematica* prints more warning messages when I specify that there is a singularity in the interval.

> *In[39]* := `NIntegrate[1/x^2, {x, -1, 0, 1}]`
> `NIntegrate::conv:`
> `    Numerical integral failed to reach specified`
> `    accuracy after 7 recursive subdivisions`
> `    near -11 -3.00859 10 for variable number 1.`
>
> `NIntegrate::conv:`
> `    Numerical integral failed to reach specified`
> `    accuracy after 7 recursive subdivisions`
> `    near -7 -2.51129 10 for variable number 1.`
>
> `NIntegrate::conv:`
> `    Numerical integral failed to reach specified`
> `    accuracy after 7 recursive subdivisions`
> `    near -0.00000734943 for variable number 1.`
>
> `General::stop:`
> `    Further output of NIntegrate::conv`
> `    will be suppressed during this calculation.`
> $$\hspace{10em} 34$$
> *Out[39]* = `9.88619 10`

Version 2.0: Notice that the warning messages in version 2.0 have been improved and `NIntegrate` returns a larger number.

```
In[39] := NIntegrate[1/x^2, {x, -1, 0, 1}]
        NIntegrate::slwcon:
            Numerical integration converging too slowly; suspect
                one of the following: singularity, oscillatory
                    integrand, or insufficient WorkingPrecision.
        NIntegrate::ncvb:
            NIntegrate failed to converge to prescribed accuracy
                after 7 recursive bisections in x near x =
                        -57
            -4.36999 10    .

                    3498
    Out[39] = 1.24066 10
```

Version 1.2: There is a package called `DefiniteIntegrate.m` designed specifically for symbolic evaluation of definite integrals with a singularity in the region of integration.

```
In[40] := Needs["Calculus'DefiniteIntegrate'"]
In[41] := Integrate[1/x^2, {x, -1, 1}]
Out[41] = Infinity
```

MS-DOS Version 1.2: The package `DefiniteIntegrate.m` is not distributed with *Mathematica*.

3.5.3 Multivariate Calculus

Mathematica can do multiple integrals (i.e., integrals involving more than one variable). Here *Mathematica* integrates first with respect to y and the result with respect to x.

```
In[42] := Integrate[x^2 Sin[y], x, y]
                3
            -(x  Cos[y])
    Out[42] = ------------
                3
```

Notice that *Mathematica* does not state the result in terms of constants of integration. So beware! This is not a problem with definite integrals.

The limits of y can be dependent on the value of x. *Mathematica* evaluates integral from the inside out. Specify $\int_0^{\pi/3} \int_0^x x^2 \sin y \; dy \; dx$ as:

In[43] := `Integrate[x^2 Sin[y], {x, 0, Pi/3}, {y, 0, x}]`

$$\text{\textit{Out[43]}} = \text{Sqrt}[3] \; - \; \frac{\text{Pi}}{3} \; - \; \frac{\text{Sqrt}[3] \; \text{Pi}}{18} \; + \; \frac{\text{Pi}}{81}$$

3.6 Limits

The function `Limit` finds the limiting value of the expression *expr* when x approaches x_0.

> `Limit[`*expr*`, x -> `x_0`]`

You can find the limit of $\sin x / x$ as x approaches 0.

In[44] := `Limit[Sin[x]/x, x -> 0]`
Out[44] = 1

Mathematica can also compute the limit when x approaches ∞.

In[45] := `Limit[1/x, x -> Infinity]`
Out[45] = 0

Version 2.0: For discontinuous functions, the limit at a particular point can depend on the direction from which you approach the point. Take for instance $1/x$. If x approaches 0 from below (a negative value) then $1/x$ approaches $-\infty$. Setting the option `Direction` to 1 instructs *Mathematica* to find the limit from below or a value less than the limiting value.

In[46] := `Limit[1/x, x -> 0, Direction -> 1]`
Out[46] = `-Infinity`

Setting the option `Direction` to -1 instructs *Mathematica* to find the limit from above or a value greater than the limiting value.

In[47] := `Limit[1/x, x -> 0, Direction -> -1]`
Out[47] = `Infinity`

3.7 Series

Power-series expansions can approximate functions. Here I obtain the power-series expansion for $\cos x$ about the point $x = 0$, up to order x^9.

```
In[48] := Series[Cos[x], {x, 0, 9}]

                  2    4     6      8
                 x    x     x      x                10
Out[48] = 1  -  --  + -- - --- + ----- + O[x]
                 2    24   720   40320
```

The term $O[x]^n$ represents a term of order x^n. In other words, the series listed above has terms that are less than or equal to some constant times x^{10} for x near 0.

To determine the value of this power series at $x = 0.004$, I must first "normalize" the power series, i.e., eliminate the O[x] term.

```
In[49] := cosSeries = Normal[%]

                  2    4     6      8
                 x    x     x      x
Out[49] = 1  -  --  + -- - --- + -----
                 2    24   720   40320
```

A rule replaces a variable with a value. With the notation /., *Mathematica* computes the value of cosSeries, applying the rule x -> 0.004 which replaces all occurrences of x with the value 0.004. Note that /. x -> 0.004 does not set x equal to 0.004 nor cosSeries equal to 0.999992, unless you write cosSeries = cosSeries /. x -> 0.004.

```
In[50] := cosSeries /. x -> 0.004
Out[50] = 0.999992
```

Instead of looking up an expansion in a book of tables or computing it yourself, you can ask *Mathematica* to compute the power-series expansion for a function.

3.8 Solving Differential Equations

The function DSolve was added to *Mathematica* in version 1.2 to enable users to solve differential equations. With DSolve, specify a differential equation or set of differential equations as well as a dependent variable and an independent variable.

```
DSolve[eqn, y[x], x]
DSolve[{eqn₁, eqn₂, ..., eqnₙ}, y[x], x]
DSolve[{eqn₁, eqn₂, ..., eqnₙ}, {y1[x], y2[x], ...}, x]
```

Here I instruct *Mathematica* to solve the differential equation:

$$y''(x) + y'(x) + y(x) = 0$$

```
In[51] := DSolve[y''[x] + y'[x] + y[x] == 0, y[x], x]

                        ((-1 - Sqrt[-3]) x)/2
Out[51] = {{y[x] -> E                          C[1] +

              ((-1 + Sqrt[-3]) x)/2
          E                          C[2]}}
```

The solution is in terms of the undetermined coefficients C[1] and C[2].

DSolve can solve a single differential equation, a set of differential equations, or a differential equation with boundary conditions.

```
In[52] := DSolve[{y'[x] + y[x] == 0, y'[0] == 2}, y[x], x]

                  -2
Out[52] = {{y[x] -> --}}
                  x
                  E
```

For differential equations that cannot be solved with DSolve, you might try finding a numerical solution with RungeKutta, a function defined in *Mathematica* version 1.2 in the package RungeKutta.m, in the directory NumericalMath or NDSolve in version 2.0.

3.9 Summary

In this chapter, you have seen how to manipulate an algebraic expression, solve a polynomial equation, solve simultaneous equations, integrate, differentiate, obtain a power-series expansion, and solve a differential equation. Many of the functions described in this chapter are listed in the following table. This is just a small set of the symbolic functions built into *Mathematica*.

Function	Description
Apart [*expr*]	Gives the partial fractions for a rational expression
Cancel [*expr*]	Cancel common factors in *expr*
Collect [*expr*, *x*]	Collect together terms involving the same power of x
Expand [*expr*]	Expand out products and positive integer powers in *expr*
ExpandAll [*expr*]	Expand out products and positive integer powers in all subexpressions of *expr*
ExpandDenominator [*expr*]	Expand the denominator
ExpandNumerator [*expr*]	Expand the numerator
Factor [*poly*]	Factors a polynomial over the rational numbers
Simplify [*expr*]	Simplifies *expr*
Short [*expr*]	Prints an abbreviated form of *expr*
Together [*expr*]	Puts an expression over a common denominator
TrigExpand [*expr*]	Expands powers and products of Sin and Cos
TrigFactor [*expr*]	Tries to write sums of trig functions as products
TrigReduce [*expr*]	Writes trig function of multiple angles as sum of products of trig functions of that angle
ComplexToTrig [*expr*]	Writes complex exponentials as trig functions
TrigToComplex [*expr*]	Writes trig functions in terms of complex exponentials
Sum [*f*, {*i*, *imax*}]	Evaluates a sum. For symbolic sums, load SymbolicSum.m (version 2.0)
GosperSum [*f*, {*i*, *min*, *max*}]	Evaluates a symbolic sum (version 1.2)
Limit [*expr*, {*x* -> x_0}]	Finds the limiting value of an expression
Integrate [*expr*, *x*]	Evaluates $\int expr\, dx$
Series [*f*, {*x*, x_0, *n*}]	Generates a power-series expansion of f about $x = x_0$ to order $(x - x_0)^n$
DSolve [*eqn*, *y[x]*, *x*]	Solves the differential equation *eqn* for *y[x]*
DSolve [{e_1, e_2}, *y[x]*, *x*]	Solves the set of differential equations e_1 and e_2 for *y[x]*

3.10 Exercises

This problem set gives you practice with *Mathematica*'s symbolic or algebraic capabilities.

3.1 Have *Mathematica* solve the following equations.

   (a) $x^2 + 2x + 1 = 0$

   (b) `Solve[ax^2 + bx + c == 0, x]`

   (c) $x + y = 5$ and $2x + 6y = 23$

3.2 (a) Make a list of the polynomial factorizations of $1 - x^n$.

      `Do[Print[1 - x^n, " == ", Factor[1 - x^n]], {n, 2, 9}]`

   (b) Do you see a pattern?

   (c) Predict the factorization for $1 - x^{11}$. Use *Mathematica* to check your prediction.

3.3 Use `Apart` to find the partial fractions for:

   (a) $x/(x^2 + 5x + 6)$

   (b) $(2x + 7)/(x^3 + 3x^2 + 3x + 1)$

3.4 Use functions in the package `Trigonometry.m` (or `Expand` and `Factor` with the option `Trig->True` in version 2.0) to simplify the expressions.

   (a) $\cos x \cos y + \sin x \sin y$

   (b) $\cos x \sin y + \cos y \sin x$

   (c) $e^{-ix} + e^{ix}$

3.5 (a) Using `Array`, generate the 2 by 2 matrix m.

      `Clear[b]`

      `m = Array[b, {2, 2}]`

   (b) Find the inverse and transpose of this matrix m.

   (c) Create the matrix n.

      `Clear[c]`

      `n = Array[c, {2, 2}]`

   (d) Calculate the values of m n and m . n. Examine the results and describe how they differ.

3.6 Integrate the quantity $1/(x^3+1)$ with respect to x. Use the D function to differentiate the result you obtained. Without using the function `Simplify`, show that the result you obtain when differentiating is equivalent to $1/(x^3 + 1)$.

Hint: See section 3.3.1 entitled *Alternatives to Simplify* on page 49.

3.7 Use *Mathematica* to compute the exact values of these integrals.

(a) $\int_0^1 \int_0^{\sqrt{1-x}} xy^2 \, dy \, dx$

(b) $\int_0^1 \int_0^{\sqrt{x}} ye^{x^2} \, dy \, dx$

3.8 Using `Series`, obtain the power-series expansion about $x = 0$ for the following expressions:

(a) e^x

(b) $1/(1 - x)$

(c) $1/(1 - x)^2$

(d) $f(x)$

3.9 See if you can experimentally discover rational expressions having the following power-series expansions. (This problem was taken from the chapter *"Computer-based Symbolic Mathematics for Discovery"* by K. D. Lane et al in the book *The Influence of Computers and Informatics on Mathematics and its Teaching*, Cambridge University Press, 1986, p. 146. [Churchhouse])

(a) $1 - x + x^2 - x^3 + x^4 - x^5 + \ldots$

(b) $1 + 2x + 4x^2 + 8x^3 + 16x^4 + 32x^5 + \ldots$

(c) $1 + 2x + 3x^2 + x^3 + 2x^4 + 3x^5 + x^6 + 2x^7 + 3x^8 + \ldots$

(d) $1 + 2x + 3x^2 + 2x^3 + x^4 + 2x^5 + 3x^6 + 2x^7 + x^8 + 2x^9 + \ldots$

3.10 *Mathematica* cannot integrate all expressions. For example, when you give *Mathematica* the following expression, it returns unevaluated.

$$\int_{-.2}^{.2} \frac{1}{1 + \sin^2 \sqrt{\pi^2 + x}} \, dx$$

Using a power-series expansion, approximate the integrand about $x = 0$. Use this expansion to calculate an approximation to the definite integral.

3.11 Use the function DSolve, available in version 1.2 and later releases of *Mathematica*, to solve each of the following differential equations:

(a) $y'(x) - y(x)\tan x = x$

(b) $y'(x) + y(x)\tan x = \sec x$

(c) $y'(x) = y(x)$ with the boundary condition $y'(0) = 1$

Note: The first argument to DSolve can be a list of equations.

(d) Vibration of a beam: $\frac{d^4 y}{dx^4} - k^4 y = 0$

(e) $y'(x)y(x) + x^2 = x$

Graphics

The graphical capabilities of *Mathematica* have contributed greatly to its success. The graphics primitives are versatile. Using *Mathematica*, you can plot functions and data in two and three dimensions, produce contour and density plots, and draw arbitrary figures and objects.

Mathematica makes decisions when producing a plot, such as how frequently to sample a function, where to position the axes and tick marks, what range of values to display, and how to shade or color the graph. This chapter describes how to make plots and how to influence the choices that *Mathematica* makes when producing graphics.

Except where noted, all plots in this chapter were produced using version 2.0.

4.1 Two-Dimensional Plots

Let me start by using `Plot` to make a two-dimensional graph of a function of one variable. The `Plot` command takes at least two arguments, an expression, *expr*, and a range. The range is a triplet (list of three elements): the variable in the expression, x, a minimum value, x_{min}, and a maximum value, x_{max}.

> `Plot[`*expr*`, {`x`, `x_{min}`, `x_{max}`}]`

The following command produces a graph of the parabola $x^2 + 5x + 6$ for x in the range $[-10, 5]$ (see figure 4.1). The semicolon at the end of the line suppresses the output line, *Out[n]* = -Graphics-, which would otherwise appear.

> *In[1]* := `Plot[x^2 + 5x + 6, {x, -10, 5}];`

Not only can *Mathematica* plot functions that have finite value, but it can also plot functions which approach ∞ or functions with singularities. Consider $\tan x$.

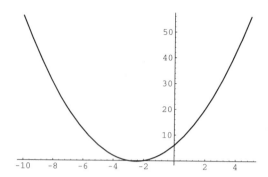

Figure 4.1: A plot of the parabola $x^2 + 5x + 6$.

Near $\pi/2 + n\pi$ for integer n, $\tan x$ approaches $\pm\infty$. None-the-less, *Mathematica* has no trouble plotting $\tan x$ (see figure 4.2).

In[2] := Plot[Tan[x], {x, 0, 10}];

As a side effect of connecting all points sampled, *Mathematica* draws approximations to the asymptotes for $\tan x$.

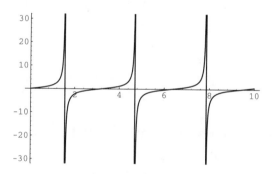

Figure 4.2: A plot of $\tan x$.

Mathematica does not always show the entire range of a plot. How does *Mathematica* select what to display? It displays the region in which the function is "interesting." Notice the plot of $\tan x$ shows the function in the range from -30 to 30. Outside this range, $\tan x$ is rather monotonous.

As another example, the plot of $\sin(x)/x$ generated with

In[3] := Plot[Sin[x]/x, {x, -20, 20}];

does not include the maximum value of the function, i.e., the point at which the function crosses the y-axis (see figure 4.3).

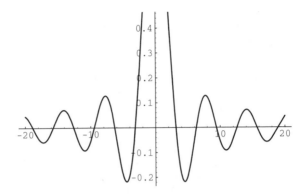

Figure 4.3: A plot of $\sin(x)/x$.

4.2 Options

When *Mathematica* plots a graph, it has to make many choices. The decisions it makes depend on the value of *options*. By using `??Plot` or the command `Options`, you can see all the options for the `Plot` function along with their default values.

```
In[4] := Options[Plot]
                                    1
Out[4] = {AspectRatio -> -----------, Axes -> Automatic,
                            GoldenRatio
          AxesLabel -> None, AxesOrigin -> Automatic,
          AxesStyle -> Automatic, Background -> Automatic,
          ColorOutput -> Automatic, Compiled -> True,
          DefaultColor -> Automatic, Epilog -> {}, Frame -> False,
          FrameLabel -> None, FrameStyle -> Automatic,
          FrameTicks -> Automatic, GridLines -> None, MaxBend -> 10.,
          PlotDivision -> 20., PlotLabel -> None, PlotPoints -> 25,
          PlotRange -> Automatic, PlotRegion -> Automatic,
          PlotStyle -> Automatic, Prolog -> {}, RotateLabel -> True,
          Ticks -> Automatic, DefaultFont :> $DefaultFont,
          DisplayFunction :> $DisplayFunction}
```

Options can be specified in any order after the required arguments.

$$\text{Plot}[expr, \{x, x_{min}, x_{max}\}, options]$$

Options are specified by giving the name of the option together with its value. An option is a rule of the form *OptionName -> OptionValue*, where *OptionName* is the name of the option and *OptionValue* is the value it is assigned. If an option is not specified, the default value is used.

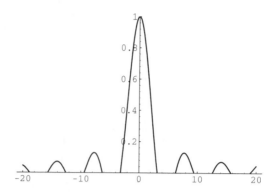

Figure 4.4: A plot of $\sin(x)/x$ in the range [0, 1].

To plot the function `Sin[x]/x` in the range [0, 1], designate {0, 1} for the option `PlotRange` (`PlotRange -> {0, 1}`).

In[5] := `Plot[Sin[x]/x, {x, -20, 20}, PlotRange -> {0, 1}];`

Note: Figure 4.4 may not be identical with what you see on your screen when you enter the input associated with *In[5]*. PostScript laser printers tend to be more accurate than *Mathematica*'s built-in PostScript interpreter.

Mathematica shows all values it sampled when the `PlotRange` is set to `All`. See figure 4.5 for the plot of $\sin(x)/x$ with `PlotRange` set to `All`.

In[6] := `Plot[Sin[x]/x, {x, -20, 20}, PlotRange -> All];`

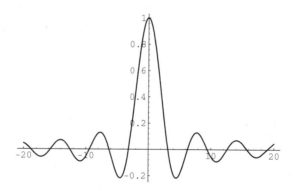

Figure 4.5: A plot of $\sin(x)/x$ with the option `PlotRange` set to `All`.

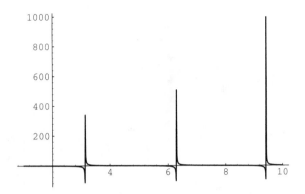

Figure 4.6: A plot of cot x with the option `PlotRange` set to `All`.

Be aware that when a function assumes a large range of values in an interval, setting `PlotRange` to `All` may not produce the effect you desire. Try making a plot of cot x using the command:

In[7] := Plot[Cot[x], {x, 1, 10}, PlotRange -> All];

The plot in figure 4.6 shows all values *Mathematica* sampled. Though the function cot x assumes all values between $-\infty$ and ∞, you might not think so from this plot.

4.2.1 Adaptive Sampling

How does *Mathematica* figure out what a function looks like? *Mathematica* takes a prescribed number of equally spaced samples. The number of samples is given by the value of the option `PlotPoints`. For a two-dimensional plot, the default number of points sampled is 25.

In[8] := PlotPoints /. Options[Plot]
Out[8] = 25

Mathematica uses an adaptive sampling algorithm to determine when and where to sample a function in addition to the above equally spaced points. *Mathematica* looks at three consecutive points along the curve. *Mathematica* then computes the angle between the line from the first point to the second point and the line from the second point to the third point. If the angle is close to 180 degrees, the line segments are drawn. Otherwise each of the intervals is subdivided until lines are drawn in each interval or an interval has been subdivided at most by the value of the option `PlotDivision`. So a section with a large curvature is sampled more frequently than a flat section of a function. Page 17 of the book *Exploring Mathematics with Mathematica* by Theo Gray and Jerry Glynn [Gray] contains a

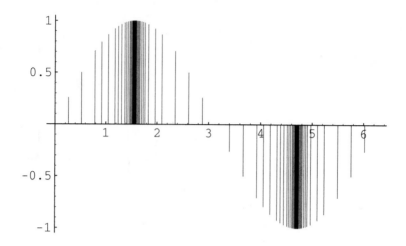

Figure 4.7: A graph showing the values that *Mathematica* uses in producing a plot of $\sin x$.

plot showing the values that *Mathematica* uses in producing a plot of $\sin x$ (see figure 4.7). The following input produces this plot.

```
In[9] := test = Plot[Sin[x], {x, 0, 2Pi},
            DisplayFunction -> Identity];
In[10] := Show[
              Graphics[{
                  Thickness[0.001],
                  Map[
                      Line[{{#[[1]], 0}, #}]&,
                      Nest[First, test, 4]
                  ]
              }],
              Axes -> Automatic
          ];
```

Let me give you an idea of how this code works. The statement labeled with *In[9]*, produces the plot of $\sin x$ but does not render it on the screen because the option DisplayFunction is set to Identity (see section 4.8.1 on page 85). The statement labeled with *In[10]*, generates a line from the x-axis to each point included in a line segment along the curve. Then these line segments are displayed together with a set of axes. (This code uses graphics primitives that are described in section 4.9 on page 87 and pure functions, described in chapter 12 on page 203.)

Though the adaptive-sampling algorithm can produce quite reasonable plots with a minimum number of sample points, it can also produce poor renditions.

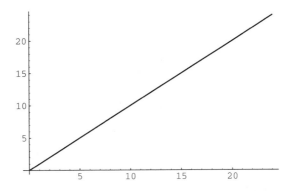

Figure 4.8: A plot of the curve $y = x + \sin(2\pi x)$, which is identical to the plot of the line $y = x$.

4.2.2 Plot Aliasing

If *Mathematica* samples a plot too infrequently, the plot may show the wrong function – an "aliased" version of the desired one.

Consider the curve $y = x + \sin 2\pi x$. Here are a list of the 25 initial sample points computed by *Mathematica*.

```
In[11] := Table[{x, x + Sin[2Pi x]}, {x, 0, 24}]
Out[11] = {{0, 0}, {1, 1}, {2, 2}, {3, 3}, {4, 4}, {5, 5}, {6, 6},
          {7, 7}, {8, 8}, {9, 9}, {10, 10}, {11, 11}, {12, 12},
          {13, 13}, {14, 14}, {15, 15}, {16, 16}, {17, 17},
          {18, 18}, {19, 19}, {20, 20}, {21, 21}, {22, 22},
          {23, 23}, {24, 24}}
```

Notice that these points lie along the line $y = x$. When you enter the following command, *Mathematica* draws the graph shown in figure 4.8.

```
In[12] := Plot[x + Sin[2Pi x], {x, 0, 24}];
```

Sampling either at a lower or at a higher frequency, you can obtain a better rendition of the function (see figure 4.9).

```
In[13] := Plot[Sin[2Pi x] + x, {x, 0, 24}, PlotPoints -> 20];
In[14] := Plot[Sin[2Pi x] + x, {x, 0, 24}, PlotPoints -> 50];
```

4.2.3 Changing the Plot Style

Using the option PlotStyle you can change the thickness, color, and style of a curve.

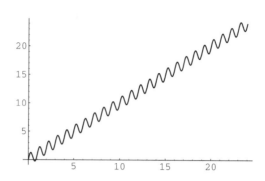

Figure 4.9: A plot of curve $y = x + \sin(2\pi x)$ with the option `PlotPoints` set to 20 or to 50.

The graphics primitive `Thickness` controls the width of a line or curve. The argument of `Thickness` is the ratio of the line width of the graph to the width of the entire plot.

$$\text{Plot}[\text{expr},\ \text{range},\ \text{PlotStyle -> Thickness}[x]]$$

Specifying the `Thickness` as 0.125 makes the curve 1/8th of the width of the entire plot (see figure 4.10).

In[15] := Plot[x, {x, 0, 10}, PlotStyle -> Thickness[0.125]];

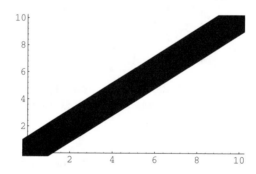

Figure 4.10: The line $y = x$ is 1/8th of the width of the entire plot.

The default setting for the `Plot` function is `Thickness[0.004]`. The graphics primitive `AbsoluteThickness`, added to version 2.0, enables you to specify the absolute or actual thickness of a line measured in printers points. One inch is approximately equal to 72 points.

With the function `RGBColor`, you can specify a color. `RGBColor` takes three arguments. The first argument is the amount of red, the second argument the amount of green, and the third argument the amount of blue. These arguments must be numbers between 0 and 1, where 1 indicates a presence of the color and

0 the absence. The three numbers need not add up to one. The package Colors.m contains definitions for a wide variety of colors. You can use GrayLevel if you want a shade of gray. The argument of GrayLevel is a number between 0 and 1, where 0 is for black and 1 is for white.

$$Plot[\text{\textit{expr}, \textit{range}, PlotStyle -> RGBColor[\textit{red}, \textit{green}, \textit{blue}]]}$$
$$Plot[\text{\textit{expr}, \textit{range}, PlotStyle -> GrayLevel[\textit{x}]]]}$$

The function Dashing makes a dashed line where successive drawn and undrawn segments are of length d_1, d_2, ..., the arguments of the function. The lengths are specified in terms of a fraction of the total width of the plot.

$$Plot[\text{\textit{expr}, \textit{range}, PlotStyle -> Dashing}[\{d_1, d_2, \ldots\}]]$$

Unlike most of the other graphics options, PlotStyle can be assigned several values, e.g., a thick dashed line. These values must be specified in a list of lists. Why a list of lists? To allow you the flexibility of drawing several curves in different styles (see section 4.3 on page 74).

$$Plot[\text{\textit{expr}, \textit{range}, PlotStyle -> } \{\{value_1, value_2, \ldots\}\}]$$

The following input produces a graph of $\sin x$ in a thick orange dashed line. See figure 4.11, but use your imagination to visualize the curved dashed line in orange.

```
In[16] := Plot[Sin[x], {x, 0, 2Pi},
        PlotStyle -> {
            { Thickness[0.01],
              RGBColor[0.8, 0.2, 0.2],
              Dashing[{0.04}]
            }
        }
    ];
```

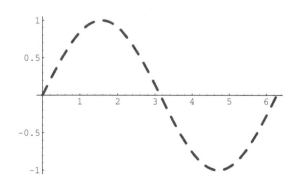

Figure 4.11: You can change the style of a curve.

4.3 Graphing Several Curves

With `Plot` and many of the other graphics commands, you can plot an expression or several expressions on one graph. The first argument to `Plot` specifies the function or functions to plot. When the first argument is a list, *Mathematica* plots more than one expression on a single graph

$$Plot\,[\{eqn_1,\ eqn_2,\ \dots\},\ range]$$

The following command produces a graph of e^x and x^e (see figure 4.12).

In[17] := `Plot[{E^x, x^E}, {x, 0, 5}];`

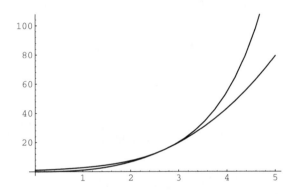

Figure 4.12: A graph of e^x and x^e.

By looking at the plot, you cannot tell if the lines cross or just touch one another. Varying the style of the lines helps distinguish several curves. The following input draws the function e^x with a thick dashed line and x^e with a thinner magenta line, which is drawn in gray in figure 4.13.

In[18] := `Plot[{E^x, x^E}, {x, 0, 5},`
`        PlotStyle -> {`
`            {Thickness[0.02], Dashing[{0.05, 0.03}]},`
`            {Thickness[0.01], RGBColor[1, 0, 1]}`
`        }`
`    ];`

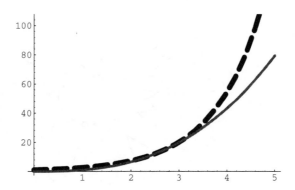

Figure 4.13: You can distinguish the curves e^x and x^e when they are drawn in different styles.

4.4 Parametric Plots

The function `ParametricPlot` plots a parametric curve, a function where the values of x and y are stated in terms of another variable such as t or time.

$$\texttt{ParametricPlot}[\{f_x[t],\ f_y[t]\ \},\ \{t,\ t_{min},\ t_{max}\}]$$

By default, a plot will be drawn so that the ratio of the height to width of the graph is 1/GoldenRatio. No axes are drawn when I set the option Axes to None (see figure 4.14).

```
In[19] := ParametricPlot[
             {
                 4 Cos[-11 t/4] + 7 Cos[t],
                 4 Sin[-11 t/4] + 7 Sin[t]
             },
             {t, 0, 8Pi},
               Axes -> None
         ];
```

By setting the option `AspectRatio` to `Automatic`, the graph is drawn to scale, i.e., one unit in the x-direction is drawn the same size as one unit in the y-direction (see figure 4.15).

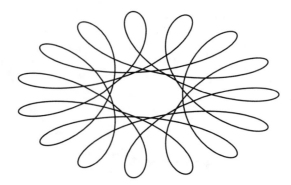

Figure 4.14: By default the ratio of the height to width of a graph is **1/GoldenRatio**.

Figure 4.15: Setting the **AspectRatio** to **Automatic** makes one unit in the x-direction equal to one unit in the y-direction.

```
In[20] := ParametricPlot[
           {
               4 Cos[-11t/4] + 7 Cos[t],
               4 Sin[-11t/4] + 7 Sin[t]
           },
           {t, 0, 8Pi},
           AspectRatio -> Automatic,
           Axes -> None
       ];
```

Wouldn't setting the **AspectRatio** to 1 produce the plot shown in figure 4.15? Yes, in this case it would since this graph is symmetric. Setting the **AspectRatio** to 1 instructs *Mathematica* to draw a plot such that the width is the same size as the height.

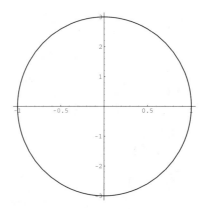

Figure 4.16: Setting the `AspectRatio` to 1 draws an ellipse as a circle.

By setting the `AspectRatio` to 1, an ellipse $x^2 + y^2/3 = 1$ appears to be a circle. Notice the scale on the x-axis is different from the scale on the y-axis in figure 4.16.

```
In[21] := ParametricPlot[{Cos[t], 3 Sin[t]}, {t, 0, 2Pi},
            AspectRatio -> 1];
```

4.5 More Options

Wolfram Research would like people to use *Mathematica* to produce graphs for journals and text books. Because many publications like to have frames drawn around figures, *Mathematica* includes the option `Frame` (Framed in version 1.2) to draw a frame around a two-dimensional plot (see figure 4.17). I have used this option in several places in this book.

```
In[22] := Plot[BesselJ[0, x], {x, 0, 20}, Frame -> True];
```

 Version 2.0: The option `GridLines` can be used to simulate graph paper (see figure 4.18).

```
In[23] := Plot[Exp[-x^2] Cos[20x], {x, -2, 2},
            GridLines -> Automatic];
```

4.6 Three-Dimensional Plots

With the function `Plot3D`, you can produce a three-dimensional plot. Its arguments are an expression and ranges for two variables.

Plot3D[*expr*, {*x*, x_{min}, x_{max}}, {*y*, y_{min}, y_{max}}, *options*]

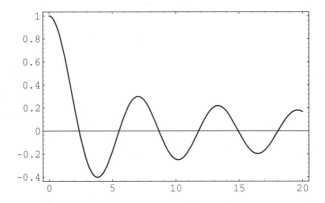

Figure 4.17: A framed plot of the Bessel function, J_0.

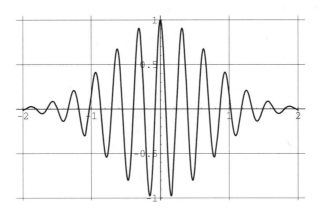

Figure 4.18: In version 2.0, the option `GridLines` can be used to simulate graph paper.

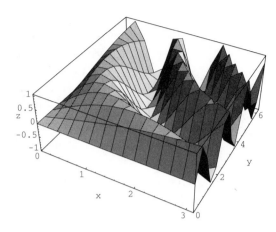

Figure 4.19: Using `Plot3D`, you can draw three-dimensional plots.

The following command plots $\sin xy$. I labeled the axes to help you figure out the orientation of the graph.

```
In[24] := Plot3D[Sin[x y], {x, 0, Pi}, {y, 0, 2Pi},
            AxesLabel -> {"x", "y", "z"}];
```

Unlike the two-dimensional plotting functions, the three-dimensional functions do not use an adaptive sampling algorithm. Instead points are sampled regularly across a rectangular grid. The number of points sampled is determined solely by the value of the option `PlotPoints`. By default, `PlotPoints` is 15, so 15^2 or 225 samples are taken. You can change `PlotPoints`, but be aware that the more points you sample, the longer it will take for *Mathematica* to render the graph.

You can view the graph from a different point of view by changing the option `ViewPoint`. The `ViewPoint` is specified relative to a bounding box whose sides are of length 1 and whose center is at {0, 0, 0}. The following table is intended to help you figure out the argument to `ViewPoint` that corresponds to a specific orientation.

ViewPoint	Position
{1.3, -2.4, 2}	Default setting
{0, -2, 0}	Directly in front
{0, 0, 2}	Directly above
{-2, -2, 0}	Left-hand corner
{2, -2, 0}	Right-hand corner
{0, -2, 2}	In front and from above

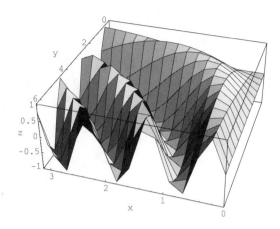

Figure 4.20: You can view a three-dimensional graphic from a different point of view, $\{-1,\ 3,\ 2\}$, using the option `ViewPoint`.

With the `Show` function you can redraw a plot, combine plots, or change the options on a plot, but you cannot change the number of points sampled. Specifying the `ViewPoint` as $\{-1,\ 3,\ 2\}$ turns the graph around so the back right corner is now on the left (see figure 4.20).

> *In[25]* := `Show[%, ViewPoint -> {-1, 3, 2}];`

Notebook Front End: To select a `ViewPoint`, I recommend using the *3D ViewPoint Selector*. With it you can select a value for `ViewPoint` interactively by positioning a cube with the mouse and/or scroll bars (see figure 4.21).

4.7 Color Plots

When the option `Lighting` is set to `True`, a graph created with `Plot3D` is shown in color using simulated illumination. The surface is treated as a white sheet of plastic lit by three colored lights: a red one, a green one, and a blue one. The command `Options[Plot3D]` returns the color and positions of these light sources, among other things. Rather than sorting through all the options, I use the command /. (the shorthand notation for `ReplaceAll`) to obtain the default value of the `LightSources`. (See section 7.3 on page 143 for a description of `ReplaceAll`.)

> *In[26]* := `LightSources /. Options[Plot3D]`
> *Out[26]* = `{{{1., 0., 1.}, RGBColor[1, 0, 0]},`
>   `{{1., 1., 1.}, RGBColor[0, 1, 0]},`
>   `{{0., 1., 1.}, RGBColor[0, 0, 1]}}`

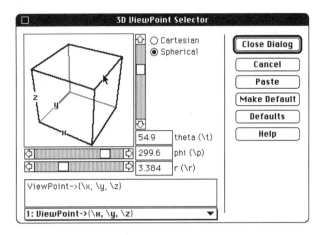

Figure 4.21: Notebook Front End users can select a value for **ViewPoint** interactively.

 Version 1.2: By default, three-dimensional plots are rendered in gray scale. A color plot is rendered when the option Lighting is set to True.

Instead of setting this option for each plot individually, you can change the default value of Lighting by using SetOptions in the current session. You can change the default value of an option with SetOptions.

> SetOptions [*plotFunction*, *OptionName* -> *NewDefaultValue*]

The following command sets the default value of the option Lighting to True.

> *In[27]* := SetOptions[Plot3D, Lighting -> True]

This option stays in effect until you quit and restart *Mathematica*, until you use SetOptions to change the option, or when you explicitly override it in a command. If you want to change the default values permanently, put a call to SetOptions in the file init.m, which is loaded automatically each time *Mathematica* starts up.

 Version 2.0: To render color three-dimensional plots automatically, the default value of the option Lighting has been changed to True in version 2.0.

4.8 Working with Data

The functions ListPlot and ListPlot3D are intended for plotting data. The argument to ListPlot can be a list of values, in which case, the x coordinates for each point are taken to be 1, 2, ... The argument can also be a list of pairs of values $\{x_n, f[x_n]\}$.

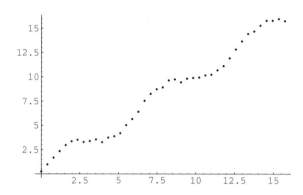

Figure 4.22: The function `ListPlot` plots data.

```
ListPlot[{f[1], f[2], ...}];
ListPlot[{{x₁, f[x₁]}, {x₂, f[x₂]}, ...}];
```

Before I show you `ListPlot`, I'll generate some data. As you learned in section 2.10 on page 32, the function `Random` gives a uniformly distributed pseudorandom real number in the range 0 to 1. In other words, if you call `Random` repeatedly, you should get a sequence of real numbers in the range (0, 1) for which all the values are statistically independent of one another. The following command generates a list of data with an upward trend, seasonal variation, and random fluctuations.

```
In[28] := bookData = N[
            Table[{x, Sin[x] + x + 0.5 Random[ ]},
            {x, 0, 5Pi, Pi/8}]
          ];
```

The function `ListPlot` plots the data (see figure 4.22).

```
In[29] := dataplot = ListPlot[bookData];
```

Besides functions for plotting data, *Mathematica* includes functions for fitting a curve to data, i.e., `Fit` and `InterpolatingPolynomial`. The function `InterpolatingPolynomial` returns a polynomial in a variable, *var*, which fits a list of data exactly.

```
InterpolatingPolynomial[data, var]
```

The data can be a list of values, {f[1], f[2], ...} or a list of pairs of values, {{x₁, f[x₁]}, {x₂, f[x₂]}, ...}.

The function `Fit` finds a least-squares fit to a list of data as a linear combination of functions of one or more variables.

```
Fit[data, functions, vars]
```

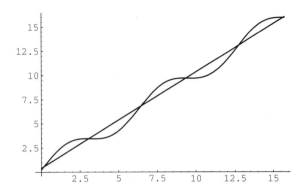

Figure 4.23: A plot of two curves generated using `Fit`.

For example, to fit a straight line, for the second argument, *functions*, specify a list consisting of a constant term, 1, and a linear term, x.

In[30] := `trend = Fit[bookData, {1, x}, x]`
Out[30] = $0.41624 + 0.995895\ x$

The second argument to `Fit` need not be a list of polynomials. By specifying `Sin[x]` and `Cos[x]` in the second argument, the result will be a curve that has a cyclic component.

In[31] := `seasonal = Fit[bookData, {1, x, Cos[x], Sin[x]}, x]`
Out[31] = $0.293631 + 0.995332\ x - 0.0383023\ Cos[x] + 1.03599\ Sin[x]$

As you saw here, `Fit` can be used to fit a list of values $\{f[1],\ f[2],\ \ldots\}$. It can also be used to fit pairs of values $\{\{x_1,\ f[x_1]\},\ \{x_2,\ f[x_2]\},\ \ldots\}$. For fitting two or more variables, you must specify more values of variables.

$$\{\{x_1,\ y_1,\ \ldots,\ f[x_1, y_1, \ldots]\},\ \{x_2,\ y_2,\ \ldots,\ f[x_2, y_2, \ldots]\},\ \ldots\}$$

The third argument to `Fit`, can be a list of values. For example, if you want to fit a surface, you would specify the third argument as a list of two variables.

`Fit[data, functions, {x, y}]`

Getting back to `bookData`, now I'll make a graph with the curves called `trend` and `seasonal` (see figure 4.23).

In[32] := `Plot[{trend, seasonal}, {x, 0, 5Pi}];`

Using the `Show` command, I plot the curves together with the data (see figure 4.24).

In[33] := `Show[dataplot, %];`

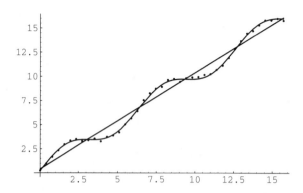

Figure 4.24: A plot of the data together with the least-squares fit curves.

If you find it difficult to see the data, you can enlarge the points by specifying a larger point size with the option PlotStyle. The following command increases the size of the data points and color them blue (see figure 4.25).

```
In[34] := ListPlot[bookData,
            PlotStyle -> {
                PointSize[0.02],
                RGBColor[0, 0, 1]
            }
        ];
```

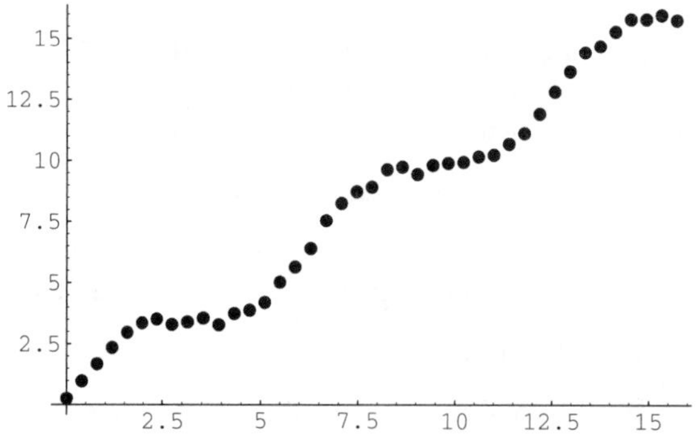

Figure 4.25: Increasing the size and coloring the data can make them more visible.

You can also connect the points by setting the option PlotJoined to True. However, it is not possible to both change the point size and connect the points because PlotJoined -> True tells *Mathematica* not to draw the points, just to draw lines connecting them.

Notice in the input line labeled *In[34]*, the value for PlotStyle is a list, not a list of lists (unlike Plot or ParametricPlot). ListPlot can plot only one set of data at a time. All data are plotted in the same style. Calling ListPlot several times with different style selections produces several plots. You can overlay or display these plots together by using Show. If you want to draw large points and connect them, produce two plots (one with large points and the other with lines between the points) and display them together using Show.

4.8.1 Suppressing Plots

Rendering plots can be time consuming. If you don't care to see the intermediate plots, you can suppress a plot by setting the option DisplayFunction to Identity. The code below plots the data in each row of a matrix in a different color: the first row in red, the second in green, and the third in blue. It also connects the data in each row of the matrix.

```
In[35] := myMatrix = Table[Random[ ], {3}, {5}]
Out[35] = {{0.27965, 0.22935, 0.975964, 0.969621, 0.699101},
           {0.233519, 0.933654, 0.790343, 0.058217, 0.784854},
           {0.929661, 0.876221, 0.969667, 0.479995, 0.292922}}

In[36] := ListPlot[myMatrix[[1]],
            PlotStyle -> RGBColor[1,0,0],
            PlotJoined -> True,
            DisplayFunction -> Identity];
In[37] := ListPlot[myMatrix[[2]],
            PlotStyle -> RGBColor[0,1,0],
            PlotJoined -> True,
            DisplayFunction -> Identity];
In[38] := ListPlot[myMatrix[[3]],
            PlotStyle -> RGBColor[0,0,1],
            PlotJoined -> True,
            DisplayFunction -> Identity];
```

Using Show with DisplayFunction set to $DisplayFunction, I display the three data plots on one graph (see figure 4.26).

```
In[39] := Show[%, %%, %%%, DisplayFunction :> $DisplayFunction];
```

I used a delayed rule (:>) instead of an immediate rule (->) to specify the value of DisplayFunction because I want *Mathematica* to replace DisplayFunction with the value of $DisplayFunction at the time it displays the plot. Suppose I wanted to save the PostScript for the graph in a file. I could change the value of $Display to a file name and then re-execute input line 39 (by typing In[39]). See section 7.3 on page 143 for a discussion of the difference between a delayed rule and an immediate rule and when it is advantageous to use each.

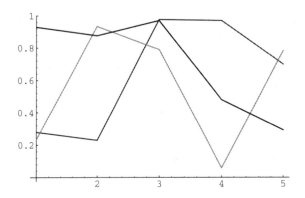

Figure 4.26: Each row of a matrix of data is connected and drawn in a different color.

4.8.2 Three-Dimensional Data

ListPlot3D does not plot points, like its two-dimensional counterpart. ListPlot3D produces a three-dimensional surface from a rectangular array of heights (see figure 4.27).

```
In[40] := array = Table[x + Sin[x] + Random[ ], {10}, {x, 1, 10}];
In[41] := ListPlot3D[array];
```

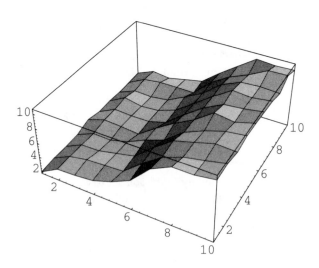

Figure 4.27: ListPlot3D produces a three-dimensional surface.

ListContourPlot generates a contour plot from a rectangular array of heights. Unfortunately, contour levels are not labeled (see figure 4.28). However, in version 2.0, levels are shaded according to their height (see figure 4.29).

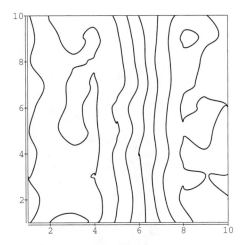

Figure 4.28: `ListContourPlot` generates a contour plot from a rectangular array of data. (This plot was produced using version 1.2.)

In[42] := `ListContourPlot[array];`

`ListDensityPlot` generates a density plot from a rectangular array of heights (see figure 4.30).

In[43] := `ListDensityPlot[array];`

4.9 Graphics Building Blocks

Besides being able to plot functions and data in two- and three-dimensions, *Mathematica* provides the capability of drawing lines, dots, circles, disks, and polygons, with the functions `Graphics` and `Graphics3D`. *Mathematica* makes the ratio of the height to the width of the graph 1/GoldenRatio. If you want a circle not to look like an ellipse, specify the option `AspectRatio -> Automatic`. Then the graph

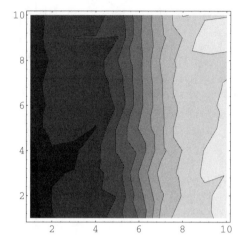

Figure 4.29: `ListContourPlot` generates a contour plot from a rectangular array of data. In version 2.0, the levels are shaded.

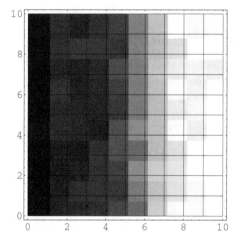

Figure 4.30: `ListDensityPlot` generates a density plot from a rectangular array of data.

will be drawn to scale; one unit in the x-direction will be drawn the same size as one unit in the y-direction (see figure 4.31).

```
In[44] := Show[
            Graphics[{
                PointSize[0.05], Point[{0, 0}], Point[{1, 0}],
                Line[{{0,0}, {1, 0}}],
                Circle[{0,0}, .1],
                Circle[{1,0}, .1]
            }],
            AspectRatio -> Automatic
        ];
```

Figure 4.31: Besides functions, *Mathematica* can plot graphic objects, e.g., circles, lines, and dots.

Let us use graphics primitives to plot some points in three-space. By default, *Mathematica* positions a box around a three-dimensional graphic (see figure 4.32).

```
In[45] := Show[
            Graphics3D[
                Point[{1, 2, 3}]
            ]
        ];
```

Here I use `Table` to generate four data points in three-dimensional space. How can you plot the points?

```
In[46] := pts = Table[Random[ ], {4}, {3}]
Out[46] = {{0.795805, 0.236892, 0.270907},
           {0.876979, 0.644491, 0.369225},
           {0.33574, 0.911239, 0.406997},
           {0.457561, 0.217424, 0.725987}}
```

Map the function `Point` onto the data points. (You will learn more about `Map` in section 6.11 on page 130.)

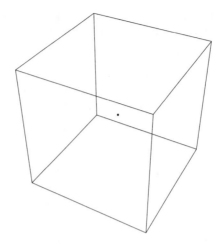

Figure 4.32: *Mathematica* positions a box around the point in three-space.

In[47] := graphicPts = Map[Point, pts]
Out[47] = {Point[{0.795805, 0.236892, 0.270907}],
        Point[{0.876979, 0.644491, 0.369225}],
        Point[{0.33574, 0.911239, 0.406997}],
        Point[{0.457561, 0.217424, 0.725987}]}

Now I use Show and Graphics3D to display the data. Because the default size of points is rather small, I enlarge the points so that you can see them better (see figure 4.33). *Note*: To change the size or color of graphic objects, specify the size and color *before* specifying the graphic objects.

In[48] := Show[
            Graphics3D[{
                PointSize[0.03],
                graphicPts
            }]
        ];

Set the option Axes to Automatic to draw tick marks on the edges of the three-dimensional box enclosing the data (see figure 4.34).

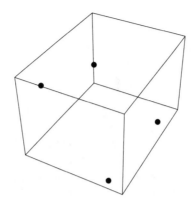

Figure 4.33: With **Show** and **Graphics3D** you can display points in three-space.

```
In[49] := Show[
            Graphics3D[{
                PointSize[0.03],
                graphicPts
            }],
            Axes -> Automatic
        ];
```

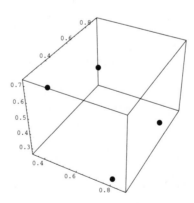

Figure 4.34: Set the option **Axes** to **Automatic** to draw tick marks on the edges of the three-dimensional box enclosing the data.

4.9.1 Converting to Graphic Objects

If you ask for the **InputForm** of a plot, you will see the graphic objects specifying the plot.

```
In[50] := simplePlot = Plot[x, {x, 0, 24}];


In[51] := InputForm[simplePlot]
Out[51] = Graphics[{{Line[{{0., 0.}, {1., 1.}, {2., 2.}, {3., 3.},
                {4., 4.}, {5., 5.}, {6., 6.}, {7., 7.}, {8., 8.},
                {9., 9.}, {10., 10.}, {11., 11.}, {12., 12.},
                {13., 13.}, {14., 14.}, {15., 15.}, {16., 16.},
                {17., 17.}, {18., 18.}, {19., 19.}, {20., 20.},
                {21., 21.}, {22., 22.}, {23., 23.}, {24., 24.}}]}},
        {PlotRange -> Automatic, AspectRatio -> GoldenRatio^(-1),
        DisplayFunction :> $DisplayFunction,
        ColorOutput -> Automatic, Axes -> Automatic,
        AxesOrigin -> Automatic, PlotLabel -> None,
        AxesLabel -> None, Ticks -> Automatic, GridLines -> None,
        Prolog -> {}, Epilog -> {}, AxesStyle -> Automatic,
        Background -> Automatic, DefaultColor -> Automatic,
        DefaultFont :> $DefaultFont, RotateLabel -> True,
        Frame -> False, FrameStyle -> Automatic,
        FrameTicks -> Automatic, FrameLabel -> None,
        PlotRegion -> Automatic}]
```

A plot is just a graphics object. This might help you to understand why you can redisplay or combine plots using the command Show. Notice you can use Show to combine a plot with graphic objects without having to render each plot separately (see figure 4.35).

```
In[52] := Show[
            Plot[Sin[x], {x, 0, 3Pi}, DisplayFunction -> Identity],
            Graphics[{
                PointSize[0.05],
                Table[Point[{n Pi, 0}], {n, 0, 3}]
            }],
            DisplayFunction -> $DisplayFunction
        ];
```

This technique can also be used to combine three-dimensional plots.

4.10 Labels

Graphics options give users the ability to show information along with a graph. The graphics packages distributed with *Mathematica* can be a good source of information on how to use graphics options.

Let me show you a few of the options for labeling plots. Using the options Ticks, you can control the placement and labels for tick marks (see figure 4.36).

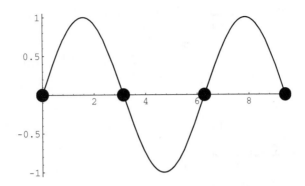

Figure 4.35: With **Show** you can combine a plot and graphic objects.

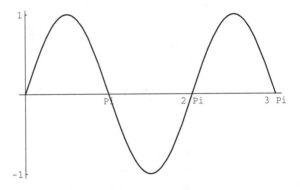

Figure 4.36: A plot of sin x with tick marks at increments of π.

```
In[53] := Plot[Sin[x], {x, 0, 3Pi},
             Ticks -> {{0, Pi, 2Pi, 3Pi}, {-1, 0, 1}}
         ];
```

Labels can span more than one line; \n starts a new line. You can vary the size of the text with FontForm (see figure 4.37).

Version 1.2: FontForm takes three arguments in version 1.2. The *fontname* can be set equal to: Bold, Italic, or Plain.

FontForm[*expr*, "*fontname*", *size*]

```
In[54] := Plot3D[Sin[x y], {x, 0, 3Pi}, {y, 0, Pi},
            PlotLabel ->
                FontForm[
                    "Plot3D[Sin[x y],\n {x, 0, 3Pi}, {y, 0, Pi}]",
                    "Bold",
                    15
                ]
            ];
```

Version 2.0: FontForm was enhanced in version 2.0 so that you can specify a name of a font, as well as a style, e.g., Helvetica-Oblique. The arguments have been changed slightly. The second and third arguments should be enclosed in braces.

```
FontForm[expr, {"fontname", size}]
```

```
In[55] := Plot3D[Sin[x y], {x, 0, 3Pi}, {y, 0, Pi},
            PlotLabel ->
                FontForm[
                    "Plot3D[Sin[x y],\n {x, 0, 3Pi}, {y, 0, Pi}]",
                    {"Courier-Bold", 15}
                ]
            ];
```

Macintosh Version 1.2: The PostScript Interpreter on the Macintosh displays text in only one size. So, though the command above instructs *Mathematica* to enlarge the label, if you use a Macintosh, to see the change, you must print the graphic.

Macintosh: To save graphics so you can put them in other documents such as page layout programs, you can copy the graphic using <*command*>-c and then select *Convert Clipboard* from the *Edit* menu or type <*command*>-m. The graphic can be saved in several different formats. If it is a PostScript graphic you can save it as an encapsulated PostScript file (EPSF) to place it in other programs or you can save it as an Adobe Illustrator file so that you can open it in Illustrator and modify the graphic. You can also save the PostScript code for the graphic in a file.

The Text command allows you to position a label centered at the coordinate specified by the second argument of the function (see figure 4.38).

```
In[56] := Show[
            Graphics[{
                Circle[{0,0}, 1],
                Text["Circle", {0,0.5}]
            }],
            AspectRatio -> Automatic
        ];
```

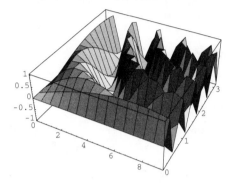

Figure 4.37: With FontForm, you can specify the size and style of text.

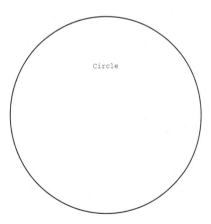

Figure 4.38: With the command Text, you can place text anywhere on a graph.

4.11 Graphics Packages

There are half a dozen graphics packages distributed with *Mathematica* version 1.2, and a dozen and a half graphics packages distributed with version 2.0. A list of the packages and the functions included in each package is included in appendix D on page 323. Look them over as they might contain functions that would be of use to you.

4.11.1 Rotating Graphics

In the package Shapes.m there are definitions of various geometric shapes as well as a function to rotate a graphic. Remember to load the package before calling functions defined in it.

There are several different ways to load a package. I prefer loading packages with Needs. If a package is already loaded, Needs will not reload it.

> *In[57]* := Needs["Graphics'Shapes'"]

or

> *In[57]* := << Graphics/Shapes.m

 or on a Macintosh

> *In[57]* := << Shapes.m

After loading the package, you can use anything defined in it. The following command plots a torus (see figure 4.39).

> *In[58]* := Show[Graphics3D[Torus[ ]]];

 Version 1.2: Torus is a Graphics3D object. To plot a torus, do not call Graphics3D; just say Show[Torus[ ]].

You can change the point from which you view an object with ViewPoint. Alternatively, you can rotate the object by using RotateShape, which rotates the object about the origin. The arguments to RotateShape are a graphics object and three Euler angles. In figure 4.40, the torus is rotated by $5\pi/6$.

> *In[59]* := Show[RotateShape[Graphics3D[Torus[ ]], 0, 5 Pi/6, 0]];

4.12 Animation

With several versions of *Mathematica* it is possible make an animation or movie. In version 1.2, the MS-DOS, Macintosh, NeXT, Sun (under SunView), and Silicon

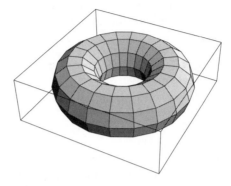

Figure 4.39: The package `Shapes.m` contains definitions for many shapes.

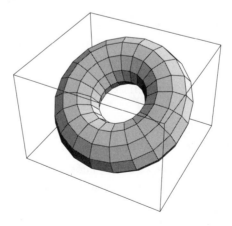

Figure 4.40: You can rotate the object using `RotateShape`.

Graphics versions of *Mathematica* support animations. In version 2.0, animations also run under X-windows.

 Unix and MS-DOS: The package `Graphics/Animation.m` contains functions for generating an animation or movie. The following command generates a movie of the function $\sin xy$ where the ranges for x and y are specified in terms of a third parameter t.

```
In[60] := Needs["Graphics`Animation`"]
In[61] := MoviePlot3D[
            Sin[x y], {x, 0, t/2}, {y, 0, t},
            {t, 1, 6, 3/4}
          ]
```

 Notebook Front End: Create a series of plots with `Do` or `Table`. Then select the cell bracket in the right margin that contains all the plots. To start the animation, type the *<control>* key and the letter y (*<control>-y*) together or select the item *Animate Selected Graphics* from the *Graph* menu. With the keys numbered 1 - 9 or by depressing the mouse on the buttons labeled with two ∧'s or two ∨'s in the status window (in the lower left corner of the window on a Macintosh and the lower right corner on a NeXT), you can control the speed at which frames are shown. See the *Macintosh* and *NeXT User's Manual for Mathematica* for more about animations.

```
In[62] := coverAnimation =
            Table[
              Plot3D[Sin[x y], {x, 0, t/2}, {y, 0, t},
                PlotPoints -> 9, Ticks -> None
              ],
              {t, 1, 6, 3/4}
            ]
```

 Version 2.0: With the function `GraphicsArray`, you can display an array of graphics plots.

```
GraphicsArray[{g₁, g₂, ...}]
GraphicsArray[{{g₁,₁, g₁,₂, ...}, ...}]
```

Figure 4.41, which is also displayed on the cover of this book, shows the frames in the animation specified in *In[62]*. It was generated with the following command.

```
In[63] := Show[
            GraphicsArray[coverAnimation],
            GraphicsSpacing -> 0.2
          ];
```

Figure 4.41: With the function `GraphicsArray`, you can create an array of graphics plots.

4.13 PostScript

PostScript is a page description language frequently used in laser printers. When producing a plot, *Mathematica* generates the PostScript and then uses a PostScript interpreter to display the graph on your screen.

The function `Display` is used to display a file on the screen. `Display` takes two arguments, *channel* and *graphic*. `Display` writes graphics in PostScript form. The first argument to `Display` is *channel*.

> `Display[`*channel*`,` *graphic*`]`

By default, *channel* is set to display graphics on the screen. In the Notebook Front End version, *channel* is set to `stdout`. For X-windows, *channel* is set to `!x11ps`. For SunView users, *channel* is set to `!sunps`. The notation `!`*command* instructs *Mathematica* to run the external command *command*. When *channel* is a file name, the PostScript is written to the file.

> *In[64]* := `expCos = Plot[Exp[-x^2] Cos[20x], {x, -2, 2}];`
> *In[65]* := `Display["graphicsForThisBook.ps", expCos]`

The file `graphicsForThisBook.m` contains hundreds of lines. To give you an idea of the contents of the file, I have printed the first few and the last few lines in the file.

```
In[66] := !!graphicsForThisBook.ps
         %!
         %%Creator: Mathematica
         %%AspectRatio: 0.61803
         MathPictureStart
         /Courier findfont 10  scalefont  setfont
         % Scaling calculations
         0.5 0.238095 0.305404 0.297915 [
         [(-2)] 0.02381 0.3054 0 2 Msboxa

                .

                .

         0.97619 0.30177 lineto
         Mfstroke
         grestore
         grestore
         % End of Graphics
         MathPictureEnd
```

Before sending this file to a PostScript printer, you will need to tack on the header of definitions. The command psfix, which is included in the *Mathematica* distribution on MS-DOS and Unix-based computers, generates the header.

Notebook Front End: To see the PostScript code for a *Mathematica* graphic, click on the graphic to select it. Then unformat the cell by simultaneously depressing the <*command* > key and the letter t or by deselecting the menu item Formatted. With the Notebook Front End, you can copy the graphic to the clipboard and then paste it into another program or into a file. If you save the graphic as an Encapsulated PostScript text file, then *Mathematica* tacks on the header of definitions so that the file can be printed on a PostScript printer.

4.14 Summary

This chapter shows some of the graphics capabilities: how *Mathematica* plots a function in two dimensions, how it plots several functions on one graph, and how to vary the style of a plot. You have also seen the three-dimensional plotting capabilities as well as some of the graphics functions defined in packages distributed with *Mathematica*.

Function	Description	Added to 2.0
Plot[*expr*, *range*]	Generates a 2D plot	
Plot[{*expr*₁, *expr*₂, ...}, *range*]	Plots several 2D functions on one graph	
ParametricPlot[{f_x, f_y}, {t, t_0, t_1}]	Produces a parametric plot	
Plot3D[*expr*, {x, x_0, x_1}, {y, y_0, y_1}]	Generates a 3D plot	
ListPlot[{y_1, y_2, ...}]	Plots a list of values	
ListPlot3D[*array*]	Plots a surface representing an array of height values	
ListContourPlot[*array*]	Generates a contour plot from an array of height values	
ListDensityPlot[*array*]	Generates a density plot from an array of height values	
ContourPlot[*expr*, {x, x_0, x_1}, {y, y_0, y_1}]	Generates a contour plot	
DensityPlot[*expr*, {x, x_0, x_1}, {y, y_0, y_1}]	Makes a density plot	
Show[*graphics*]	For displaying or redisplaying graphics	
Graphics[*prim*]	For representing 2D graphical images	
Graphics3D[*prim*]	For representing 3D graphical images	
GraphicsArray[{g_1, g_2, ...}]	Represents an array of graphic objects	yes

The following table describes some of the graphics options.

Function	Description	Example	Added to 2.0
Axes	Where axes should be drawn	Axes -> {2, 1}	
Axes	How axes should be drawn	Axes -> Automatic	yes
AxesOrigin	Where axes should cross	AxesOrigin -> {2, 1}	yes
AspectRatio	The ratio of height to width for a plot	AspectRatio -> Automatic	
Background	Background color	Background -> GrayLevel[.7]	yes
Frame	To draw a frame around a plot	Frame -> True	yes
Framed	Only in version 1.2	Framed -> True	
GridLines	To specify grid lines	GridLines -> Automatic	yes
Ticks	Tick marks for axes	Ticks -> {{0, 5}, None}	
AxesLabel	Labels for the axes	AxesLabel -> {"x","y","z"}	
FontForm	Print expr in specified font and style (version 1.2)	FontForm[expr, "Bold", 9]	
FontForm	Print expr in specified font and style	FontForm[expr, {"Bold", 9}]	yes
PlotLabel	The label for a graph	PlotLabel -> "My Graph"	
Dashing	A dashed line	Dashing[{.04,.02}]	
GrayLevel	A shade of gray 0 for black, 1 for white	GrayLevel[0.5]	
RGBColor	A color	RGBColor[0, 1, 1]	
Thickness	The thickness of a line	Thickness[0.001]	
PlotJoined	To join the points	PlotJoined -> True	
DisplayFunction	A function to apply to graphics to display/suppress them	DisplayFunction -> Identity	
Lighting	Use simulated lighting Renders a surface in color	Lighting -> True	

4.15 Exercises

This problem set is designed to give you practice with the graphical capabilities of *Mathematica*.

4.1 Plot the function $\sin x$ for x in the range $[0, 6\pi]$.

- Change the `AspectRatio` so that the width of the plot is twice its height.
- Using `PlotLabel`, give the plot the label or title `"Sin[x]"`.
- With the option `AxesLabel`, label the x axis `"x"` and the y axis `"y"`.
- Using `Axes` in version 1.2 or `AxesOrigin` in version 2.0, instruct *Mathematica* to draw axes that cross at $x = 2\pi, y = 1/2$.

4.2 (a) Estimate the roots of the equation by plotting the function
$$f(x) = 2x^3 - 7x^2 - 17x + 10$$
for x in the range [-6, 6]. Verify your estimations by using `Solve`.

   (b) Find the two roots of the Bessel function $J_0(x)$ (`BesselJ[0,x]`) to 3 places of accuracy for x in the range [8,12] by graphing the function.

4.3 As I mentioned in section 2.13 on page 37, `FindRoot` uses Newton's method to obtain a root, given a function and a starting value. Produce a plot that contains the curve $y = J_0(x)$ (`BesselJ[0, x]`) for x from 0 to 20 together with seven line segments. Each of those line segments should have endpoints $\{x, J_0(x)\}$ and $\{r, 0\}$ where r is the root returned by `FindRoot` when given the starting value x.

4.4 In problem 10 on page 62, you were asked to find a power-series expansion to approximate the expression

$$\frac{1}{1 + \sin^2 \sqrt{\pi^2 + x}}$$

about $x = 0$. Use `Normal` to convert the power-series expansion to an expression, which you can then plot. Draw a graph of the function together with its approximation. Looking at the graph, determine in what region the power-series expansion closely approximates the expression.

4.5 (a) Plot the function $x^2 + \cos 22x$ for x in the range $[-5, 5]$.

   (b) Make the same graph with the option `PlotPoints` set to 70 (`PlotPoints->70`). Notice any difference between this plot and the plot in problem 5a?

4.6 With a Spirograph set, you can make graphs that look like flowers. Make the following polar plots.

(a) `ParametricPlot[ {Cos[4t] Cos[t], Cos[4t] Sin[t]}, {t, 0, 2Pi}, AspectRatio -> Automatic];`

(b) `ParametricPlot[ {Cos[7t] Cos[3t], Cos[7t] Sin[3t]}, {t, 0, 2Pi}, AspectRatio -> Automatic];`

(c) `ParametricPlot[ {Cos[7t] Cos[11t], Cos[7t] Sin[11t]}, {t, 0, 2Pi}, AspectRatio -> Automatic];`

4.7 Load the package `Polyhedra.m`, which contains the definitions of various polyhedra. Plot a regular icosahedron (a 20-faced polyhedron) and a stellated icosahedron (an icosahedron with a tetrahedron on each of its faces). With the stellation ratio of 3, you get the "great stellated dodecahedron," which has 12 star-shaped intersecting faces.

(a) `Show[Graphics3D[Icosahedron[ ]]];`

(b) `Show[Graphics3D[Stellate[Icosahedron[ ], 3]], Boxed -> False];`

4.8 If you have a color monitor, produce a color plot of $\sin xy$ by setting the option `Lighting` to `True` (`Lighting->True`). In version 2.0 this option is selected by default.

4.9 (a) Simulate a color density plot of $\sin xy$ by producing a graph with the command `Plot3D` and viewing it from directly overhead.

(b) Change the viewpoint to simulate viewing the graph from farther away. What sad effect does this have on the colors in the graph?

4.10 Make a contour plot and a density plot of $\sin xy$.

4.11 Plot a set of concentric ellipses $x^2 + 2y^2 = n$ using `ContourPlot`.

4.12 (a) Make a list of the first 10 primes, i.e., 2, 3, 5, ... Plot them by using `ListPlot`.

(b) Specify the option `PlotJoined->True` when calling `ListPlot` to connect the points.

(c) Fit a quadratic (second-degree) polynomial to the points.

(d) Plot the polynomial obtained in part 12c.

(e) Display the curve together with the points representing the primes.

(f) Compute the error, i.e., the difference between the points and the curve.

(g) Plot the error together with the data and the curve.

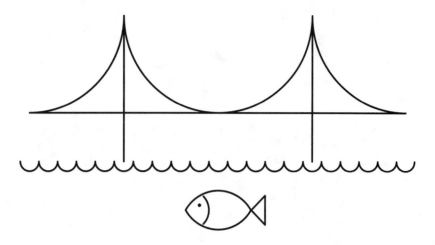

Figure 4.42: A fish swimming under the Golden Gate Bridge drawn using *Mathematica*.

4.13 Use graphics primitives such as Point, Disk, Line, and Circle to draw a face or a fish (see figure 4.42).

4.14 Using the graphics primitives, draw a triangle. Color the vertices red, green and blue. Connect the midpoints of the sides to form another triangle. Color its vertices magenta, yellow, and cyan (mixtures of the colors of the vertices of which each is the midpoint).

4.15 Draw colored dots along the curve $\cos x^2 - x \sin x$ so that it appears to vary in color from blue to green.

5

In[1]:=Plot[Sin[x], {x, 0, 2Pi}];

Getting Around with *Mathematica*

By now you should feel comfortable using *Mathematica* interactively to perform numerical computations, to manipulate expressions, and to plot functions and data. This chapter describes how to get around with *Mathematica*: how to change the width of the printout, reference previous inputs and results, edit inputs, results, and definitions, access the on-line help when entering input, suppress results, and time your calculations.

5.1 Setting the Page Width

When you results are too wide to fit on the screen or on a page, consider resetting the width of a page. With the following commands you can reset the page width of your *Mathematica* output so that no more than 45 characters will be printed on a line.

or

```
ResetMedium[PageWidth -> 45]
```
                                                                    Version 1.2

```
SetOptions[$Output, PageWidth -> 45]
```
                                                                    Version 2.0

5.2 Listing Previous Commands and Results

Sometimes it may be useful to see previous inputs and outputs from a session.

Notebook Front Ends: Because users most commonly want to reenter or edit the previous input line, if you simultaneously depress the *<command>* key and the letter L, *Mathematica* retypes the previous input line. Try it out.

MS-DOS: The previous input line may be recalled by pressing the up arrow key.

More generally, the `Recall` function returns one or more input lines.

Macintosh: Before you can recall input lines by using `Recall`, load the package `Edit.m`. (`Edit.m` is included in version 1.2 but is not distributed with version 2.0.)

Version 1.2: Here I request input lines 1, 2, and 3. These inputs are shown in section 1.5 on *Mathematica Dialogs*, on page 8.

> *In[100]* := `Recall[1, 2, 3]`
>
>   10
> *Out[100]* = `In[1]  :> 5`
>
>   1/10
>   `In[2]  :> Out[1]`
>
>   `In[3]  :> % + a`

Version 2.0: The function `InString`, like `Recall`, returns the input associated with one or more input lines. However, unlike `Recall`, the input is returned as a string.

> *In[101]* := `InString[{1, 2, 3}]`
> *Out[101]* = `{5^10, %1^(1/10), % + a}`

You can re-execute input line number n by typing `In[n]`. Here I re-execute input line 1.

> *In[102]* := `In[1]`
> *Out[102]* = `9765625`

You can get a listing of all your inputs for the current session by typing `??In`. This gives a list of all the rules associated with the symbol `In`.

>   `??In`

Similarly, you can get a listing of all results or output for the current session by typing

>   `??Out`

It is not possible to save the output of the operator `??` in a file.

Version 1.2: Input lines can be saved to the file `math.record` by loading the package `Utilities/Record.m`.

You can also save a *Mathematica* session by using the `Save` command. The command `Save` writes the rules associated with one or more symbols to a specified file. (If the file already exists, the contents are not destroyed. The new information is appended to the file.) Here I save all our inputs and results in a file called `mySession.m`.

In[103] := Save["mySession.m", In, Out]

Invoking !! followed by the name of a file displays the contents of that file. The exclamation marks, !!, must be the first characters in the line. To look at the contents of the file mySession.m, type:

!!mySession.m

MS-DOS: You can save an entire session up to the time you save it by hitting the function key **F10** and *<return>*. By default, it is saved in the file math.log unless you type in a different file name before hitting *<return>*.

5.3 Editing (Unix and MS-DOS)

The functions Edit, EditIn, and EditDefinition (EditDef in version 1.2) are intended for editing expressions, input, and definitions using your favorite editor. After you exit from the editor, the contents of the editor are taken as input to *Mathematica*.

NeXT: These editing functions are not available from the Notebook Front End.

On Unix systems, *Mathematica* invokes the editor specified by the environment variable $EDITOR, which defaults to the visual editor vi.

The command Edit[*expr*] invokes an editor on the result of *expr*. For example Edit[Expand[(x + 2y)^2]] puts you in the editor with the expression:

x^2 + 4 x y + 4 y^2

The command EditIn[*n*] invokes the editor on the input line *n*. For example, EditIn[100] invokes the editor with the buffer containing the expression specified by *In[100]*, as shown on page 108.

Recall[1, 2, 3]

The commands EditDefinition[*function*] in version 2.0 and EditDef[*function*] in version 1.2 invokes an editor on the definition of *function*.

For example, if you had defined nThirty as shown on page 29, the command EditDefinition[nThirty] in version 2.0 (EditDef[nThirty] in version 1.2) starts up the editor with the following lines in the buffer:

```
(* nThirty *)
Clear[nThirty]
nThirty/:  nThirty[x_] := N[x, 30]
```

Remember (* and *) are delimiters for comments that are ignored by *Mathematica*. The command Clear[nThirty] clears all values associated the symbol nThirty. The next line states the current definition of nThirty. The notation nThirty/: indicates that the definition nThirty[x_] := N[x, 30] is associated with the symbol nThirty. See section 9.5 and 9.6 on page 172 for more on /: (TagSet).

Upon exiting the editor, the contents of the buffer are taken as input to *Mathematica*.

5.4 Asking for On-Line Help (MS-DOS and Unix)

You can access the on-line help even when you are in the middle of writing some code. For example, suppose you want the power-series expansion of the cosecant of x. If you type the incomplete expression Series[Csc[x], and then a carriage return, immediately followed by ?Series and a carriage return, *Mathematica* prints the usage statement for Series and then retypes the input. This works only if your input is incomplete, i.e., if *Mathematica* cannot evaluate the input before the carriage return.

```
In[104] := Series[Csc[x],
           ?Series
           Series[f, {x, x0, n}] generates the power series expansion
               for f about the point x = x0 to order (x - x0)^n.
               Series[f, {x, x0, nx}, {y, y0, ny}] successively
               finds series expansions with respect to y, then x.

In[104] := Series[Csc[x],
```

Being able to see a usage statement along with your input should help you understand how to complete your input.

5.5 A Space Can Mean *Or*

A space is interpreted as *or* when used with the ? operator. Here I ask for the commands that begin with the letter X or the letter Z.

```
In[105] := ?X* Z*
           Xor    ZeroTest    Zeta
```

5.6 List of Symbols

The output of the ? operator cannot be saved. It just prints on your screen. While the command ?W* prints symbols that begin with the letter W, the function Names returns a list of strings containing those symbols. Output from Names can be referenced, manipulated, or saved.

In[106] := Names ["W*"]
Out[106] = {Which, While, WorkingPrecision, Write, WriteString,
        WynnDegree}

5.7 Different Ways to Invoke a Function

You can call a function by enclosing its argument in brackets. This is known as *prefix* notation.

In[107] := N[Sqrt[2]/2]
Out[107] = 0.707107

In *postfix* notation, the expression to the left of // is taken as the argument of the function to its right.

In[108] := Sqrt[2]/2 // N
Out[108] = 0.707107

Like Unix pipes, you can string together several commands. The output of one command can be used as input to another command.

In[109] := "W*" // Names // Length
Out[109] = 6

5.8 Suppressing Output

Operations followed by a semicolon are performed, but the output is not printed. Though the output is suppressed, % refers to the result.

In[110] := BesselJ[0, 5.7];

In[111] := %
Out[111] = 0.05992

Using semicolons, you can list several commands on a single line. In this case, the output of the first two commands is suppressed (and cannot be recalled with %).

In[112] := x = 5; y = x + 37; y
Out[112] = 42

5.9 Timing

The Timing function prints out the amount of CPU time taken to perform a function. Knowing the timing of one calculation may be useful in predicting the time required to perform other similar types of calculations. Here I compute π

to 500 decimal places. Because I put a semicolon after the command, the output, i.e., the expansion of π, is suppressed, and in its place, *Mathematica* returns the value Null.

In[113] := Timing[N[Pi, 500];]
Out[113] = {4.48333 Second, Null}

Note: Timing *Mathematica* calculations can be somewhat tricky. For instance, if you ask for a decimal expansion of π to 400 places after asking for a decimal expansion of π to 500 places, it will take no time because *Mathematica* saves the most accurate value of π calculated in a session.

5.10 Interrupting Calculations

It is impossible for *Mathematica* to predict how long a calculation will take. However, it is sometimes possible to interrupt a calculation by pressing the *<command>* key along with "." on a Macintosh or NeXT, by depressing the *<control>* key along with the letter C (control-C) on a Unix system, or by depressing the *<control >* key together with *<break>* key under MS-DOS. When the calculation is interrupted, the following options are available to you:

Command	Description	Added to 2.0
Continue	Continue the calculation	
Step	Take one step	
Trace	Show what *Mathematica* is doing	
Inspect	Inspect the current state	yes
Abort	Abort the calculation	
Quit	Exit *Mathematica* completely	

The speed with which a calculation is interrupted depends upon how the code was written. Some parts of the code interrupt much more quickly than other parts. Not all operations are interruptible.

5.11 Global Variables

Certain values are stored in variables whose names start with $. These variables, which are used by *Mathematica*, are known as global variables. For example, the global variable $Line is set to the number of the current input line.

In[114] := $Line
Out[114] = 114

The global variable $Version is a string that indicates the version of *Mathematica* is being used.

In[115] := $Version
Out[115] = Macintosh 2.0 (June 21, 1991)

The global variable $VersionNumber is a real number that indicates the version number of *Mathematica* begin used.

In[116] := $VersionNumber
Out[116] = 2.

5.12 Special Forms

Mathematical symbols and other special forms are aliases for functions built into *Mathematica*. On the inside back cover of this book is a table of the special forms that can be used as input to *Mathematica*.

5.13 Summary

In this first part of the book, you have seen how to use *Mathematica* interactively. This chapter described how to reference, edit, and save previous input and output, how to ask for on-line help in the middle of your input, how to suppress output, how to time a calculation, and how to interrupt a calculation that is in progress. The following table lists many of the functions described in this chapter.

Command	Description	Added to 2.0
Recall[*n*]	List the rule for input line *n*.	
InString[*n*]	Input line *n* (a string).	yes
??In	List all inputs for the current session.	
??Out	List all results or output for the current session	
Save["*file*", *s*]	Save rules associated with the symbol *s* in *file*.	
!!*file*	Display the contents of *file*	
Edit[*expr*]	Allows one to edit *expr*	
EditIn[*n*]	Allows one to edit input line *n*.	
EditDef[*f*]	Allows one to edit rules attached to the symbol *f*.	
Names["*string*"]	Gives a list of the symbols which match *string*.	
arg // *f*	Postfix notation equivalent to *f*[*arg*].	
expr;	The semicolon suppresses output of *expr*.	
Timing[*expr*]	Returns the CPU time taken to evaluate *expr*.	

5.14 Exercises

The following exercises should give you experience with the capabilities presented in this chapter.

5.1 List the input lines in your current session by using `??In`. Note: The `??` must be the first two characters on the line.

5.2 Find all the commands that contain the word `Matrix` or `Power` in their names. Are there any duplicates in the list?

5.3 (a) Determine how much CPU time it takes to invert a 3-by-3 matrix on the computer you are using. Use postfix notation (i.e., specify the timing function to the right side of its argument).

   (b) Find out how much CPU time it takes to invert a 10-by-10 matrix.

5.4 (a) Use the following command to ask *Mathematica* to compute five factorials.

        `Do[Print[i!], {i, 5}]`

   (b) Now change the 5 to a 250 and re-execute the command. Interrupt the command. Then abort the calculation.

      Notebook Front End: Remember you can instruct *Mathematica* to retype the previous input line by typing <*command*>–L.

Part II:
Programming

If there is not a function in *Mathematica* to satisfies your needs, you can write your own. The general form of a function definition is:

$f[arg1\_, arg2\_, \ldots] := body$

Below is the definition for the function `square` that returns the square of its argument.

In[1] := `square[x_] := x^2`

In[2] := `square[y]`

```
         2
Out[2] = y
```

In defining the function, I used the notation `x_`, a named pattern and `:=`, a delayed assignment. *Mathematica* provides many of the constructs found in procedural languages such as C and Pascal. Like APL, *Mathematica* provides primitives for array manipulation.

In the following chapters you will learn about these constructs as well as others that are typically used in programming in *Mathematica*.

Chapter	Description
6	Array and list manipulation.
7	Assignment statements, rules, and equality.
8	Data types and how expressions are represented internally.
9	Writing simple functions.
10	Procedural programming.
11	Programming using pattern matching.
12	Anonymous (pure) functions.
13	Common traps and pitfalls, and debugging techniques.
14	Input/Output – importing and exporting data.
15	How to use and write packages.

6

1. 109810987
2. 09823987632
3. 9873894563
4. 76387623562
5. 737638712441

ThingsTo Do
Insert[]
Length[]
Join[]
Sort[]

1.
2.
3.
4.
5.

1. 109810987
2. 09823987632
3. 9873894563
4. 76387623562
5. 737638712441

A. {1}
B. {3, 5, 7}
C. {6, 3, 1}
D. {9}

19287398723
1239892871
2139813
1398712398719
129387198756

List Manipulation

Lists provide a mechanism for representing arrays (both regular and irregular), vectors, matrices, and for grouping together objects such as data, variables, or expressions. A list is a collection of objects whose symbols are enclosed in braces, { }, and separated by commas.

$$\{item_1, \ item_2, \ item_3, \ \ldots, \ item_n\}$$

Members of the list do not have to be of the same type. The following list contains an integer, a real, some symbols, a polynomial, and a rule.

```
{4, 6.7, a, 7x + 8, Sin[x], D, I, Integer, x -> E}
```

Often the most efficient and cleanest way to approach a problem is by using lists. *Mathematica* uses lists frequently. Lists are used both as input to and as output from functions. For example, for solving a set of simultaneous equations, the equations are specified in a list, and the solution is returned as a list of lists of rules.

```
In[1] := Solve[{2x + 5y == 19, 3x + 7y == 27}]
Out[1] = {{x -> 2, y -> 3}}
```

Why is the solution enclosed in double braces? Because Solve returns a list of solutions, each of which is enclosed in braces. The pair {x -> 2, y -> 3} is one solution. Though this is the only solution, *Mathematica* encloses this solution in braces. So this single solution is enclosed in double braces.

When you ask for the options for a function, such as NIntegrate or a graphics command, *Mathematica* returns a list.

In[2] := Options[NIntegrate]
Out[2] = {AccuracyGoal -> Infinity, Compiled -> True,
        GaussPoints -> Automatic, MaxRecursion -> 6,
        Method -> Automatic, MinRecursion -> 0,
        PrecisionGoal -> Automatic, SingularityDepth -> 4,
        WorkingPrecision -> 19}

A list can bring together several values. To use *Mathematica* effectively, you need to know how to manipulate lists. This chapter describes functions for making lists, rearranging the elements, referencing elements, and selecting elements.

6.1 Making Lists

You can construct a list by enclosing a set of values in braces and separating them with commas or by using the functions Range, Table, and Array.

6.1.1 Range

The function Range produces a list of consecutive numbers or equally spaced numbers. With one argument, Range[n] returns a list of the numbers 1 through Floor[n], the greatest integer less than or equal to n.

In[3] := Range[5]
Out[3] = {1, 2, 3, 4, 5}

In[4] := Range[6.5]
Out[4] = {1, 2, 3, 4, 5, 6}

If you want to generate a list of consecutive numbers not necessarily starting with 1, consider using Range[m,n]. It generates the list $\{m, m+1, m+2, \ldots, m+k\}$ where $m + k \leq n$.

In[5] := Range[2, 7]
Out[5] = {2, 3, 4, 5, 6, 7}

In[6] := Range[2.6, 7.8]
Out[6] = {2.6, 3.6, 4.6, 5.6, 6.6, 7.6}

If you want a list of equally spaced numbers differing by quantities other than 1, you can use Range[m,n,d]. It returns the list $\{m, m+d, m+2d, \ldots, m+kd\}$, where $m + kd \leq n$.

In[7] := Range[2.1, 14, 3.2]
Out[7] = {2.1, 5.3, 8.5, 11.7}

6.1.2 Table

The function `Table` is more versatile than `Range`. Like the functions `Product`, `Sum`, and `Do`, `Table` requires an iterator.

> `Table[expr, iterator]`

The iterator indicates the number of elements to be generated. Iterators can take several forms, as was mentioned in section 2.11 on page 34. The simplest iterator, a single number enclosed in curly braces, e.g., $\{n\}$, instructs *Mathematica* to make a list of `Floor[n]` items.

> *In[8]* := `Table[i, {5}]`
> *Out[8]* = `{i, i, i, i, i}`

With an iterator of the form $\{i, \, imax\}$, `Table` computes a list of values with i assuming consecutive values from 1 to `Floor[imax]`. Below I construct a list whose values are `i!` `(i(i-1)(i-2)...1)`, where `i` runs from 1 to 5.

> *In[9]* := `Table[i!, {i, 5}]`
> *Out[9]* = `{1, 2, 6, 24, 120}`

Besides being able to specify a maximum value for the index variable, an iterator can specify a minimum value, *imin*, for the index variable with an iterator of the form $\{i, \, imin, \, imax\}$. Here I construct a list of multiples of 3.

> *In[10]* := `Table[3i, {i, 5, 11}]`
> *Out[10]* = `{15, 18, 21, 24, 27, 30, 33}`

When an iterator includes a step size or increment $\{i, \, imin, \, imax, \, istep\}$, the difference between successive values is *istep* instead of 1. Here I construct a list based on values of i that are 6 units apart.

> *In[11]* := `Table[i, {i, 5, 50, 6}]`
> *Out[11]* = `{5, 11, 17, 23, 29, 35, 41, 47}`

If the first argument is a list, `Table` generates a list of lists or matrix.

> *In[12]* := `Table[{i, i^2}, {i, 3}]`
> *Out[12]* = `{{1, 1}, {2, 4}, {3, 9}}`

`Table` can take more than one index variable and iterator. With two iterators for two index variables, I obtain a matrix.

> *In[13]* := `Table[a[i] + b[j], {i, 1, 3}, {j, 4, 6}]`
> *Out[13]* = `{{a[1] + b[4], a[1] + b[5], a[1] + b[6]},`
> `{a[2] + b[4], a[2] + b[5], a[2] + b[6]},`
> `{a[3] + b[4], a[3] + b[5], a[3] + b[6]}}`

In[14] := MatrixForm[%]

Out[14] = a[1] + b[4]   a[1] + b[5]   a[1] + b[6]

a[2] + b[4]   a[2] + b[5]   a[2] + b[6]

a[3] + b[4]   a[3] + b[5]   a[3] + b[6]

Notice that one iterator can depend on the values of another. Here the initial value of j depends on the value of i.

In[15] := Table[a[i] + b[j], {i, 1, 3}, {j, i, 4}]

Out[15] = {{a[1] + b[1], a[1] + b[2], a[1] + b[3], a[1] + b[4]},
        {a[2] + b[2], a[2] + b[3], a[2] + b[4]},
        {a[3] + b[3], a[3] + b[4]}}

Table is a much more flexible command than Range for creating lists.

6.1.3 Array

The function Array is for constructing lists or matrices of symbolic values. Here I make a matrix with elements a[*i*, *j*].

In[16] := Array[a, {2, 3}]

Out[16] = {{a[1, 1], a[1, 2], a[1, 3]},
        {a[2, 1], a[2, 2], a[2, 3]}}

6.2 Rearranging Lists

There are several functions for rearranging the terms in a list including: Reverse, Sort, RotateLeft, and RotateRight.

To demonstrate some of the list-manipulation capabilities, I construct a list of random integers, which I call listA.

In[17] := listA = Table[Random[Integer, {0, 15}], {10}]

Out[17] = {12, 7, 4, 12, 2, 5, 2, 5, 10, 3}

The Sort function sorts elements into canonical order, putting numbers in increasing order. Union sorts elements as well as eliminating duplicates (see section 6.5 on page 124).

In[18] := Sort[listA]

Out[18] = {2, 2, 3, 4, 5, 5, 7, 10, 12, 12}

The Reverse function reverses the order of elements in a list.

In[19] := Reverse[listA]

Out[19] = {3, 10, 5, 2, 5, 2, 12, 4, 7, 12}

Mathematica provides two functions for rotating lists: RotateLeft and RotateRight. With these functions, you can rotate a list so that a particular element is moved to the beginning or end of the list. Here I rotate the list such that the first three elements get cycled to the end of the list.

In[20] := RotateLeft[%, 3]
Out[20] = {2, 5, 2, 12, 4, 7, 12, 3, 10, 5}

Here I rotate the list such that the last four elements are cycled from the end of the list to the beginning of the list.

In[21] := RotateRight[%, 4]
Out[21] = {12, 3, 10, 5, 2, 5, 2, 12, 4, 7}

A negative argument to RotateLeft is equivalent to RotateRight with the absolute value of the argument.

The function Permutations gives a list of all permutations of a list.

In[22] := Permutations[{a, b, c}]
Out[22] = {{a, b, c}, {a, c, b}, {b, a, c},
         {b, c, a}, {c, a, b}, {c, b, a}}

Version 1.2: The function Permutations does not notice if elements in the original list are the same. For example, Permutations[{a, a, a}] gives 3! or 6 copies of the same list.

In[23] := Permutations[{a, a, a}]
Out[23] = {{a, a, a}, {a, a, a}, {a, a, a}},
         {a, a, a}, {a, a, a}, {a, a, a}}

6.3 Changing the Number of Elements in Lists

Mathematica provides functions that generate a list based on a list given as input: Append, AppendTo, Drop, Insert, Prepend, PrependTo, Rest, and Take. In this section I work with ListA, which I generated in the last section.

In[24] := listA
Out[24] = {12, 7, 4, 12, 2, 5, 2, 5, 10, 3}

The command Rest returns a list with the first element removed.

In[25] := Rest[listA]
Out[25] = {7, 4, 12, 2, 5, 2, 5, 10, 3}

Drop is intended for dropping elements off the front of a list, the end of the list (if the second argument is negative), or the middle of the list.

In[26] := Drop[listA, 5]
Out[26] = {5, 2, 5, 10, 3}

In[27] := Drop[listA, -5]
Out[27] = {12, 7, 4, 12, 2}

You can drop a single element or several elements from the middle of a list. Here I drop just the 3rd element from listA.

In[28] := Drop[listA, {3}]
Out[28] = {12, 7, 12, 2, 5, 2, 5, 10, 3}

Here I drop the 3rd through 8th elements from listA.

In[29] := Drop[listA, {3, 8}]
Out[29] = {12, 7, 10, 3}

You can take a set of elements from the beginning of the list or the end of the list (if the second argument is negative), or from the middle of the list.

In[30] := Take[listA, 4]
Out[30] = {12, 7, 4, 12}

In[31] := Take[listA, -4]
Out[31] = {2, 5, 10, 3}

In[32] := Take[listA, {4, 6}]
Out[32] = {12, 2, 5}

You can append an element to the end of the list. Here I append the number 4 to the end of the list.

In[33] := Append[listA, 4]
Out[33] = {12, 7, 4, 12, 2, 5, 2, 5, 10, 3, 4}

You can prepend an element to the beginning of the list. Here I prepend the number 5 to the front of the list.

In[34] := Prepend[listA, 5]
Out[34] = {5, 12, 7, 4, 12, 2, 5, 2, 5, 10, 3}

You can insert a number into a list at a specified position. Here I insert a 9 at position 3.

In[35] := Insert[listA, 9, 3]
Out[35] = {12, 7, 9, 4, 12, 2, 5, 2, 5, 10, 3}

Neither Append, Prepend, nor Insert change the list listA. The functions AppendTo and PrependTo are intended for that purpose.

> *In[36] :=* AppendTo[listA, 4]
> *Out[36] =* {12, 7, 4, 12, 2, 5, 2, 5, 10, 3, 4}

Notice a 4 is appended to listA.

> *In[37] :=* listA
> *Out[37] =* {12, 7, 4, 12, 2, 5, 2, 5, 10, 3, 4}

Besides being able to rearrange the order of elements in a list, you can access a subset of the elements of a list. You can add elements to a list or drop elements from a list.

6.4 Counting

The functions Length and Dimensions are for determining the size of a list. Length returns the number of elements while Dimensions is intended for nested rectangular lists, i.e., a list with sublists all the same length.

> *In[38] :=* Length[{3, d, 4, t, a^2}]
> *Out[38] =* 5

A 2-by-5 matrix consists of a list of two lists, each containing 5 elements. Notice that Length tells us that such a list has 2 elements.

> *In[39] :=* Length[{{3, d, 4, t, a^2}, {1, 2, 3, 4, 5}}]
> *Out[39] =* 2

Dimensions gives more detailed information about this matrix.

> *In[40] :=* Dimensions[{{3, d, 4, t, a^2}, {1, 2, 3, 4, 5}}]
> *Out[40] =* {2, 5}

6.5 Combining Lists

The functions Complement, Intersection, Join, and Union are for combining lists. The functions Complement, Intersection, and Union eliminate duplicates and always return sorted lists.

Complement returns a list of the elements in *list1* that are not in *list2, list3, ...*

> Complement[*list1, list2, list3, ...*]

For example, those elements that are in {1, 4, 2, 3} that are not in {2, 3}.

In[41] := Complement[{1, 4, 2, 3}, {2, 3}]
Out[41] = {1, 4}

Intersection returns elements common to all arguments.

In[42] := Intersection[{1, 4, 2, 3}, {6, 5, 4, 3}]
Out[42] = {3, 4}

The Union function returns a sorted list of all distinct elements.

In[43] := Union[{1, 4, 2, 3}, {6, 5, 4, 3}]
Out[43] = {1, 2, 3, 4, 5, 6}

The functions Union, Intersection, Complement, and Join can take one or more arguments. The Union (or Complement or Intersection) of one argument, eliminates duplicates.

In[44] := Union[{1, 5, 3, 3, 2, 8, 4, 8, 5}]
Out[44] = {1, 2, 3, 4, 5, 8}

Notice that Join just joins or merges lists. The order is preserved and duplicate entries are left unchanged.

In[45] := Join[{1, 2, 3, 4}, {3, 4, 5, 6}]
Out[45] = {1, 2, 3, 4, 3, 4, 5, 6}

The functions Complement, Intersection, and Union sort the elements in their arguments in the process of determining the result. Consequently they all return sorted lists.

6.6 Changing the Shape of a List

The functions Flatten and Partition are for changing the shape of a list. With Range, I create a vector and name it vectorA.

In[46] := vectorA = Range[8]
Out[46] = {1, 2, 3, 4, 5, 6, 7, 8}

I partition vectorA into two sets to form a matrix with two rows and four columns, called matrixA.

In[47] := matrixA = Partition[vectorA, 4]
Out[47] = {{1, 2, 3, 4}, {5, 6, 7, 8}}

This partitioned vector can be displayed as a matrix.

In[48] := MatrixForm[matrixA]
Out[48] = 1 2 3 4

5 6 7 8

Partitioning can be useful when you are working with data that have some structure to it. For instance, if you have data that represent points in three-space, you might want to partition your data into sets of three.

In[49] := Partition[{1, 34, 456, 2, 33, 453, 3, 36, 435}, 3]
Out[49] = {{1, 34, 456}, {2, 33, 453}, {3, 36, 435}}

The third argument of Partition specifies an offset. Here I form lists of three elements with an offset of one.

In[50] := Partition[{a, b, c, d, e, f, g}, 3, 1]
Out[50] = {{a, b, c}, {b, c, d}, {c, d, e}, {d, e, f}, {e, f, g}}

How would you take a list of points in three-space and draw lines between neighboring points? By specifying an offset of one, you can get a list of pairs consisting of the end points for each line segment.

In[51] := Partition[
            {{1, 2, 3}, {4, 5, 6}, {7, 8, 9}, {10, 11, 12}},
            2, 1
          ]
Out[51] = {{{1, 2, 3}, {4, 5, 6}}, {{4, 5, 6}, {7, 8, 9}},
            {{7, 8, 9}, {10, 11, 12}}}

The function Flatten eliminates nested lists. It returns a single flat list.

In[52] := Flatten[matrixA]
Out[52] = {1, 2, 3, 4, 5, 6, 7, 8}

Partition constructs a matrix from a vector or list, and Flatten returns a vector or list when given a matrix.

The function Transpose transposes a matrix, converting rows into columns and columns into rows.

In[53] := Transpose[{{a, b, c}, {d, e, f}}]
Out[53] = {{a, d}, {b, e}, {c, f}}

6.7 Referencing Elements

With *Mathematica*, you can reference a single element or a list of elements with First, Last, or Part. Here I construct a list named myList, and then pick out the first and last elements of that list.

```
In[54] := myList = {a, b, c, d, e}
Out[54] = {a, b, c, d, e}
```

```
In[55] := First[myList]
Out[55] = a
```

```
In[56] := Last[myList]
Out[56] = e
```

Double brackets [[ ]], an alias for the function Part, are for referencing an element or several elements from a list. Unlike the C programming language, *Mathematica* starts numbering with 1. Obtain the fourth element with myList[[4]].

```
In[57] := myList[[4]]
Out[57] = d
```

In addition to being able to reference a single element, the function Part can be used to reference several elements in a list. To obtain a list of elements, specify a list of indices. Here I use Range to generate the list of indices {2, 3, 4}.

```
In[58] := myList[[ Range[2,4] ]]
Out[58] = {b, c, d}
```

The *n*th row of a matrix is just the *n*th element of the matrix, which can be referenced by using Part. I generate a 2-by-2 matrix.

```
In[59] := myArray = Array[a, {2, 2}]
Out[59] = {{a[1, 1], a[1, 2]}, {a[2, 1], a[2, 2]}}
```

```
In[60] := myArray[[2]]
Out[60] = {a[2, 1], a[2, 2]}
```

To reference an element of a matrix, specify the row and the column in double brackets.

```
In[61] := myArray[[1, 2]]
Out[61] = a[1, 2]
```

Using Part, you can select data if you know the position of the data in a list or matrix.

6.8 Selecting Data

If you want to test if data have certain properties, e.g., they are greater than a certain value, what can you do? The function MemberQ tells you if an item is in a list. Using MemberQ, I find out whether the number 3 is in listA (defined in section 6.2 on page 120).

In[62] := MemberQ[listA, 3]
Out[62] = True

The Select function is designed to pick values that meet a given criterion. The Select function takes two arguments: a list of data and *criterion*.

Select[{e_1, e_2, ..., e_n}, *criterion*]

The Select function returns a list of elements e_i where *criterion*[e_i] returns True. The following example returns a list of items that are positive, i.e., those items that are greater than 0. Notice that you do not specify the argument of the criterion.

In[63] := Select[{-3, 2, 4.5, 7, a, 5, -5}, Positive]
Out[63] = {2, 4.5, 7, 5}

A criterion is just a function that returns the values True and False. If the criterion returns a value other than True, Select interprets the result as False. Notice that Positive[x] returns neither True nor False. So Select[{x}, Positive] does not return x.

In[64] := Select[{x}, Positive]
Out[64] = {}

The following table contains some of the criteria built into *Mathematica*.

Criteria	Returns True when	Added to 2.0
DigitQ[*string*]	all characters in *string* are digits in the range 0 – 9	yes
IntegerQ[*expr*]	*expr* is an integer	
LetterQ[*string*]	all the characters in *string* are letters	yes
LowerCaseQ[*string*]	all the characters in *string* are lower-case letters	yes
MachineNumberQ[*expr*]	*expr* is a machine-precision real number	yes
MatrixQ[*expr*]	*expr* is a list of lists of equal length (a matrix)	
Negative[*expr*]	*expr* a negative number	
NonNegative[*expr*]	*expr* a non-negative number	
NumberQ[*expr*]	*expr* is a number	
NameQ[*string*]	there are any symbols whose names match *string*	
OddQ[*expr*]	*expr* is an odd integer	
Positive[*expr*]	*expr* a positive number	
PrimeQ[*expr*]	*expr* is a prime integer	
UpperCaseQ[*string*]	all the characters in *string* are upper-case letters	yes
ValueQ[*expr*]	a value has been defined for *expr*	
VectorQ[*expr*]	*expr* is a list, none of the elements are themselves lists	

The criterion can be user-defined. The criterion exact returns True if its argument is considered exact.

In[65] := exact[x_] := Precision[x] === Infinity

Using this criterion, you can determine which values *Mathematica* considers exact.

In[66] := Select[{-3, Pi, a, 4.5}, exact]
Out[66] = {-3, Pi, a,}

6.9 Calculating with Lists

This section discusses how to work with lists effectively. Suppose you have some data you want to sum. You can instruct *Mathematica* to add up the numbers by using Sum.

In[67] := Sum[i^2, {i, 5}]
Out[67] = 55

It is not always possible to generate your data by using a formula.

In[68] := myData = {3.5, 6.4, 4.2};

These numbers could be summed by referencing each element in the list.

In[69] := Sum[myData[[i]], {i, Length[myData]}]
Out[69] = 14.1

Referencing individual elements is inefficient and thus impractical for huge data sets. A better approach would be to call the Plus operator directly with the arguments being the elements of the list.

In[70] := Plus[a, b, c]
Out[70] = a + b + c

How can you instruct *Mathematica* to apply the Plus operator to the elements of our list? Notice that, if you give the list as the argument of Plus, you get back our list. This is not surprising since, because Plus is Listable, you are asking *Mathematica* to add up a single element, a list. Section 6.10 on page 129 describe the attribute Listable.

In[71] := Plus[{a, b, c}]
Out[71] = {a, b, c}

You can sum the elements in a list by applying the Plus operator to the list.

In[72] := Apply[Plus, {a, b, c}]
Out[72] = a + b + c

It is often faster to perform an operation on a list than to perform the operation on each element of the list. Notice that it is more than twice as fast to add the first 500 integers by applying the Plus command to a list as adding the numbers by using Sum. These timing measurements were run on a Macintosh II with 8 megabytes of memory.

In[73] := Timing[Apply[Plus, Range[500]]]
Out[73] = {0.583333 Second, 125250}

In[74] := Timing[Sum[i, {i, 500}]]
Out[74] = {1.2 Second, 125250}

6.10 Listable

With a list, you can perform an operation on a set of values. Many arithmetic functions operate on lists, viz., those that have the attribute Listable. When you ask for the Log of a list, you obtain the Log of each element of the list.

In[75] := Log[{2, 4, 5, 3}]
Out[75] = {Log[2], Log[4], Log[5], Log[3]}

Using the function N, you obtain numerical approximations to these values.

In[76] := N[%]
Out[76] = {0.693147, 1.38629, 1.60944, 1.09861}

A function specifies an operation to be performed. Functions have properties or attributes. A function with the attribute Listable applies the function to each element of the list. If you call Sin of a list, the function is applied to each element of the list.

In[77] := Sin[{2, 4, 5, 3}]
Out[77] = {Sin[2], Sin[4], Sin[5], Sin[3]}

Since Plus is Listable, I can add two vectors.

In[78] := {1, 2, 3} + {a, b, c}
Out[78] = {1 + a, 2 + b, 3 + c}

Many functions have the attribute Listable.

In[79] := Attributes[{Exp, Log, Sin, Plus}]
Out[79] = {{Listable, Protected}, {Listable, Protected},
        {Listable, Protected},
        {Flat, Listable, OneIdentity, Orderless, Protected}}

The reason I was able to obtain the attributes of each of the elements in the list {Exp, Log, Sin, Plus} is that the function Attributes has the attribute Listable.

In[80] := Attributes[Attributes]
Out[80] = {HoldAll, Listable, Protected}

6.11 Listable and Map

There are two ways to get *Mathematica* to apply a function to each element of a list: (1) map the function onto each element of the list or (2) give the function the attribute Listable. Since the function f does not have the attribute Listable, *Mathematica* does not map f onto each element of the list {2, 4, 5, 3}.

In[81] := f[{2, 4, 5, 3}]
Out[81] = f[{2, 4, 5, 3}]

The command Map lets you apply a function to each element of a list or an expression.

In[82] := Map[f, {2, 4, 5, 3}]
Out[82] = {f[2], f[4], f[5], f[3]}

Notice that a function can also be mapped onto an expression.

In[83] := Map[f, a + b x]
Out[83] = f[a] + f[b x]

If you assign the attribute Listable to the function f, then call f, it is applied to each element.

In[84] := AppendTo[Attributes[f], Listable]
Out[84] = {Listable}

In[85] := f[{2, 4, 5, 3}]
Out[85] = {f[2], f[4], f[5], f[3]}

Let us look at what happens when a Listable function is given more than one argument.

In[86] := f[{a, b, c}, {d, e, f}]
Out[86] = {f[a, d], f[b, e], f[c, f]}

Mathematica threads the function over over lists that appear as its arguments.

6.12 Map Versus Apply

Map, which is also represented with /@, applies a function to each element of a list or expression. Apply, which is also represented with @@, changes the "head" of an expression. Experimentation can help you to understand what a particular function does. If you can't remember whether you want Map or Apply, experiment with the two functions.

```
In[87] := Map[f, {a, b, c}]
Out[87] = {f[a], f[b], f[c]}

In[88] := f /@ {a, b, c}
Out[88] = {f[a], f[b], f[c]}

In[89] := Apply[f, {a, b, c}]
Out[89] = f[a, b, c]

In[90] := f @@ {a, b, c}
Out[90] = f[a, b, c]
```

The functions Map and Apply are useful for performing functions on lists.

6.13 Formatting Lists

In addition to manipulating lists, you may wish to include a list in a paper or a viewgraph. There are several print forms for displaying lists including: ColumnForm, MatrixForm, and TableForm. These forms are only for display purposes; i.e., you cannot perform computations on their outputs. ColumnForm makes a list appear as a column. I define the function pascal so that it returns the nth row of Pascal's triangle. Using ColumnForm, I display each row on a separate line.

```
In[91] := pascal[n_] := Table[Binomial[n, i], {i, 0, n}]
In[92] := ColumnForm[Table[pascal[m], {m, 0, 5}]]
Out[92] = {1}
          {1, 1}
          {1, 2, 1}
          {1, 3, 3, 1}
          {1, 4, 6, 4, 1}
          {1, 5, 10, 10, 5, 1}
```

The optional second argument of ColumnForm specifies the horizontal alignment of the columns: Left, Right, or Center. By default, the columns are left-justified. Specifying Center as the second argument to ColumnForm, you can display Pascal's triangle as it is commonly appears.

In[93] := `ColumnForm[Table[pascal[m], {m, 0, 5}], Center]`
Out[93] =   {1}
                  {1, 1}
               {1, 2, 1}
            {1, 3, 3, 1}
         {1, 4, 6, 4, 1}
      {1, 5, 10, 10, 5, 1}

6.14 Summary

Mathematica makes extensive use of lists. Being able to work with lists is a skill that will help you in working with other types of expressions in *Mathematica*. Lists are a mechanism for grouping terms together. *Mathematica* provides utilities for rearranging elements, inserting elements, removing elements, performing operations on the entire list or a subset of the list, referencing elements, and formatting lists.

Function	Description
Range[*min*, *max*, *step*]	Generates a list (arithmetic progression)
Table[*expr*, *iterator*]	Generates a list (more general)
Array[*s*, *dim*]	Generates a list of length *dim*
Sort[*list*]	Sorts elements of *list*
Reverse[*list*]	Reverses elements in *list*
RotateLeft[*list*, *n*]	Cycles the elements *n* positions to the left
RotateRight[*list*, *n*]	Cycles the elements *n* positions to the right
Permutations[*list*]	Generates a list of all possible permutations of the elements of *list*
Drop[*list*, *n*]	Drops the first *n* elements from *list*
Take[*list*, *n*]	Takes the first *n* elements from *list*
First[*list*]	Gives the first element of *list*
Last[*list*]	Gives the last element of *list*
list[[*n*]] or Part[*list*, *n*]	Gives the *n*th element
Rest[*list*]	Returns all but the first element of *list*
Select[*list*, *crit*]	Picks out elements in *list* which meet the criterion *crit*
Append[*list*, *elem*]	Returns a list with *elem* appended to the end of *list*
AppendTo[*list*, *elem*]	Changes *list* by appending *elem* to the end
Prepend[*list*, *elem*]	Returns a list with *elem* added to the front of *list*
PrependTo[*list*, *elem*]	Changes *list* by adding *elem* to the front
Insert[*list*, *elem*, *n*]	Inserts *elem* at position *n* in *list*
Length[*list*]	Gives the number of elements in *list*
Dimensions[*list*]	Gives the dimensions of a list or expression
Complement[*list*$_1$, *list*$_2$, ...]	Gives the complement, i.e., those elements in *list*$_1$ but not in *list*$_2$, ...
Intersection[*list1*, *list2*, ...]	Gives a sorted list of all distinct elements
Union[*list*$_1$, *list*$_2$, ...]	Gives a sorted list of the distinct elements
Join[*list*$_1$, *list*$_2$, ...]	Joins or concatenates lists together
Partition[*list*, *n*]	Partition *list* into sublists of length *n*
Flatten[*list*]	Flattens out nested lists, i.e., eliminates nested lists
Transpose[*list*]	Transpose
Apply[*f*, *list*]	Replaces the head of *list* with *f*
Map[*f*, *list*]	Applies *f* to each element in *list*
Listable	An attribute, if set, automatically maps a function onto a list
ColumnForm[*list*]	Prints *list* as a column
MatrixForm[*list*]	Prints elements in *list* in a regular array

6.15 Exercises

This problem set is designed to give you practice in working with lists.

6.1 Create a list of the first 10 odd positive integers (i.e., 1, 3, 5, ..., 19) by using:

(a) `Range`

(b) `Table`

6.2 Obtain the first four elements and the last four elements of the list you created in problem 1 with the commands:

(a) `Take`

(b) `Drop`

6.3 Call the functions `Dimensions` and `Length` on the matrices m and n.

$$m = \{\{2, 4, 6\}, \{5, 7, 9\}\} \qquad n = \{\{1, 2, 3\}, \{4, 5\}\}$$

6.4 (a) Using `Table` and `Random`, create two lists of ten random integers in the range [0, 10].

(b) Sort the elements in one of the lists.

(c) Append a 5 to the end of one of the lists.

(d) Find the set of elements included in both lists, i.e., find the intersection set.

(e) Join the two lists together.

(f) Make a list of the distinct elements in the two lists.

(g) List the elements that are in list 1 but not in list 2.

(h) Are there any elements in `Range[10]` that are not in list 1 nor list 2?

6.5 Given a list named `myList`, how would you check whether all the elements in the list are the same by using only list-oriented primitives? Test your answer on the following two lists:

$$\{x^2 -1, \ x^2 - 1, \ x^2 - 1, \ x^2 - 1, \ (x - 1)(x + 1)\}$$
$$\{\{-1,-1,2\}, \ \{-1,-1,2\}, \ \{-1,-1,2\}, \ \{-1,-1,2\}\}$$

6.6 (a) Generate a list of 16 integers between 0 and 100. Assign a name to the list.

(b) Partition the list into four sets of four integers by using `Partition`.

(c) List the third row of the 4-by-4 matrix you created in problem 6b.

(d) List the third column of the 4-by-4 matrix. *Note*: This is a bit tricky.

(e) Convert the matrix back into a list by using the function `Flatten`.

(f) Find the mean (average) and median of the 16 numbers. The median is the middle element of a sorted list or the average of the middle two elements if the list has an even number of elements.

6.7 Use the `Select` command to pick out integers that exceed 50 from the list of random integers you generated in problem 6.

Hint: Use the function `greater50`, which returns `True` if its argument is greater than 50.

```
greater50[x_] := x > 50
```

6.8 Determine what *Mathematica* returns when executing the following commands with

```
myList = {{a, b}, {c, d}}.
```

(a) `Apply[f, myList]`

(b) `Map[f, myList]`

(c) Use the on-line help (`?MapAt` and `?MapAll`) to obtain brief descriptions of the commands `MapAt` and `MapAll`.

(d) `MapAt[f, myList, {2}]`

(e) `MapAll[f, myList]`

6.9 In a town there are three stores selling 5 popular toys. Store A sells the toys for $15, $17, $18, $32, and $29 and store B sells the same 5 toys for $14, $18, $22, $29, and $26. The policy of store C is to match the most competitive price in town. Write a *Mathematica* expression to determine store C's selling prices for the 5 toys.

6.10 Generate 80 points in three-space. Plot the points using `Show` and `Graphics3D` in color according to their location, so points that are close together should have nearly the same color.

7

Assignments and Rules

Programs usually consist of a series of statements in which values are computed, assigned names, and used in further calculations. This chapter describes how to assign a name to a value or to an operation and how to replace symbols with values in an expression. At the end of the chapter, I describe the functions for testing equality.

7.1 Assignments

You can assign a name to a result. Names are made up of alphanumeric characters and/or the $ character. Names can contain numbers, but the first character must be a letter or the $ character. By convention, user defined names start with a lower-case letter. Names of built-in global variables typically start with the $ character, e.g., $Display, $Context. The length of a name is not restricted. Here I assign the value 3 to the symbol a.

In[1] := a = 3
Out[1] = 3

Now all occurrences of a are replaced by the value 3.

In[2] := a + 7
Out[2] = 10

Symbolic expressions can also be assigned names. Assigning a new value to a name discards the old value. I assign a the value 2x + y.

In[3] := a = 2x + y
Out[3] = 2 x + y

When I ask for 1/a, *Mathematica* substitutes the most recently assigned value in place of a.

```
In[4] := 1 / a

          1
Out[4] = -------
         2 x + y
```

Setting a name equal to . unassigns the value.

```
In[5] := a =.
```

Now a has no value assigned to it. When I ask for a, *Mathematica* simply returns the symbol a.

```
In[6] := a
Out[6] = a
```

Sometimes users forget about having assigned a value to a variable. It is prudent to unassign values when you anticipate no longer needing to refer to the value by name.

7.1.1 Assignments: Immediate Versus Delayed

If an expression uses = or the Set function, *Mathematica* immediately replaces the variable with the value assigned to it.

```
In[7] := random1 = Random[ ]
Out[7] = 0.495874
```

Here the variable random1 is assigned the value 0.495874. Whenever it is called, random1 returns this value.

I define random2 with := or SetDelayed. A value is assigned to random2 when it is called. The function to the right of := is executed when random2 is invoked.

```
In[8] := random2 := Random[ ]
```

No value is returned when the assignment is made.

Notice random1 always returns the same value whenever I refer to it.

```
In[9] := Table[random1, {5}]
Out[9] = {0.495874, 0.495874, 0.495874, 0.495874, 0.495874}
```

Every time random2 is called, *Mathematica* calls the function Random, which returns a random number. So random2 returns a different value each time it is called.

```
In[10] := Table[random2, {5}]
Out[10] = {0.02327, 0.71788, 0.430938, 0.862531, 0.128657}
```

Let us look at two functions that are identical except that one is specified by using an immediate assignment (=) and the other with a delayed assignment (:=). The function f[x] computes the value of x + b for b = 3, while g[x] computes x + b for the current value of b. I assign the value 3 to b and set up these two definitions.

```
In[11] := b = 3

In[12] := f[x_] = x + b
Out[12] = 3 + x

In[13] := g[x_] := x + b
```

Let us change the value of b.

```
In[14] := b = 5
```

The functions f and g now return different results because they are based on different values of b.

```
In[15] := f[4]
Out[15] = 7

In[16] := g[4]
Out[16] = 9
```

Values are assigned names with = and delayed assignments defined with := are used for specifying procedures or functions. Using the ? operator, you can see the definitions of f and g.

```
In[17] := ?f
         Global'f
         f[x_] = 3 + x

In[18] := ?g
         Global'g
         g[x_] := x + b
```

7.1.2 Multiple Assignments

Several assignments can be made with a single statement. *Mathematica* evaluates the statement c = d = e from right to left. The variable d is set equal to e or to the value of e. The variable c is set equal to the value returned by d = e, i.e., the value of e.

In[19] := c = d = e

Out[19] = e

Now c and d refer to the same value.

Using lists, you can assign several values.

In[20] := {r, s} = {3, 5}

Out[20] = {3, 5}

Using lists, you can swap two values.

In[21] := {r, s} = {s, r}

Out[21] = {5, 3}

7.1.3 Recursive Functions

It is possible to construct a look-up table of values by using multiple assignments. This is particularly useful when defining a recursive function, a function defined in terms of itself. Look at this definition of factorial. When factorial[n] is calculated, it is stored.

In[22] := factorial[1] = 1;

In[23] := factorial[n_] := factorial[n] = n factorial[n-1]

Try to figure out what assignments are made when you ask for factorial[3]. Ask *Mathematica* for information on factorial (?factorial) both before and after executing factorial[3]. If you ask for factorial[m] and you have already computed factorial[n] for $n \geq m$, *Mathematica* simply returns the value it has stored. No computations are performed.

7.2 Unassigning Values

Section 7.1 on page 138, mentions that *name* =. removes rules defined for *name*. You can use this notation for removing function definitions. However, *name* =. does not remove rules for *name*[x_]. When using Unset (=.), the left-hand-side must be identical to the left-hand-side of the definitions that you want to remove. For example, to clear the definition of factorial as specified in the previous section, you need to unset each rule.

```
In[24] := factorial[1] =.
In[25] := factorial[n_] =.
```

If you have already called `factorial`, these two statements may not be enough to clear out all the definitions.

For functions with many rules, this can be tedious. Luckily there are other functions specifically intended to clearing function definition. The `Clear` function clears all values associated with the symbol.

When defining a function, it is advisable first to clear the function of any old definition. Thus you can protect against inadvertently invoking an old definition.

```
In[26] := cube[x_] := x^3
```

After clearing cube, notice that when I ask for information on cube, *Mathematica* returns only the symbol.

```
In[27] := ?cube
         Global`cube
         cube[x_] := x^3

In[28] := Clear[cube]
In[29] := ?cube
         Global`cube
```

The `Clear` function clears values defined for the symbol but it does not remove the symbol nor does it remove the symbol's attributes.

```
In[30] := Attributes[cube] = {Listable}

In[31] := Clear[cube]
In[32] := ?cube
         Global`cube
         Attributes[cube] = {Listable}
```

The function `ClearAll` clears definitions as well as any attributes.

```
In[33] := ClearAll[cube]
In[34] := ?cube
         Global`cube
```

The function `Remove` removes the symbol completely so the name is no longer recognized by *Mathematica*. It also removes the attributes.

```
In[35] := Remove[pascal]
In[36] := ?pascal
         Information::notfound: Symbol pascal not found.
```

If the symbol has the attribute `Protected`, its rules are not cleared or removed. Most functions built into *Mathematica* have the attribute `Protected` to ensure that you don't inadvertently clear them or change their definition.

```
In[37] := Remove[Apply]
          Remove::rmptc:
             Symbol Apply is Protected and cannot be removed.
```

When would you want to remove a symbol? When there are two instances of a symbol. When you call a function before loading the package in which it is defined, *Mathematica* creates the symbol in the current context. (Section 15.2 on page 247 describes contexts.) Then if you load the package containing the definition, another symbol with the same name may be created. When you call the function, *Mathematica* invokes the symbol in the current context. Only after you remove the symbol in the current context, will you be able to access the function specified in the package. Consider, for example, if you call the function `CMYColor` before loading the package `Colors.m`. *Mathematica* cannot find `CMYColor` so it creates the symbol. This symbol does not have any rules attached to it.

```
In[38] := Show[
              Graphics[{
                  CMYColor[0.7, 0.5, 0.3],
                  Point[{0,0}]
              }]
          ]
          Graphics::gprim:
             Unknown Graphics primitive CMYColor[0.7, 0.5, 0.3]
                encountered.
```

When you load the package, there will be two symbols named `CMYColor`, i.e., `Global'CMYColor` and `Graphics'Color'CMYColor`.

```
In[39] := Needs["Graphics'Colors'"]
```

```
In[40] := ?*'CMYColor
          CMYColor      Graphics'Colors'CMYColor
```

When I call `CMYColor`, I reference the symbol in the current context, not the one that is defined in the package `Colors.m`. Notice when I ask for information on `CMYColor`, *Mathematica* does not show the usage statement in the package `Graphics.m`.

```
In[41] := ?CMYColor
          Global'CMYColor
```

After removing the symbol `CMYColor`, I can access the definition and usage statement specified in the package `Colors.m`.

In[42] := `Remove[CMYColor]`

In[43] := `?CMYColor`
    `CMYColor[c,m,y]` represents a color in the CMY
    (cyan-magenta-yellow) system.

You can also use `Remove` to discard variables and definitions you no longer need. Notice that I defined `cube` and `pascal` with a lower-case c and a lower-case p. If you follow the convention that all your own function and variable names start with a lower-case letter, the command

    `Remove["Global`@*"]`

removes all those symbols in the context `Global`. The meta character `@` refers to one or more characters that are lower-case letters.

Version 2.0: The meta character `@` has been changed so that it refers to non-upper-case characters. In addition to lower-case characters, `@` also refers to the character `$`. So the command `Remove["Global`@*"]` attempts to remove the variables whose names start with a `$` or a lower-case letter. I do not advise using the command `Remove["@*"]` because it removes the values of global variables that are not protected. (For examples of global variables, see section 5.11 on page 112.)

7.3 Rules

Rules are a mechanism for replacing a variable with a value in an expression. The operator `/.` (no space between the `/` and the `.`) or `ReplaceAll` applies a rule or list of rules after evaluating the expression. Think of `/.` as meaning *given that* and `->` as meaning *goes to*. So the expression `x + 5y /. x -> 2` can be interpreted as `x + 5y` given that x goes to 2.

In[44] := `x + 5y /. x -> 2`
Out[44] = `2 + 5 y`

Using a list of rules, you can perform several replacements. Here I specify two replacement rules in a list.

In[45] := `x + 5y /. {x -> 2, y -> 3}`
Out[45] = `17`

The expression to the left of the `/.` is evaluated before any replacements are made.

In[46] := 2x + 3x /. {2x -> y, 3x -> 3}
Out[46] = 5x

The left hand-side gets evaluated; 2x + 3x gets replaced by 5x. Neither rule applies to this result, so neither rule is invoked.

7.3.1 Delayed Rules

Just as there are two types of assignments, set (=) and delayed set (:=), *Mathematica* includes two types of rules, immediate rules (->) and delayed rules (:>).

In the following example, x gets replaced by the value returned by Random[ ] when the rule is specified. So I obtain a list consisting of five identical values.

In[47] := Table[x, {5}] /. x -> Random[ ]
Out[47] = {0.7724, 0.7724, 0.7724, 0.7724, 0.7724}

Rules do not make assignments. Though the rule x -> 2 causes *Mathematica* to replace x with 2 in an expression, the value 2 is not assigned to x. If you ask *Mathematica* about x, notice that it has not been assigned a value.

In[48] := x
Out[48] = x

Delayed rules are used when the expression to the right of the rule should be evaluated after the rule is invoked. Using a delayed rule to replace x with Random[ ], I obtain a list of five different random real numbers.

In[49] := Table[x, {5}] /. x :> Random[ ]
Out[49] = {0.653039, 0.289855, 0.14162, 0.617554, 0.566551}

7.3.2 Replace Repeated

The notation //. applies a rule repeatedly.

In[50] := log[a b c d] /. log[x_ y_] -> log[x] + log[y]
Out[50] = log[a] + log[b c d]

In[51] := log[a b c d] //. log[x_ y_] -> log[x] + log[y]
Out[51] = log[a] + log[b] + log[c] + log[d]

7.3.3 Graphics Options

Let us look at how rules are used.

The options for graphics commands, such as Plot and ContourPlot, are specified with rules. Most of the options are specified by using immediate rules (->). Only the options DefaultFont and DisplayFunction are specified with a delayed rule. A graphic is displayed by using the values of the global variables `$DisplayFunction` and `$DefaultFont` at the time the plotting command is invoked. All other options have fixed values.

```
In[52] := Options[ContourPlot]
Out[52] = {AspectRatio -> 1, Axes -> False, AxesLabel -> None,
          AxesOrigin -> Automatic, AxesStyle -> Automatic,
          Background -> Automatic, ColorFunction -> Automatic,
          ColorOutput -> Automatic, Compiled -> True,
          ContourLines -> True, Contours -> 10,
          ContourShading -> True, ContourSmoothing -> None,
          ContourStyle -> Automatic, DefaultColor -> Automatic,
          Epilog -> {}, Frame -> True, FrameLabel -> None,
          FrameStyle -> Automatic, FrameTicks -> Automatic,
          PlotLabel -> None, PlotPoints -> 15,
          PlotRange -> Automatic, PlotRegion -> Automatic,
          Prolog -> {}, RotateLabel -> True,
          Ticks -> Automatic, DefaultFont :> $DefaultFont,
          DisplayFunction :> $DisplayFunction}
```

7.3.4 Labeling Plots

In some versions of *Mathematica*, graphs and plots are put in a separate window or screen from the input command. To help users pair up plots and input commands, I instruct *Mathematica* to label each plot with the command that generated it.

The global variable `$Line` specifies the number of the current input line. Try it out.

```
In[53] := $Line
Out[53] = 53
```

The function `Recall[`*n*`]` returns the rule for input line *n*.

Version 1.2 Macintosh: Most non-Macintosh versions of *Mathematica* automatically load the package `Edit.m`. On the Macintosh, you need to load it manually for the following example to work properly. In version 1.2, `Edit.m` is in the `Packages` directory or folder in the `StartUp` subdirectory or folder. Load the package with the command `Needs["Edit`"]` or `<< Edit.m`.

```
In[54] := << Edit.m
```

`Recall[$Line]` returns your current line.

```
In[55] := Recall[$Line]
Out[55] = In[55] :> Recall[$Line]
```

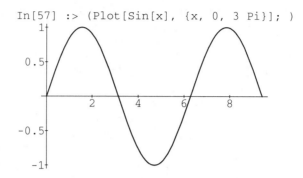

```
In[57] :> (Plot[Sin[x], {x, 0, 3 Pi}]; )
```

Figure 7.1: After setting the option **PlotLabel** (see *In[57]*), a plot is labeled with the command that was used to generate it.

With a delayed rule (:>), set the option **PlotLabel** equal to **Recall[$Line]** to label a graph produced with **Plot** with the command used to generate the plot.

```
In[56] := SetOptions[
         Plot,
         PlotLabel :> ToString[Recall[$Line]]
       ];
```

Version 2.0: **Recall** has been eliminated. The more useful function **InString** has been added. **InString** returns the string, which when parsed, produces the expression returned by *In[n]*. So input *In[56]* (shown above) can be rewritten as[1]:

```
In[56] := SetOptions[
         Plot,
         PlotLabel :> StringJoin[
             "In[",
             ToString[$Line],
             "] :> ",
             InString[$Line]
           ]
       ];
```

After the option **PlotLabel** is set, the plot is labeled with the command that was used to generate the plot. The following command generates the plot shown in figure 7.1.

```
In[57] := Plot[Sin[x], {x, 0, 3Pi}];
```

---

[1]I wish to thank the editorial staff of *The Mathematica Journal* for suggesting the use of **InString**. See Volume 1, Issue 4, Spring 1991, page 48.

7.3.5 Simplification of Trigonometric Expressions

Rules transform expressions. The package Trigonometry.m contains functions designed for transforming trigonometric expressions. In version 1.2, the package Trigonometry.m contains the following definition of TrigReduce. Notice two rules are applied to the argument.

```
TrigReduce[e_] :=
    FixedPoint[(# /. TrigCanonicalRel /. TrigReduceRel)&, e]

'TrigCanonicalRel = {
    (* reduce arguments of the form n Pi / m *)
    Sin[x_. + r_Rational Pi] :> Cos[x] /; EvenQ[r-1/2],
    Sin[x_. + Pi] :> -Sin[x],
    Sin[x_. + n_Integer?OddQ Pi] :> -Sin[x]
}
```

What is this code doing? The definition of TrigReduce uses anonymous or pure functions, which are described in chapter 12 on page 203. The function FixedPoint applies the rules TrigCanonicalRel and TrigReduceRel to the argument of TrigReduce until the result no longer changes.

Let us look at the first rule in TrigCanonicalRel, i.e.,

```
Sin[x_. + r_Rational Pi] :> Cos[x] /; EvenQ[r-1/2]
```

In the expression above, the pattern x_. instructs *Mathematica* to assign the value 0 to x if no value is specified. (See section 9.4 on page 171 for a description of how to specify default values.) The rule on the left-hand side of /; is evaluated if the condition to the right (EvenQ[r-1/2]) is met. (See section 9.3 on page 170 for more on conditional evaluation.) Notice that TrigReduce transforms Sin[x + Pi].

```
In[58] := Needs["Algebra'Trigonometry'"]

In[59] := TrigReduce[Sin[x + Pi]]
Out[59] = -Sin[x]
```

7.3.6 A List of Values

Rules can be used to indicate a correspondence between symbols or names and values. Notice how the function DispersionReport returns a list of rules specifying values of certain variables. The function DispersionReport is defined in the package DescriptiveStatistics.m. In version 2.0 this package located in the directory or folder named Statistics. In version 1.2 the package DescriptiveStatistics.m can be found in the directory or folder named DataAnalysis.

In[60] := Needs ["Statistics`DescriptiveStatistics`"]
In[61] := dReport = DispersionReport [{3, 5, 5, 3, 2, 6, 3, 2, 8, 4}]

$$
Out[61] = \{\text{Variance} \to \frac{329}{90}, \text{StandardDeviation} \to \frac{\text{Sqrt}[\frac{329}{10}]}{3},
$$

$$
\text{SampleRange} \to 6, \text{MeanDeviation} \to \frac{38}{25},
$$

$$
\text{MedianDeviation} \to \frac{3}{2}, \text{QuartileDeviation} \to 1\}
$$

Using /. (ReplaceAll), you can obtain the values of any of the symbols in the list. For example, MeanDeviation /. dReport returns the value MeanDeviation.

In[62] := MeanDeviation /. dReport

$$
Out[62] = \frac{38}{25}
$$

7.3.7 Replacement Rules

Functions that return replacement rules include: FindRoot, Options, and Solve. The function Solve attempts to solve an equation or set of equations specified in a list. When solutions can be found, Solve returns a list of lists of rules, i.e., a nested list.

In[63] := theRoots = Solve[x^2 + 15x + 42 == 0]

$$
Out[63] = \{\{x \to \frac{-15 + \text{Sqrt}[57]}{2}\}, \{x \to \frac{-15 - \text{Sqrt}[57]}{2}\}\}
$$

Using the replacement mechanism, you can verify the solution by substituting the values obtained into the original equation.

In[64] := x^2 + 15x + 42 == 0 /. theRoots

$$Out[64] = \{42 + \frac{15\ (-15 + Sqrt[57])}{2} + \frac{(-15 + Sqrt[57])^2}{4} == 0,$$

$$42 + \frac{15\ (-15 - Sqrt[57])}{2} + \frac{(-15 - Sqrt[57])^2}{4} == 0\}$$

Simplifying the result, you can see that the roots do satisfy the equation.

In[65] := Simplify[%]
Out[65] = {True, True}

By using Part or [[ ]], I can substitute one root into another expression.

In[66] := x + 5 /. theRoots[[1]]

$$Out[66] = 5 + \frac{-15 + Sqrt[57]}{2}$$

7.4 Equality

Just like in the C programming language, a double equal sign, ==, is for comparisons and for specifying equations.

In[67] := Expand[(x + y)^2] == x^2 + 2 x y + y^2
Out[67] = True

If you were to use a single equal sign = instead of a double equal sign == when testing equality, would you change the value of a function or operator?

In[68] := a + b = c
          Set::write: Tag Plus in a + b is Protected.
Out[68] = c

Mathematica protects itself against such accidental assignments. Symbols built into *Mathematica* are protected. If a user was to change the definition of a built-in function, that function and other functions that depend on it may stop working properly. So the developers of *Mathematica* made it difficult to change the built-in functions accidentally. Most built-in functions are protected; they have the attribute Protected. If you want to change, add, or delete a rule, first unprotect the function or symbol. In the following example, I unprotect Out, so that I can clear it.

In[69] := Unprotected[Out]

In[70] := Clear[Out]
In[71] := Protect[Out]

Now I won't be able to refer to any of the results that I calculated in this session, i.e., those results with labels *Out[1])* through *In[71])*.

7.4.1 Converting from Equality to Rules

The command NRoots returns a logical statement with equations. The equations can be converted to rules with ToRules.

In[72] := NRoots[x^3 - 3 x^2 - 17 x + 51 == 0, x]
Out[72] = x == -4.12311 || x == 3. || x == 4.12311

In[73] := ToRules[%]
Out[73] = ({x -> -4.12311}, {x -> 3.}, {x -> 4.12311})

7.4.2 More on Equality

There are several functions for testing equality and inequality including: == (Equals), === (SameQ), != (Unequal), and =!= (UnsameQ).

The symbol == is an attempt at mathematical equality. *Mathematica* returns True if the left-hand side is equal to the right-hand side. If the quantities have different precision, *Mathematica* checks whether they are equal to the precision of the number with lower precision.

In[74] := N[Pi, 3] == N[Pi, 30]
Out[74] = True

The expression is returned unevaluated if *Mathematica* cannot determine whether the expressions are equal. The variable y could be equal to x if x and y refer to the same value. Consequently, *Mathematica* is not able to say whether this statement is true or false; so it is returned unevaluated.

In[75] := x == y
Out[75] = x == y

The notation != tests whether the quantity on the left hand side is not equal to the quantity on the right hand side.

In[76] := 1 != 2
Out[76] = True

On the other hand, === returns True if the expressions are syntactically identical (or to the precision of the number of lesser precision) and always returns False otherwise.

In[77] := N[Pi, 3] === N[Pi, 30]
Out[77] = True

In[78] := N[Pi, 3] =!= N[Pi, 30]
Out[78] = False

In[79] := x === y
Out[79] = False

In[80] := x =!= y
Out[80] = True

7.5 Summary

Often it is convenient to refer to a value or to a procedure by name. Immediate-assignment statements allow you to assign names to values. Delayed assignments are used for specifying procedures or functions. Rules are used when you want to replace a variable with a value only in an expression. *Mathematica* includes several functions for testing equality.

Notation	Command	Description
=	Set	Immediate assignment
:=	SetDelayed	Delayed assignment
->	Rule	Immediate rule
:>	RuleDelayed	Delayed rule
/.	ReplaceAll	For applying a rule or list of rules
//.	ReplaceRepeated	For applying rules repeatedly
==	Equal	Test equality
!=	Unequal	Test for inequality
===	SameQ	Test if syntactically the same
=!=	UnsameQ	Test if not the same

7.6 Exercises

This problem set is designed to give you experience with assignment statements and rules.

7.1 Find the value of f[3 + a] and g[3 + a] given the following definitions. Describe the operations *Mathematica* performed to arrive at the result.

```
f[x_] = x /. a -> 7        f[x_] = x + %
g[x_] := x /. a -> 7       g[x_] := x + %
```

```
f[x_] = N[x]               f[x_] = Expand[2x]
g[x_] := N[x]              g[x_] := Expand[2x]
```

7.2 Explain why *Mathematica* uses := (SetDelayed) in each input line *(In[n] := x)* and = (Set) for each output line *(Out[n] = y)*.

7.3 (a) Given the pairs of data, use the rule below to double the second element in each pair.

{{1, 1}, {2, 2}, {3, 3}} /. {x_, y_} :> {x, 2y}

(b) Given the pairs of data, why doesn't the rule {x_, y_} :> {x, 2y} double the second element in each pair? What does this rule do?

{{1, 1}, {2, 2}} /. {x_, y_} :> {x, 2y}

7.4 Write a rule which, when applied to points specified in three-space, {x,y,z}, returns pairs of {x,y}. *Hint:* See problem 3.

7.5 Write a rule that takes a list of pairs, $\{x_i, y_i\}$ and a list of values z_i for $i = 1$ to 4 and transforms the two lists into a single list of triplets $\{x_i, y_i, z_i\}$.

7.6 (a) Why doesn't the rule y z_ -> y Expand[z] expand the term (x - 2)(x + 2) in the expression y(x - 2)(x + 2)?

y (x + 2)(x - 2) /. y z_ -> y Expand[z]

(b) Write a rule that will expand (x - 2)(x + 2).

7.7 In the package Trigonometry.m distributed with version 1.2, TrigFactor contains the following rule.

a_. Cos[x_] Cos[y_] + a_. Sin[x_] Sin[y_] :> a Cos[x - y]

Why doesn't it also contain the rule

a_. Cos[x_ - y_] :> a Cos[x] Cos[y] + a Sin[x] Sin[y]?

7.8 Use DSolve to find the solution to the differential equation $y'(x) = y(x)$. Then use rules to substitute the solution back into the equation to verify that it is correct.

Data Types

In *Mathematica*, there is no need to declare the types of variables or functions as is required in C or FORTRAN. *Mathematica* handles data more like the programming language APL; it figures out the type of your data on the basis of how they are being used. This chapter describes the different types of expressions and how they are stored internally. Understanding how *Mathematica* represents expressions will help you to use *Mathematica* more effectively.

8.1 Atomic Types

Though you do not need to declare data types when programming in *Mathematica*, each expression is composed of objects of one or more of the following atomic types: Integer, Real, Rational, Complex, Symbol, and String. The table below gives descriptions and examples of each of these indivisible types.

Type	Description	Example
Integer	An integer	3
Real	A real of the form nn.mm	3.4
Rational	A rational number a/b, for integers a and b	3/4
Complex	A complex number of the form r + I c	3 + 4.2I
Symbol	A variable or value represented by a symbol	v, Pi
String	A character string	"red"

The function Head returns the type of an atomic expression.

```
In[1] := Head[53]
Out[1] = Integer

In[2] := Head[5.7]
Out[2] = Real
```

In[3] := Head[2 + 3I]
Out[3] = Complex

In[4] := Head[a]
Out[4] = Symbol

In[5] := Head[Pi]
Out[5] = Symbol

In[6] := Head["title"]
Out[6] = String

8.2 Other Types and Predicate Functions

In addition to the atomic types, *Mathematica* knows about other types of expressions. A value is considered a number if it is one of the following: an integer, a floating-point number, a rational, or a complex number. A vector is a list. There are predicate functions for checking if an expression is of a certain type. A predicate function returns True or False.

In[7] := NumberQ[3 + 4 I / 7]
Out[7] = True

In[8] := VectorQ[{a, b, c}]
Out[8] = True

The names of most of the predicate functions end with the letter Q. Exceptions to this rule are the functions LegendreQ and PolynomialQ, which end with the letter Q but are not predicate functions, and the functions Negative, NonNegative, and Positive, which are predicate functions. Some of these predicate functions are described in section 6.8 on page 127.

In[9] := ?*Q

AtomQ	MatrixQ	PartitionsQ	StringMatchQ
EvenQ	MemberQ	PolynomialQ	TrueQ
FreeQ	NameQ	PrimeQ	UnsameQ
IntegerQ	NumberQ	ProbablePrimeQ	ValueQ
LegendreQ	OddQ	SameQ	VectorQ
MatchQ	OrderedQ		

Version 2.0: More predicate expressions have been added to version 2.0.

```
In[10] := ?*Q
        AtomQ              MachineNumberQ      PolynomialQ
        DigitQ             MatchLocalNameQ     PrimeQ
        EllipticNomeQ      MatchQ              SameQ
        EvenQ              MatrixQ             StringMatchQ
        FreeQ              MemberQ             StringQ
        HypergeometricPFQ  NameQ               SyntaxQ
        IntegerQ           NumberQ             TrueQ
        LegendreQ          OddQ                UnsameQ
        LetterQ            OptionQ             UpperCaseQ
        ListQ              OrderedQ            ValueQ
        LowerCaseQ         PartitionsQ         VectorQ
```

Predicate functions are typically used in programming, as you will see in section 9.2 on page 168.

8.3 *Mathematica's* **Internal Representation**

The basic form of an expression is f [x, y, ...] where f is a function and x, y, ... are arguments. The arguments (and even the functions) can be arbitrary expressions.

Expressions, including those that use special symbols, such as /@, or mathematical symbols such as + or /, are represented in *Mathematica* by functions. It can be useful to see how *Mathematica* represents an expression. The functions FullForm, FullForm[Hold[*expr*]], and TreeForm show how *Mathematica* internally stores a result.

```
In[11] := FullForm[2/3]
Out[11] = Rational[2, 3]

In[12] := FullForm[2 + 3I]
Out[12] = Complex[2, 3]

In[13] := FullForm[h[x, y]]
Out[13] = h[x, y]

In[14] := FullForm[a b^c]
Out[14] = Times[a, Power[b, c]]

In[15] := TreeForm[a b^c]
Out[15] = Times[a, |                ]
                    Power[b, c]
```

Mathematica evaluates an expression when it can. Instead of showing us the internal representation of $2 + 7$, *Mathematica* shows us the internal representation of the result, which is simply 9.

In[16] := FullForm[2 + 7]
Out[16] = 9

8.3.1 Not Evaluating or Forcing Evaluation

If you want to see an expression before it is evaluated, wrap the function Hold around the expression.

In[17] := FullForm[Hold[2 + 7]]
Out[17] = Hold[Plus[2, 7]]

Sometimes *Mathematica* does not evaluate an expression or a subexpression. The functions Release (version 1.2), ReleaseHold (version 2.0), or Evaluate an expression to be evaluated.

The function ReleaseHold removes Hold or HoldForm in its argument, *arg*.

In[18] := ReleaseHold[Hold[2 + 7]]
Out[18] = 9

The function Evaluate evaluates its argument, *arg*, immediately, even if an attribute of *f* indicates the argument should be held.

    f [Evaluate[*arg*]]

Let aList be a list consisting of names of two commands.

In[19] := aList = {"Abs", "And"};

Notice that when I ask for the attributes of aList, I obtain the attributes of the symbol aList, not the attributes of the list of symbols to which it refers.

In[20] := Attributes[aList]
Out[20] = {}

Wrapping Release (version 1.2) or Evaluate (version 2.0) around aList causes *Mathematica* to replace aList with its value {Abs, And}.

In[21] := Attributes[Evaluate[aList]]
Out[21] = {{Listable, Protected}, {Listable, Protected}}

8.3.2 The Head of An Expression

You saw above that Head returns the type of an expression. For nonatomic expressions, FullForm may help you to understand what Head returns.

In[22] := FullForm[a + b]
Out[22] = Plus[a, b]

In[23] := Head[a + b]
Out[23] = Plus

In[24] := FullForm[{a, b}]
Out[24] = List[a, b]

In[25] := Head[{a, b}]
Out[25] = List

In[26] := FullForm[Sin[x + 3x^2]]
Out[26] = Sin[Plus[x, Times[3, Power[x, 2]]]]

In[27] := Head[Sin[x + 3x^2]]
Out[27] = Sin

In an expression of the form $h[arg_1, arg_2]$, the symbol h is the head of the expression, and arg_1 and arg_2 are considered arguments.

8.3.3 Changing Heads

Notice that the internal representation of the list {a, b, c} (List[a, b, c]) is quite similar to the internal representation of the sum a + b + c (Plus[a, b, c]).

In[28] := FullForm[{a, b, c}]
Out[28] = List[a, b, c]

In[29] := FullForm[a + b + c]
Out[29] = Plus[a, b, c]

Using a replacement rule, you can replace the head of a list with Plus and thus transform a list into a sum. However, this is not recommended. In nested lists, the head of the sublists would also turn into Plus.

In[30] := {a, b, c} /. List -> Plus
Out[30] = a + b + c

Apply replaces the head of *expr* with *f*.

Apply[*f*, *expr*]

If you want to add up elements of a list, use Apply[Plus, $\{e_1, e_2, \ldots, e_n\}$].

In[31] := Apply[Plus, {a, b, c}]
Out[31] = a + b + c

In[32] := Apply[Plus, Range[100]]
Out[32] = 5050

8.4 Referencing Parts of Expressions

Just as you could reference an element of a list, you can also reference an element in an expression.

In[33] := expr = 3 + a + Sin[2Pi x^y]

$$Out[33] = 3 + a + Sin[2\ Pi\ x^y]$$

In[34] := TreeForm[expr]
Out[34] = Plus[3, a, |]
                   Sin[|]
                        Times[2, Pi, |]
                                      Power[x, y]

In[35] := expr[[3]]

$$Out[35] = Sin[2\ Pi\ x^y]$$

In[36] := expr[[3, 1]]

$$Out[36] = 2\ Pi\ x^y$$

In[37] := expr[[3, 1, 2]]
Out[37] = Pi

The function Position gives the list of positions where a symbol is found.

In[38] := expr2 = Expand[(x + y)^3]

$$Out[38] = x^3 + 3\ x^2\ y + 3\ x\ y^2 + y^3$$

In[39] := Position[expr2, x]
Out[39] = {{1, 1}, {2, 2, 1}, {3, 2}}

The result {2, 2, 1} indicates that there is an x in the first argument of the second term of the second term in expr2.

In[40] := { expr2[[2]], expr2[[2, 2]], expr2[[2, 2, 1]] }

$$Out[40] = \{3\ x^2\ y,\ x^2,\ x\}$$

8.5 Infinity and Other Such Quantities

Infinite quantities are treated differently from finite quantities. There are some fundamental rules built into *Mathematica*, such as 0 x = 0 for finite x. *Mathematica* knows not to apply this rule when x is an infinite quantity.

In[41] := 0 x
Out[41] = 0

In[42] := 0 Infinity
      Infinity::indt:
         Indeterminate expression 0 (Infinity) encountered.
Out[42] = Indeterminate

Mathematica differentiates between huge quantities that are positive, negative, and complex.

In[43] := Limit[1/x, x -> 0]
Out[43] = ComplexInfinity

In[44] := Limit[Log[1/x], x -> 0]
Out[44] = Infinity

In[45] := -3 Infinity
Out[45] = -Infinity

Mathematica prints error messages when you divide a quantity by 0.

In[46] := 4/0

                                 1
      Power::infy: Infinite expression - encountered.
                                 0

Out[46] = ComplexInfinity

In[47] := 0/0

                                 1
      Power::infy: Infinite expression - encountered.
                                 0

      Infinity::indt:
         Indeterminate expression 0
         ComplexInfinity encountered.
Out[47] = Indeterminate

The following table lists types of infinities known to *Mathematica*.

Symbol	Description
Infinity	A positive real infinite quantity.
-Infinity	A negative real infinite quantity.
ComplexInfinity	A quantity with infinite magnitude, but undetermined complex phase.
Indeterminate	A numerical quantity whose magnitude cannot be determined.

8.6 How *Mathematica* Stores Values

The function `MemoryInUse` returns the number of bytes *Mathematica* is currently using. With this function, you can determine how much memory *Mathematica* uses to store values.

```
In[48] := before = MemoryInUse[ ];
In[49] := Table[Random[ ], {1000}];
In[50] := after = MemoryInUse[ ];

In[51] := N[after - before] / 1000
Out[51] = 37.312
```

If you examine how much memory is used when storing a list of 1000 random integers that are less than 200 and a list of 1000 random integers that are greater than 500, you will notice that significantly less memory is used when storing integers that are less than 200. Real-valued numbers stored to the precision of the floating point hardware of the machine that you are using similarly use less memory than real numbers stored with more precision.

8.6.1 Sharing Memory

Mathematica tries to be somewhat efficient about storing expressions. If you create an array a, then set b equal to a, *Mathematica* does not create an array for b. Instead b points to the value of a, so a and b share values. Only one instance of the array is created.

```
In[52] := (
            Clear[a, b];
            beforeA = MemoryInUse[ ];
            a = Table[Random[ ], {1000}];
            afterA = MemoryInUse[ ];
            b = a;
            afterB = MemoryInUse[ ];
            {afterA - beforeA, afterB - afterA}
        )
Out[52] = {36020, 0}
```

Notice that the memory used by b is 0. If you change or delete a, then the old value of the array a is copied to b.

The function Share is intended for decreasing memory use. With Share, you can force *Mathematica* to share common subexpressions in storing a result and thus decrease the amount of memory used.

In the following example, I create an array of 1000 random integers between the values of 10,000 and 10,010. Because the array will contain duplicates, Share can decrease the amount of memory used to store the 1000 numbers.

```
In[53] := (
          Clear[c];
          beforeStore = MemoryInUse[ ];
          c = Table[Random[Integer, {10000, 10010}], {1000}];
          afterStore = MemoryInUse[ ];
          c = Share[c];
          afterShare = MemoryInUse[ ];
          {afterStore - beforeStore, afterShare - beforeStore}
        )
Out[53] = {24020, 4020}
```

The function ByteCount gives the number of bytes used by *Mathematica* to store an expression. Unfortunately, it assumes that no subexpressions are shared.

```
In[54] := ByteCount[a]
Out[54] = 36020
```

```
In[55] := ByteCount[{a, b}]
Out[55] = 72068
```

The following table contains the number of bytes used to store different types of expressions on a Macintosh II.

Type	Example	Bytes Used
Integer	3	20
Real	4.5	32
Rational	2/3	68
Complex	4 + 6 I	68
String	"red"	20

8.7 Summary

Like many other computer languages, *Mathematica* supports various data types. Unlike many other computer languages, you need not declare the type of a variable before using it. By understanding how *Mathematica* represents expressions, you will be better able to use *Mathematica* effectively.

8.8 Exercises

8.1 Determine how *Mathematica* internally represents the following expressions.

   (a) 35a

   (b) a35

   (c) -x

   (d) -3

   (e) x - 3

   (f) 3 - x

   (g) Sqrt[5]

   (h) Series[Tan[x], {x, 0, 9}]

   (i) Normal[Series[Tan[x], {x, 0, 9}]]

8.2 (a) If you ask *Mathematica* to evaluate 2^3^4, will it compute 2^(3^4) or (2^3)^4?

   (b) Compare the FullForm of (x^y)^z with the FullForm of x^(y^z).

8.3 The function MemoryInUse gives the number of bytes of memory used to store data in the current session of *Mathematica*. See how much memory *Mathematica* uses storing a list of 1000 random integers that are between 100 and 200, 1000 integers that are between 300 and 400, 1000 floating-point numbers with the default level of precision, and 1000 floating-point numbers with 30 places of precision. Can you draw any conclusions from your study?

8.4 Suppose you have 4 megabytes memory available on your machine. One magabyte is equal to 2^{20} bytes. Suppose *Mathematica* requires 32 bytes to store a floating point number. What is the largest square matrix that you can store on your machine, assuming all the memory can be used to store the matrix.

9

pascal[n_Integer] := Table[Binomial[n, i

Writing Functions

Mathematica may not have a function for what you want to do. In such cases, you can write a function yourself. The pattern-matching capabilities of *Mathematica* allow you flexibility in specifying the arguments of a function. This chapter starts by showing you the simplest specification of an argument to a function. It goes on to show how you can restrict a function to work only on certain types of arguments or arguments that meet certain conditions. This chapter also describes ways to document your code.

9.1 A Simple Function

Let us write a function to compute the square of its argument. I call `Clear` before defining the square function so that other definitions of `square` will not be invoked inadvertently.

```
In[1] := Clear[square];
In[2] := square[x] := x^2
```

This function returns x^2 when given x as an argument.

```
In[3] := square[x]

          2
Out[3] = x
```

However, notice that `square` does not work for any other argument. The function is defined only for the argument x.

```
In[4] := square[y]
Out[4] = square[y]
```

The cube function computes the cube of its argument, provided it is a single expression.

In[5] := Clear[cube];
In[6] := cube[x_] := x^3

The _ or Blank appearing after x tells *Mathematica* to assign the name x to the argument of cube. The cube function works when given any expression as an argument.

In[7] := cube[9 + 4x^2]

$$Out[7] = (9 + 4 x)^{2\ 3}$$

The general form of a function definition is:

$$f[arg1_, arg2_, ...] := body$$

The symbol *f* is to be associated with the function definition. The formal parameters, *arg1, arg2, ...*, are the names used within the body of the procedure to refer to the corresponding arguments of the procedure. The name preceding the [is the symbol to be associated with the function definition. The *body* is an expression that yields the value of the procedure application when the formal parameters are replaced by the actual arguments to which the procedure is applied. The *body* can be a single expression or several expressions that are grouped together. The function polarTransform consists of three statements grouped together with parentheses.

```
In[8] := polarTransform[r_, theta_] := (
            x = r Cos[theta];
            y = r Sin[theta];
            {x, y}
        )
```

If you want polarTransform to transform a pair of values (a list of two elements), specify a function whose argument is a pair.

In[9] := polarTransform[{r_, theta_}] := polarTransform[r, theta]

9.2 Type Checking

The notation f[*arg_type*] is used to specify the function to work only when Head[*arg*] === *type*.

Here is the function pascal, defined for integer-valued arguments.

```
In[10] := Clear[pascal];
In[11] := pascal[n_Integer] := Table [Binomial[n, i], {i, 0, n}]

In[12] := pascal[5]
Out[12] = {1, 5, 10, 10, 5, 1}
```

Notice pascal is not evaluated when given a real-valued argument.

```
In[13] := pascal[5.5]
Out[13] = pascal[5.5]
```

The following definition of mean works when given a list as an argument.

```
In[14] := mean[x_List] := Apply[Plus, x]/Length[x]

In[15] := mean[{1, 2, 3, 4}]

          5
Out[15] = -
          2
```

The notation h[*x_type*] cannot be used to check whether the argument is positive or a polynomial. Instead you can use the notation h[*x_?test*] to specify that the function h is invoked only if *test*[*x*] returns True.

I could have written the pascal function with the predicate function for checking if an expression is integer-valued pascal[n_?IntegerQ] but this takes more time to evaluate than pascal[n_Integer].

The function half is defined only for even-valued arguments.

```
In[16] := Clear[half];
In[17] := half[x_?EvenQ] := x / 2
```

Since 5 is odd, half[5] does not return half the value of 5.

```
In[18] := half[5]
Out[18] = half[5]
```

The number 14 is even and thus satisfies the test EvenQ.

```
In[19] := half[14]
Out[19] = 7
```

For type checking, you can define rules for different types of arguments. The signum function is equal to 1 if its argument is positive and -1 if its argument is negative.

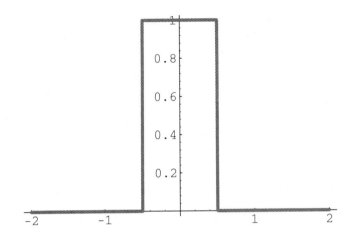

Figure 9.1: The `rect` function as specified in *In[23]* and *In[24]*.

In[20] := `signum[x_Positive] := 1`
In[21] := `signum[x_Negative] := -1`

9.3 Conditional Evaluation

In *Mathematica* it is possible to apply a rule if a specified condition is met. Here I define the `rect` function to be 1 in the interval [-1/2, 1/2]. The notation `/;` can be interpreted as meaning *such that*. The rule is evaluated provided the condition on the right-hand side is met. I define `rect[x]` with two rules. The first rule is used when $-1/2 \le x \le 1/2$. This condition could have been written by using the `Abs` function as was done with the second rule.

In[22] := `Clear[rect];`
In[23] := `rect[x_] := 1 /; (-1/2 <= x && x <= 1/2)`
In[24] := `rect[x_] := 0 /; Abs[x] > 1/2`

 Version 2.0: Constraints or conditions can be specified for patterns.

In[22] := `Clear[rect];`
In[23] := `rect[x_/; (-1/2 <= x && x <= 1/2)] := 1`
In[24] := `rect[x_/; Abs[x] > 1/2] := 0`

To distinguish the curve representing the function from the lines representing the axes, I draw the function in a thick (`Thickness[0.01]`) gray (`GrayLevel[0.05]`) line. The graph is shown in figure 9.1.

```
In[25] := Plot[rect[x], {x, -2, 2},
            PlotStyle -> {{
                Thickness[0.01],
                GrayLevel[0.5]
            }}
        ];
```

Why did I specify `PlotStyle` with two braces, {{ }}, instead of just one, { }? If I had used just one, then the graph would have been drawn with a thick line, not a thick gray line. By using double braces, I am able to specify two styles.

Notice that though this function is not built into *Mathematica* and it is not continuous, you can use `NIntegrate` to find the area under the curve.

```
In[26] := NIntegrate[rect[x], {x, -2, 2}]
Out[26] = 1.
```

9.4 Default Values

Mathematica assigns a default value for an argument specified with the patterns x_-. and $x_-:value$. With the notation x_-., the default value depends on the default value assigned to a function. The default value is designed to keep the value of the expression unchanged. In the pattern x_-. + y_-. $z_-\hat{}e_-$., the variable x defaults to 0 because x + y z^e is equal to y z^e when x is set equal to 0. Using a similar sort of reasoning, you can see why the default values for y and for e are 1. Below I write a function that returns the default values of x, y, and e, along with the value of z.

```
In[27] := Clear[f]
In[28] := f[x_. + y_. z_^e_.] := {x, y, z, e}

In[29] := f[4]
Out[29] = {0, 1, 4, 1}
```

The pattern $x_-:val$ assigns the value *val* to *x* when no value is specified.

With the argument `first_:0`, the call `myRange[n]` returns a list of consecutive numbers starting with 0. The argument is assigned the name `last`.

```
In[30] := Clear[myRange]
In[31] := myRange[first_:0, last_] := Range[first, last]

In[32] := myRange[3]
Out[32] = {0, 1, 2, 3}

In[33] := myRange[2, 5]
Out[33] = {2, 3, 4, 5}
```

In packages that are distributed with *Mathematica*, defaults are sometimes assigned with additional rules. In `Laplace.m` distributed with version 1.2, the following rule handles the case where only one argument is passed to `Laplace`.

```
Laplace[e_] := Laplace[e, t, s]
```

I recommend assigning default values by using the notation *var_:value* to make it obvious to those reading your code what default values arguments will take on.

9.5 The Order of Evaluation of Rules

In *Mathematica*, you can specify one or more rules. *Mathematica* attempts to evaluate more specific rules before more general rules. Using the ? operator, you see the order in which *Mathematica* tries rules.

```
In[34] := Clear[r]
In[35] := r[x_] := x^2
In[36] := r[x_Integer] := x
In[37] := r[2] := 16
In[38] := ?r
        r/: r[2] := 16
        r/: r[x_Integer] := x
        r/: r[x_] := x^2

In[39] := r[2]
Out[39] = 16

In[40] := r[4]
Out[40] = 4
```

The notation *f/: lhs := rhs* associates the assignment *lhs := rhs* with the symbol *f*. By default *f[...] := ...* is associated with *f*. How can you make use of this notation?

9.6 Tagging Rules

Notice that *Mathematica* does not let you assign `f[x_] + g[x_] := h[x]` because the symbol `Plus` is write protected.

```
In[41] := f[x_] + g[x_] := h[x]
        Set::write:
            Symbol Plus is write protected.
```

Each rule, either built-in or user-defined, is associated with a symbol. The built-in symbols, such as Plus, Integrate, and Plot are write-protected so that users cannot easily change the definitions of these symbols by accident. Using the notation *symbol/*: before specifying a rule or assignment, instructs *Mathematica* to associate the rule or assignment with *symbol*.

Here I associate the assignment f[x_] + g[x_] := h[x] with the symbol f.

In[42] := f/: f[x_] + g[x_] := h[x]

Notice that this rule does not match the expression f[3].

In[43] := f[3]
Out[43] = f[3]

The rule simplifies the expression f[3] + g[3].

In[44] := f[3] + g[3]
Out[44] = h[3]

9.7 Documenting Your Own Functions

If you use the ? operator on a function defined in *Mathematica*'s own programming language, it returns the definition.

In[45] := ?pascal
        pascal
        pascal/: pascal[n_Integer] := Table[Binomial[n, i],
            {i, 0, n}]

You can write usage statements for your functions by using the notation:

function::usage = "*function*[*arg1*, *arg2*, ...] *returns something*."

For example, here I specify the usage statement for our pascal function.

In[46] := pascal::usage = "pascal[n] lists the nth row of Pascal's
            triangle."
Out[46] = pascal[n] lists the nth row of Pascal's triangle.

Notice I obtain this usage statement if I ask for information on pascal.

In[47] := ?pascal
        pascal[n] lists the nth row of Pascal's triangle.

If I ask for additional information, *Mathematica* shows the usage statement together with the definition of pascal.

```
In[48] := ??pascal
        pascal[n] lists the nth row of Pascal's triangle.
        pascal/: pascal[n_Integer] := Table[Binomial[n, i],
            {i, 0, n}]
```

9.8 Attributes

As you saw in section 6.11 on page 130, a function can be assigned the attribute Listable. Other attributes that can be assigned to functions include: Constant, Flat, HoldAll, HoldFirst, HoldRest, Locked, Orderless, Protected, and ReadProtected. Section 11.6 on page 195 shows an example of pattern matching with a function assigned the attribute Orderless. Attributes are not user extendible.

You can see the attributes of a function by calling the function Attributes. The ?? operator will also show you any attributes that have been assigned.

```
In[49] := Attributes[Table]
Out[49] = {HoldAll, Protected}
```

Most functions built into *Mathematica* have the attribute Protected so that users will not inadvertently change their meaning or add rules to the function. Below is a table of some of the Attributes that are built into *Mathematica*.

Attribute	Description
Constant	Indicates zero derivative of a symbol with respect to all parameters.
Flat	All expressions involving nested functions should be flattened out.
HoldAll	All arguments to a function are to be maintained in an unevaluated form.
HoldFirst	The first argument to a function is to be maintained in an unevaluated form.
HoldRest	All but the first argument to the function are to be maintained in an unevaluated form.
Listable	The function should automatically be threaded over a list, i.e., f[{a, b, c}] gets transformed to {f[a], f[b], f[c]}.
Locked	Prevents modification of any attribute of a symbol.
Orderless	The elements ei in expressions of the form f[e1, e2, ...] should automatically be sorted into canonical order.
Protected	Protects a symbol so that it cannot be changed unless it is unprotected.
ReadProtected	Prevents any values associated with a symbol from being printed.

9.9 Evaluation

How does *Mathematica* evaluate an expression? It depends on the expression and the attributes of the functions in the expression.

Mathematica first evaluates the head of an expression. Then it evaluates each element of the expression. If an element consists of non-atomic expression (expressions that are not one of the atomic types), then *Mathematica* recursively applies this same evaluation procedure.

However, if any element of the expression has the attribute `HoldFirst`, `HoldAll`, or `HoldRest` or a call to `Release` (version 1.2), `Evaluate` (version 2.0), or `ReleaseHold` (version 1.2), then its arguments are evaluated in a slightly different order. If a function has the attribute `HoldFirst`, then the first argument of the function is not evaluated. If a function has the attribute `HoldAll`, all arguments to the function are maintained in unevaluated form. The functions `Plot`, `Table`, and `Attributes` have the attribute `HoldAll`. If a function has the attribute `HoldRest` then all arguments except for the first are maintained in unevaluated form. The functions `Release` (version 1.2) and `Evaluate` (version 2.0) cause an argument to be evaluated even if it is in a "held" position. Consider, for example, the function `Table`, which has the attribute `HoldAll`. By forcing *Mathematica* to evaluate `Random`, I obtain three copies of the same random number.

```
In[50] := Table[Evaluate[Random[ ]], {3}]
Out[50] = {0.56175, 0.56175, 0.56175}

In[51] := Table[Random[ ], {3}]
Out[51] = {0.659713, 0.468764, 0.232585}
```

Mathematica applies rules to transform an expression until the result no longer changes.

9.10 Summary

In this chapter you learned how to write a simple function. The pattern-matching mechanism enables you to restrict functions to work only when provided with certain types of arguments or with arguments that meet certain conditions.

Pattern	Description
$x\_$	A pattern that matches any single expression. The matched expression is given the name x
x_type	A pattern that matches a single expression whose Head is *type*.
$x\_?test$	A pattern that matches a single expression that yields True when *test* is applied to the expression.
$x\_/\,;condition$	A pattern that matches a single expression for which *condition* evaluates to True (Version 2.0).
$x\_:v$	A piece of a pattern with default value v.
$x\_.$	A piece of a pattern with a globally defined default value designed to not change the value of the complete expression.

9.11 Exercises

This problem set is designed to give you experience with writing functions.

9.1 After specifying the following assignments and rules,

```
f[2] = 3
f[u] := 2u^2
f[v_] := 1/v
u = 2
```

what is f[u]?

9.2 Write the function middle[x] that returns the integer-valued result (x + 1)/2 for odd values of x.

9.3 Write a function that takes a pair, {x, y}, and returns {x, 2y}. Map this function onto the list of data points {{1, 1}, {2, 2}}.

9.4 Define a function triangle[x] to be equal to 1 - Abs[x] when Abs[x] < 1, and is equal to 0 otherwise as in figure 9.2. Plot your triangle function.

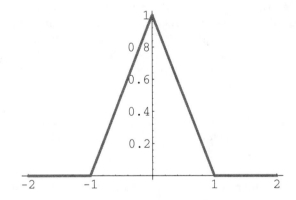

Figure 9.2: The triangle function.

9.5 Write the signum function, sgn[x], which is equal to 1 if x is positive and is equal to −1 if x is negative (see figure 9.3). Plot your sgn function. Specify sgn[0.] = 0 by convention, as 0 is neither positive nor negative. Plot your signum function.

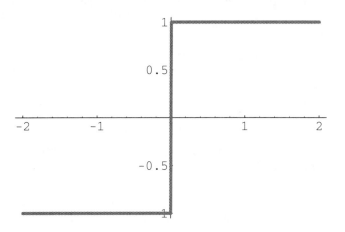

Figure 9.3: The signum function.

9.6 Rewrite the function myRange listed on page 171 so that, when given a single positive-valued argument n, it returns the list of consecutive integers from 0 to n. If it is given two arguments, n and m such that n < m, it returns the list of consecutive integers from n to m. If it is given three arguments, n, m, and d > 0 with n ≤ m, it returns the list {n, n + d, n + 2d, ...} for n + kd ≤ m.

9.7 Notice that the rule s[- x_] :> - s[x] transforms s[-a] to -s[a] but it does not transform s[-3]. What do you think this rule will do to s[1 - x] and why?

9.8 Write the recursive function piByFour[n_] to compute an approximation to $\pi/4$ using the formula:
$$\pi/4 \approx 2*4*4*6*6*8*8*10*10\ldots2n/(3*3*5*5*7*7*9*9\ldots(2n+1)$$
That is,

```
piByFour[1] = 2/3
piByFour[2] = 2 * 4 * 4 / (3 * 3 * 5)
piByFour[2] = piByFour[1] * 4 * 4 / (3 * 5)
piByFour[3] = 2 * 4 * 4 * 6 * 6 / (3 * 3 * 5 * 5 * 7)
piByFour[3] = piByFour[2] * 6 * 6 / (5 * 7)
piByFour[4] = piByFour[3] * 8 * 8 / (7 * 9)
```

9.9 Determine the functions whose names begin with the letters A – E that have the attribute `Listable`. *Hints*: The function `Names` returns a list of names (strings) of symbols that match the string specified as an argument. The function `MemberQ` returns `True` if an element is in a list. You might consider writing a function which when given a symbol returns `True` if the symbol is `Listable`.

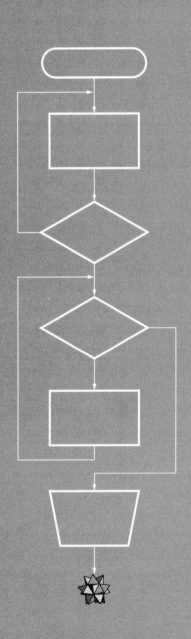

10

Local Variables & Procedural Programming

This chapter discusses what happens when you try to use the name of a variable that has already been assigned a value. Mechanisms are described for declaring variables local to a procedure. Functions are also shown for iterating and for writing conditional expressions. The chapter concludes with an example that employs some of the constructs it presents.

10.1 Colliding Global Variables (Version 1.2)

Let us look at what happens if you use a variable name that has already been used. The functions f and g both use i as an index variable.

```
In[1] := f[n_] := Table[g[i], {i, n}]
In[2] := g[m_] := Table[Log[i], {i, m}]
```

Mathematica prints error messages when g tries to use i since f assigned a value to i.

In[3] := f [3]

    General::itervar:
       In iterator {i, 1}, variable i already
       has a value.

    General::itervar:
       In iterator {i, 2}, variable i already
       has a value.

    General::itervar:
       In iterator {i, 3}, variable i already
       has a value.

    General::stop:
       Further output of General::itervar will
       be suppressed during this calculation.

Out[3] = {{0}, {0, Log[2]}, {0, Log[2], Log[3]}

On the other hand, no error messages are printed if f and g use different index variables.

In[4] := f[n_] := Table[g[i], {i, n}]
In[5] := g[m_] := Table[Log[j], {j, m}]

In[6] := f [3]
Out[6] = {{0}, {0, Log[2]}, {0, Log[2], Log[3]}}

When you write a function, you do not know what variables may have been set by users of your function. Consequently, it is advisable to use local or private variables instead of global variables.

10.2 Local Variables

Variables can be declared to be local to a procedure by using Block (or Module in version 2.0). Though both f and g use the same index variable, now there is no collision since the index variables i have been declared local to f and local to g.

In[7] := f[n_] := Block[{i}, Table[g[i], {i, n}]]

In[8] := g[m_] := Block[{i}, Table[Log[i], {i, m}]]

In[9] := f [3]
Out[9] = {{0}, {0, Log[2]}, {0, Log[2], Log[3]}}

How does Block handle local variables? If the symbol i is defined when f is called, its value is stored and put aside so that it cannot interfere with the local variable i. When f finishes, the global value of i is restored. Thus if a variable is declared globally and locally, you cannot access the global value from within the Block or any function called from within the Block. The functions Module and With in version 2.0 address this particular shortcoming of the Block command. These commands are an attempt to support lexical binding. (See *Structure and Interpretation of Computer Programs* by Abelson and Sussman for a description of lexical binding.) Module creates a new symbol to represent each of its local variables every time it is called. For the local variable x, a symbol is created with name $x\$n$, where n is the current value of the global variable $ModuleNumber.

In[10] := Module[{x}, x]
Out[10] = x$1

Instead of using x as a local variable, a new symbol is created that does not conflict with the global definition of x. So the global definition of x and the local specification of x are accessible simultaneously. In version 2.0, Module can be used in place of Block.

Section 15.2 on page 247 describes contexts, another mechanism for avoiding variable collisions.

10.3 Procedural Programming

In *Mathematica* you can write procedural programs, i.e., define a sequence of steps to be executed. As with C and Pascal, with *Mathematica* you can perform a calculation repeatedly by using: Do, For, or While. The *Mathematica* language includes the conditional constructs: If, Which, and Switch.

10.3.1 Changing Values of Variables

There are a couple of shorthand notations for incrementing a variable by 1. The notation ++i increments i by 1 and returns the new value of i. On the other hand, the notation i++ returns the value of i and then increments it.

In[11] := i = 1
Out[11] = 1

In[12] := ++i
Out[12] = 2

In[13] := i++
Out[13] = 2

In[14] := i
Out[14] = 3

The notation x += dx adds dx to x and returns the new value of x. Similarly, the notation x -= dx subtracts dx from x and returns the new value of x, the notation x *= c multiplies x by c and returns the new value of x, and the notation x /= c divides x by c and returns the new value of x. This notation can only be used after x has been assigned a value.

```
In[15] := x  = 3
Out[15] = 3

In[16] := x += 4
Out[16] = 7

In[17] := x -= 5
Out[17] = 2

In[18] := x *= 6
Out[18] = 12

In[19] := x /= 4
Out[19] = 3
```

10.3.2 Iterative or Looping Constructs

The functions Do, For, and While are used to instruct *Mathematica* to do something repeatedly. In the following examples, I compute the square of the first three positive integers.

The function Do behaves identically with Table except that it always returns Null instead of a list. It is used for its side effects. With the function Print, you can display results.

```
In[20] := Do[Print[i^2], {i, 3}]
            1
            4
            9
```

For and While are more general. With For, specify an initial value, a test, a formula for incrementing the index variable, and a body.

```
For[start, test, incr, body]
```

```
In[21] := For[i = 1, i <= 3, ++i, Print[i^2]]
            1
            4
            9
```

With While, specify a test and the statements to be evaluated.

```
While[test, body]
```

```
In[22] := i = 1;
In[23] := While[i <= 3, (Print[i^2]; i++)]
        1
        4
        9
```

10.3.3 Logic

A test is specified in If, For, and While statements. *Mathematica* supports several logical functions including And (represented by &&), Or (||), Not (!), and Xor. Here is a logical statement that returns True if x is greater than 17 or x is odd and less than 5.

$$(x > 17) \ || \ (x < 5) \ \&\& \ \text{OddQ}[x]$$

In what order does *Mathematica* evaluate clauses? I'll write an example in which one clause evaluates to True and the other clause, if evaluated, generates an error message.

```
In[24] := (3 > 2) || (1/0 > 5)
Out[24] = True
```

Mathematica only evaluated the first clause. The second clause was not evaluated.

```
In[25] := (1/0 < 5) || (3 > 2)
        Power::infy:
                              1
             Infinite expression - encountered.
                              0

        Less:nord:
             Comparison with complex number
             ComplexInfinity attempted.

Out[25] = True
```

Both clauses were evaluated. *Mathematica*, like C, evaluates its argument involving && and || from left to right and stops as soon as the result is known.

10.3.4 Conditionals

Using a conditional expression, you can instruct *Mathematica* to perform an operation only if a condition is met. With the functions If, Switch, and Which, you can run some test and then instruct *Mathematica* to take some action based on its value.

The function If is a mechanism for specifying two possible alternatives. If *test* evaluates to True then *true–body* is evaluated. If *test* evaluates to False then *false–*

body is evaluated. If *test* evaluates to neither True nor False then *neither–body* is evaluated. The arguments *false–body* and *neither–body* are optional.

If[*test*, *true–body*, *false–body*, *neither–body*]

Here I instruct *Mathematica* to call the option Framed when using using a version of *Mathematica* less than 2, otherwise to use the option Frame.

```
In[26] := If[$VersionNumber < 2.0,
            Plot[Exp[-x^2] Cos[20x], {x, -2, 2}, Framed ->True],
            Plot[Exp[-x^2] Cos[20x], {x, -2, 2}, Frame -> True]
         ]
```

For specifying more than two alternatives, you can nest sets of If statements. Alternatively, you could use the functions Switch or Which, intended for specifying several alternatives. The function Switch evaluates an expression, *expr*, then compares the result with each of the forms *form$_i$* in turn, evaluating and returning *value$_i$* corresponding to the first match found.

Switch[*expr*, *form$_1$*, *value$_1$*, *form$_2$*, *value$_2$*, ...]

With the function Which, you supply a series of tests that are evaluated in turn. It returns the value corresponding to the first test that yields True.

Which[*test$_1$*, *value$_1$*, *test$_2$*, *value$_2$*, ...]

```
In[27] := sign[x_] :=
            Which[
                x < 0., -1,
                x == 0., 0,
                x > 0, 1
            ]
```

```
In[28] := sign[3]
Out[28] = 1
```

10.3.5 Spaghetti Code

The primitives Goto, Label, Throw, and Catch allow you to write code whose flow of control may not be obvious to those who read it. Most code written with these constructs can be written more clearly without them. These constructs may not work as you would expect, even if you are familiar with similar constructs in another language because *Mathematica*'s notion of evaluation is different.

10.3.6 Median: An Example

The median is the middle element if the length of the list is odd and the average of the middle two elements otherwise. In the function below, the variables sl and len are declared to be local to the procedure. These variables are not known outside the Block. Statements are indented to show the structure of the code and to make the code readable and easier to debug.

```
In[29] := median[list_List]  :=
        Block[{
                sl,
                len
            },
            len = Length[list];
            sl = Sort[list];
            If[
                OddQ[len],
                sl[[ (len + 1)/2 ]],
                (sl[[len/2]] + sl[[len/2 + 1]])/2
            ]
        ]
In[30] := median[{76, 56, 23, 78, 34}]
Out[30] = 56
```

10.4 Summary

This chapter describes different ways of declaring variables. Because of the problems associated with colliding variables, when writing functions, it is advisable not to use variables that are already in use. With Block or Module (version 2.0), you can declare variables to be local to a procedure.

Like languages such as C, FORTRAN, and Pascal, with *Mathematica* you can write procedural programs using loops, flow control, and conditional statements.

Constructs	Description	Added to 2.0
Do[*expr*, {*n*}]	Evaluate *expr* n times.	
For[*start*, *test*, *incr*, *body*]	For looping or iterating	
While[*test*, *body*]	For looping or iterating	
++, +=, --, -=, *=, /=	Changing values of variables	
If[*condition*, *t*, *f*]	Evaluates *t* if *condition* is True and *f* if False	
Switch[*expr*,f_1,v_1,f_2,v_2,...]	Conditional branching	
Which[$test_1$,v_1,$test_2$,v_2,...]	Conditional branching	
Block[{var_1, var_2}, *body*]	For declaring local variables.	
Module[{var_1, var_2}, *body*]	Lexical scoping.	yes
With[{$x = x_0$, $y = y_0$}, *expr*]	For defining local constants.	yes

10.5 Exercises

This problem set is short because most functions that can be written procedurally can be written more succinctly by using rule-based programming, a technique described in the next chapter.

10.1 Determine the number of iterations required to obtain an approximation to $\sqrt{2}$ to 30 decimal places using Newton's method. Starting with the value 2, approximate $\sqrt{2}$ by using the formula:

$$x_{i+1} = (x_i + 2/x_i)/2$$

10.2 Define a function that takes three numbers as arguments and returns the sum of the squares of the two largest numbers. (This problem is taken from exercise 1.2 on page 19 of *Structure and Interpretation of Computer Programs* by Harold Abelson and Gerald Jay Sussman, MIT Press and McGraw-Hill, 1985).

10.3 Suppose families have children until they have a boy. Run a simulation with 1000 families and determine how many children a family will have on average. On average, how many daughters and how many sons will there be in a family?

10.4 (a) In a *perfect shuffle*, the dealer splits the deck exactly in half and then reorders the deck by interleaving cards from each half, making sure that the first card from the first half is placed down first. For example, if you had a deck of 10 cards, initially arranged in ascending order, i.e., $\{1, 2, 3, 4, 5, 6, 7, 8, 9, 10\}$, after one perfect shuffle, the deck would be ordered $\{1, 6, 2, 7, 3, 8, 4, 9, 5, 10\}$. Write the function, perfectShuffle, that simulates the perfect shuffle of a list of an even number of cards.

(b) Write the function, returnToOrder, that computes the number of perfect shuffles to return a deck of n cards to its original order. Use returnToOrder to determine the number of perfect shuffles you need to return a deck of 52 cards to its original order.

10.5 This problem attempts to help you understand the difference between `Block` and `Module`.

Look at the following examples. They are identical except the first uses `Block` while the second uses `Module`. Explain why *Mathematica* returns different results.

```
In[31] := a = i;
In[32] := i = 3;
In[33] := Block[{i},
              Table[a, {i, 2}]
          ]
Out[33] = {1, 2}
```

Version 2.0

```
In[34] := a = i;
In[35] := i = 3;
In[36] := Module[{i},
              Table[a, {i, 2}]
          ]
Out[36] = {3, 3}
```

11

Pattern Matching

The pattern-matching capabilities built into *Mathematica* are powerful. As you saw in chapter 9 on page 167, patterns are used to represent types of expressions. A simple named pattern is *var_* that stands for any expression. The variable preceding the _ is the name assigned to the expression. Other patterns include *var_type* and *var_?test*. Each of these patterns matches a single expression. This chapter discusses patterns that match a sequence of zero or more expressions and shows examples of their use.

11.1 Matching a Sequence

There are times when you want a function to be able to apply to a single argument or to multiple arguments. How would you write a function for computing the mean of a sequence of numbers? Here are rules for computing the mean of one, two, or three elements.

```
In[1] := mean[a_]  :=  a
In[2] := mean[a_, b_]  :=  (a + b) / 2
In[3] := mean[a_, b_, c_]  :=  (a + b + c) / 3
```

Instead of writing rules for specific numbers of arguments, you can write a rule that applies to one or more arguments with the pattern __ (2 underscores). The pattern ___ (3 underscores) matches any sequence of zero or more expressions. A sequence differs from a list in that the symbols for its elements are separated by commas but are not surrounded by braces. With these patterns, you can write a function that takes a variable number of arguments. The following definition computes the mean of one or more quantities.

```
In[4] := mean[x__]  :=  Plus[x]/Length[{x}]
```

In[5] := mean[a, b, d, c, e]

$$Out[5] = \frac{a + b + c + d + e}{5}$$

The foregoing definition does not compute the average of a list of elements. After adding the rule mean[{x__}] := mean[x], the function computes the average of a list.

In[6] := mean[{x__}] := mean[x]
In[7] := mean[{1, 2, 3, 4, 5}]
Out[7] = 3

11.2 Destructuring

Assigning names to elements, you can easily implement functions that select a specified element. The following examples show how the functions First, Last, and Head can be implemented using pattern-matching.

In[8] := {a, b, c, d, e} /. {x_, y___} :> x
Out[8] = a

In[9] := getFirst[{x_, y___}] := x
In[10] := getFirst[{a, b, c, d, e}]
Out[10] = a

In[11] := {a, b, c, d, e} /. {x___, y_} :> y
Out[11] = e

In[12] := getLast[{x___, y_}] := y
In[13] := getLast[{a, b, c, d, e}]
Out[13] = e

In[14] := {a, b, c, d, e} /. h_[x___] :> h
Out[14] = List

In[15] := getHead[h_[x___]] := h
In[16] := getHead[{a, b, c, d, e}]
Out[16] = List

With pattern-matching, you can reorder elements. The rule {x_, y_} :> {y, x} swaps the terms in a pair.

In[17] := {{1, 1}, {2, 4}, {3, 9}} /. {x_, y_} :> {y, x}
Out[17] = {{1, 1}, {4, 2}, {9, 3}}

11.3 Polymorphic Definitions

With pattern matching, you can specify definitions for a function that depends on the type or value of its argument(s). For instance, pascal could be defined to return the *n*th row of Pascal's triangle when *n* is an integer and *n*! when *n* is a floating-point number.

In[18] := pascal[n_Integer] :=
        Table[Binomial[n, i], {i, 0, n}]

In[19] := pascal[n_Real] := n!

11.4 Naming an Expression

In addition to being able to name pieces of expressions, you can assign a name to the complete expression. The pattern

   x:pattern

assigns the name *x* to an expression matching *pattern*. Below the symbol a refers to the entire expression and the symbols x, y, z refer to subexpressions.

In[20] := 3 + 4 Sin[x] /.
        a:(x_ + y_ Sin[z_]) :>
            {{"a", a}, {"x", x}, {"y", y}, {"z", z}}

Out[20] = {{a, 3 + 4 Sin[x]}, {x, 3}, {y, 4}, {z, x}}

11.5 Finding Expressions that Match Patterns

It is important to understand how *Mathematica* represents expressions if you want to take advantage of the pattern-matching capability of *Mathematica*. The command Cases lists the expressions that match a specified pattern.

   Cases[$\{e_1, e_2, \ldots, e_n\}$, *pattern*]

For example, here I ask for the expressions that match the pattern x_.

In[21] := Cases[{1, 2.2, {a, b}, x^2 + 5, x + y + z}, x_]

Out[21] = {1, 2.2, {a, b}, 5 + x^2, x + y + z}

With the pattern x_Integer, I obtain a list of the integer-valued elements.

In[22] := Cases[{1, 2.2, {a, b}, x^2 + 5, x + y + z}, x_Integer]

Out[22] = {1}

Version 2.0: You can check for two or more patterns by using | (Alternatives) between each pattern. Here I ask for all integer-valued or real-valued expressions, i.e., floating-point numbers.

In[23] := Cases[{1, 2.2, {a, b}, x^2 + 5}, (x_Integer | x_Real)]
Out[23] = {1, 2.2}

Here I ask for all elements in the list that are themselves lists.

In[24] := Cases[{1, 2.2, {a, b}, x^2 + 5}, x_List]
Out[24] = {{a, b}}

As mentioned in section 8.2 on page 156, a number is a value composed of integers, floating-point numbers, rationals, and/or complex numbers. Using the predicate NumberQ, I obtain a list consisting of numbers.

In[25] := Cases[{1, 2.2, Pi, {a, b}, x^2 + 5}, x_?NumberQ]
Out[25] = {1, 2.2}

This could have been done more directly using Select.

In[26] := Select[{1, 2.2, Pi, {a, b}, x^2 + 5}, NumberQ]
Out[26] = {1, 2.2}

Here I ask for expressions that are a sum of two expressions. Notice the pattern a_ + b_ matches the expression x + y + z.

In[27] := Cases[{1, 2.2, {a, b}, x^2 + 5, x + y + z}, a_ + b_]

$$Out[27] = \{5 + x^2, x + y + z\}$$

What if you want to pick out all complex expressions? Without examining how *Mathematica* represents a complex expression, you might incorrectly suspect that the pattern r_ + I i_ would match a complex expression.

In[28] := Cases[{3, 5.5, 3 + 4I, 22I}, r_ + I i_]
Out[28] = {}

Understanding how *Mathematica* represents a complex expression may give you some ideas on why the pattern r_ + I i_ does not match the complex expression 3 + 4I.

In[29] := FullForm[3 + 4I]
Out[29] = Complex[3, 4]

Complex, like Rational, is an atomic type. To obtain all complex elements, ask for all expressions whose heads are Complex.

In[30] := Cases[{3, 5.5, 3 + 4I, 22I}, x_Complex]
Out[30] = {3 + 4 I, 22 I}

11.6 The Attribute Orderless

As you saw in section 9.8 on page 174, you can assign Attributes or general properties to a function. How can Attributes be used with pattern-matching? Let's look at an example.

Here I define a function, f, which takes three arguments.

In[31] := f[a_Integer, b_Complex, c_Real] := {a, b, c}

Only if I call f with three arguments, an integer followed by a complex number and then a real number, will *Mathematica* return an evaluated expression.

In[32] := f[2, 1 + 3 I, 4.7]
Out[32] = {2, 1 + 3 I, 4.7}

In[33] := f[1 + 3 I, 4.7, 2]
Out[33] = f[1 + 3 I, 4.7, 2]

When a function has the attribute Orderless, the arguments are sorted into "*standard*" order. If you assign the attribute Orderless, the order in which arguments are specified is not important.

You must specify the attribute Orderless before you define the function. I clear out the previous definition of f, and any attributes that have been assigned to it, with ClearAll.

In[34] := ClearAll[f]

Then I assign the attribute Orderless and redefine the function.

In[35] := SetAttributes[f, Orderless]
In[36] := f[a_Integer, b_Complex, c_Real] := {a, b, c}

The function is evaluated even when arguments are specified in a different order than in the definition of f.

In[37] := f[4.7, 1 + 3 I, 2]
Out[37] = {2, 1 + 3 I, 4.7}

In addition to Orderless, the attributes Flat, HoldAll, HoldFirst, HoldRest, and Listable must be assigned before you attach any rules to the symbol. Neglecting to do this will result in random behavior.

11.7 Examples That Use Pattern Matching

Most people have little experience with rule-based programming, i.e., writing code that uses pattern matching. In this section are several examples of this programming style.

11.7.1 Selected Expand

A variation of the following question was posted to the Usenet newsgroup (an electronic bulletin board) sci.math.symbolic.

> We are trying to get *Mathematica* to perform a seemingly simple, though subtle, function. We want this function to expand the terms in only one part of an expression: Only the operand of the Log function in an expression. If anybody can think of a simple way of constructing this function, please let us know. We want a function that would transform
>
>   (1-x)^2 Log[-(1 - a)^2]
>
> to
>
>   (1 - x)^2 Log[-1 + 2 a - a^2]

Using a rule and pattern matching, I write the function expandLogArg to expand the argument of Log.

In[38] := expandLogArg[x_] := x /. Log[a_] :> Log[Expand[a]]

In[39] := expandLogArg[(1 - x)^2 Log[-(1 - a)^2]]

```
                 2                    2
Out[39] = (1 - x)  Log[-1 + 2 a + a ]
```

11.7.2 Removing Excess Braces

Mathematica output sometimes contains more braces than necessary. For example, suppose you want to map RGBColor onto a list of triplets. The function RGBColor takes three arguments, not a list of three values. Using a rule, you eliminate extra sets of braces.

In[40] := Map[RGBColor, {{.1,.1, .3}, {.3, .2, 0.}}] /.
                RGBColor[{x__}] :> RGBColor[x]

Out[40] = {RGBColor[.1, .1, .3], RGBColor[.3, .2, 0.]}

11.7.3 A Recursive Definition of Map

Recursion can be used to replace iterative constructs such as Do, For, and While.

How would you implement the Map function if it were not built into *Mathematica*? Using recursion (a function that calls itself) you can write the solution in just a few lines of code. With this definition, one element is picked off the list each time myMap is called, until the list is empty.

```
In[41] := myMap[f_, { }] := { }
In[42] := myMap[f_, {a_, b___}] := Prepend[myMap[f, {b}], f[a]]
```

```
In[43] := myMap[g, {1, 2, 3}]
Out[43] = {g[1], g[2], g[3]}
```

11.7.4 Counting Numbers of Digits

Consider the problem of finding six consecutive 9's in the decimal expansion of π out to 770 places. We want to know how many digits past the decimal point they are.

Convert the decimal expansion to a list of characters. Then look for six consecutive "9"s.

The function ToString converts an expression to a string, and the function Characters takes a string and converts it to a list of characters.

```
In[44] := Characters[ToString[12345]]
Out[44] = {1, 2, 3, 4, 5}
```

```
In[45] := characterList = Characters[ToString[N[Pi, 770]]];
In[46] := findNines[
            {
                "3", ".", a___,"9","9","9","9","9","9",___
            }] :=
            Length[{a}]
```

```
In[47] := findNines[characterList]
Out[47] = 761
```

Just after the 761st place after the decimal point in the decimal expansion of π there are six 9's in a row.

11.7.5 Passing Options

Suppose you want a log-log plot of a function. The function LogLogPlot in the package Graphics.m in the directory Graphics is designed specifically for this purpose. This function calls the built-in ParametricPlot function specifying that tick marks on the x- and y-axes are on a log scale. With LogLogPlot, the user can specify options to be passed to the ParametricPlot function. Notice that options are specified by using BlankNullSequence (___ or three underscores). This allows the function LogLogPlot to work when supplied with a sequence of zero or more options (i.e., no options, one option, or several options). There is one exception.

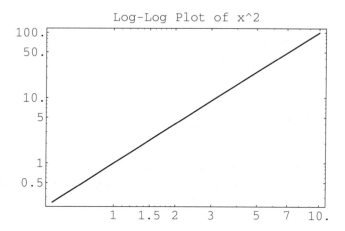

Figure 11.1: A log-log plot of x^2.

If the user specifies a value for Ticks, it is ignored since LogLogPlot sets Ticks to {LogScale, LogScale} after using the user-supplied options.

```
In[48] := Needs["Graphics`Graphics`"]

         LogLogPlot[f_, {x_, xmin_, xmax_}, opts___] :=
           ParametricPlot[
               {Log[10,x], Log[10,f]},
               {x, xmin, xmax},
                Ticks -> {LogScale, LogScale},
               opts
           ]
```

After loading Graphics.m, the following command produces a log-log plot, as shown in figure 11.1.

Version 1.2:

```
In[49] := LogLogPlot[x^2, {x, 0.5, 10},
             PlotLabel -> "Log-Log Plot of x^2",
             Framed -> True
         ];
```

Version 2.0:

```
In[49] := LogLogPlot[x^2, {x, 0.5, 10},
             PlotLabel -> "Log-Log Plot of x^2",
             Frame -> True
         ];
```

11.8 Summary

With the pattern-matching capabilities, you can specify a sequence of patterns and actions that tell *Mathematica* what patterns to look for and what actions to take when a match is found. Though procedural programming is far more common, many types of problems can be solved faster and more efficiently using rule-based programming or pattern matching. Since values are assigned to names, it is often easy to understand how a function works that is defined using pattern matching.

Pattern	Description	Added to 2.0
$x\_\_$ (2 _ chars)	A pattern that matches one or more expressions. The matched expression is given the name x.	
$x\_\_\_$ (3 _ chars)	A pattern that matches zero or more expressions.	
$x:pattern$	A pattern given the name x.	
$pattern_1 \mid pattern_2$	A pattern that matches at least one of the $pattern_i$.	yes

11.9 Exercises

This problem set is designed to give you experience in writing rule-based programs using the pattern-matching capabilities of *Mathematica*.

11.1 Write a function, geometricMean, that returns the geometric mean of a list of numbers. The geometric mean of {a, b, c, d, e} is:

$$a^{1/5} \quad b^{1/5} \quad c^{1/5} \quad d^{1/5} \quad e^{1/5}$$

Use pattern matching and recursion to solve the next two problems. Each of these problems can be solved in only a few lines of code.

11.2 Show how you would implement the Join function if it were not built into *Mathematica*.

11.3 (a) Implement the function fold as described here.

```
fold::usage = "fold[f, base, list] gives
    f[...[f[f[base, x1], x2], ..., xn]
    where list is {x1, x2, ... xn}"
```

(b) Describe what fold[Plus, 0, list] returns.

(c) Describe what fold[Max, -Infinity, list] returns.

The following problems are more difficult than all earlier problems.

11.4 A Programming Language, or APL, is a powerful but terse interactive language. Functions that might take a page to program in a conventional language can often be represented in a single line of APL.

Write the APL Deal function in *Mathematica*. I recommend implementing it recursively. The function Deal is represented by ? in APL and L?R selects L integers at random from the population Range[R] without replacement. In other words, once you select one of the numbers, it is taken out of the set. Use the following usage message for the function.

```
deal::usage="deal[n, r] selects n integers
    without replacement at random from the
    list Range[r]."
```

11.5 You can use the pattern x___List to specify a function that takes a variable number of lists for its argument. How can you find the length of each list?

11.6 This encoding-decoding problem was taken from the *Mathematica* Programming Competition at the 1990 *Mathematica* Conference. Construct the best *Mathematica* functions for run-length encoding and decoding. The function RunEncode should take a list of integers and return a list of pairs, each representing a "run" of contiguous identical integers in the original list. Each pair contains an integer, together with the length of the run in which it occurs. For example,

RunEncode[{2, 2, 1, 1, 1, 3, 1, 1, 2}]

should return {{2, 2}, {1, 3}, {3, 1}, {1, 2}, {2, 1}}. The function RunDecode should take the output of RunEncode and reconstruct the original list.

11.7 Rework problem 9 on page 135 by defining a function with the attribute Listable.

In a town there are three stores selling 5 popular toys. Store A sells the toys for $15, $17, $18, $32, and $29 and store B sells the same 5 toys for $14, $18, $22, $29, and $26. The policy of store C is to match the most competitive price in town. Write a *Mathematica* expression to determine store C's selling prices for the 5 toys.

Anonymous (Pure) Functions

Suppose you want to perform some operation just once. If you don't anticipate using the operation often, consider specifying the operation with an anonymous function. An anonymous function is an operation with no name assigned to it. In *Mathematica*, such functions are called pure functions. This chapter shows you how to define and use anonymous functions.

12.1 Function

An anonymous function is specified by using Function. The first argument specifies the formal parameters and the second argument the body of the function.

```
Function[var, body]
```

The anonymous function Function[x, x^2] computes a square. As with other functions, the arguments of an anonymous function are enclosed in brackets. I apply this anonymous function to the value 5 and to the list {1, 2, 3}.

```
In[1] := Function[x, x^2][5]
Out[1] = 25

In[2] := Function[x, x^2][{1, 2, 3}]
Out[2] = {1, 4, 9}
```

The remainder of this chapter presents examples involving anonymous functions.

12.2 Selecting Data

On page 135, in problem 7 you were asked to select data with values greater than 50 by using the function greater50.

> *In[3]* := greater50[x_] := x > 50

> *In[4]* := data = Table[Random[Integer, {0, 100}], {15}]
> *Out[4]* = {68, 50, 9, 3, 21, 31, 23, 25, 84, 97, 22, 7, 40, 25, 19}

> *In[5]* := Select[data, greater50]
> *Out[5]* = {68, 84, 97}

Now let us replace the function greater50 with an anonymous function.

Function[x, x > 50] is an anonymous function that returns the value of x > 50. It returns True for arguments > 50.

> *In[6]* := Function[x, x > 50][64]
> *Out[6]* = True

> *In[7]* := Function[x, x > 50][3]
> *Out[7]* = False

I replace the function greater50 with an equivalent anonymous function.

> *In[8]* := Select[data, Function[x, x > 50]]
> *Out[8]* = {68, 84, 97}

There are more compact ways of writing anonymous functions. The symbol # represents the formal arguments of an anonymous function.

> *In[9]* := Select[data, Function[# > 50]]
> *Out[9]* = {68, 84, 97}

You can write the solution even more compactly by using &, which is an alias for Function.

> *In[10]* := Select[data, (# > 50)&]
> *Out[10]* = {68, 84, 97}

12.3 Thirty Places of Precision

On page 29, I defined the function nThirty to compute decimal approximations to 30 places of precision.

```
In[11] := nThirty[x_] := N[x, 30]
In[12] := $Post = nThirty
```

The previous two lines of code could be rewritten in a single line with an anonymous function.

```
In[13] := $Post := N[#, 30]&
```

12.4 Transforming Pairs into Rules

If you have two lists, {x1, x2, ..., xn} and {y1, y2, ..., yn}, how can you produce a list of pairs of values {x1, y1}, {x2, y2}, ..., {xn, yn}?

```
In[14] := list1 = {x1, x2, x3, x4, x5};
In[15] := list2 = {y1, y2, y3, y4, y5};
```

Answer:

```
In[16] := Transpose[{list1, list2}]
Out[16] = {{x1, y1}, {x2, y2}, {x3, y3}, {x4, y4}, {x5, y5}}
```

Suppose listA is a list of variables, {a, b, c}, and listB is a list of values, {8, 10, 12}.

```
In[17] := listA = {a, b, c}; listB = {8, 10, 12};
```

Then using the function Transpose, you can form pairs consisting of a variable and a value.

```
In[18] := Transpose[{listA, listB}]
Out[18] = {{a, 8}, {b, 10}, {c, 12}}
```

Using an anonymous function, I set up a list of rules, a correspondence between variables and values.

```
In[19] := Map[(#[[1]] -> #[[2]])&, Transpose[{listA, listB}]]
Out[19] = {a -> 8, b -> 10, c -> 12}
```

12.5 Multiple Arguments

Multiple arguments can be passed to an anonymous function. The first argument to Function can be a parameter or a list of parameters.

```
Function[{x₁, x₂, ...}, body]
```

The anonymous function below takes two arguments.

```
In[20] := Function[{x, y}, x > y][a, 2]
Out[20] = a > 2
```

If you pass less than two arguments to this function, *Mathematica* prints a warning message and returns the input expression unevaluated.

```
In[21] := Function[{x, y}, x > y][a]
          Function::fpct:
                Too many parameters in {x, y} to be filled from
                Function[{x, y}, x > y][a].
Out[21] = Function[{x, y}, x > y][a]
```

If you pass more than two arguments to this function, the extra arguments are ignored.

```
In[22] := Function[{x, y}, x > y][a, 2, z]
Out[22] = a > 2
```

You can refer to the *n*th argument of an anonymous function with #*n*. The notation # is short for #1.

```
In[23] := (#1 > #2)&[a, 2]
Out[23] = a > 2
```

12.6 Filtering Data

Taking a weighted average of an element and its neighbors reduces the amount of noise or randomness in a time series. I obtain a weighted average of values by using myFilter.

```
In[24] := myFilter = {.1, .8, .1};
In[25] := myData = {3.1, 3.3, 4.2, 3.7, 1.7, 3.5, 3.3, 6.7};
```

By specifying an offset to Partition, I partition myData into sets, each of which consists of an element together with its right and left neighbors.

```
In[26] := Partition[myData, Length[myFilter], 1]
Out[26] = {{3.1, 3.3, 4.2}, {3.3, 4.2, 3.7}, {4.2, 3.7, 1.7},
          {3.7, 1.7, 3.5}, {1.7, 3.5, 3.3}, {3.5, 3.3, 6.7}}
```

I filter the data by taking the dot product of the filter with the partitioned data.

```
In[27] := Map[myFilter . #&,
            Partition[myData, Length[myFilter], 1]
        ]
```

I combine these steps in the function `simpleConvolve`.

```
In[28] := simpleConvolve[filter_List, data_List] :=
            Map[filter . #&,
                Partition[data, Length[filter], 1]
            ]
```

Now I'll try out this function.

```
In[29] := simpleConvolve[myFilter, myData]
Out[29] = {3.37, 4.06, 3.55, 2.08, 3.3, 3.66}
```

12.7 Summary

An anonymous function is for performing an operation without assigning a name to it. Anonymous functions are often used in conjunction with `Select`, `Map`, and `Apply`.

This table shows notations used in writing anonymous functions.

Notation	Description
`Function[x, `*body*`] [`*arg* `]`	The result of evaluating *arg* is substituted for all occurrences of *x* in *body* and the resulting expression is evaluated and returned.
`Function[{`x_1`, `x_2`, ...},` *body*`] [`arg_1`, `arg_2`, ...]`	The result of evaluating arg_i is substituted for all occurrences of x_i in *body* and the resulting expression is evaluated and returned.
`Function[`*body*`] [`*arg* `]`	The result of evaluating *arg* is substituted for all occurrences of **#** in *body* and the resulting expression is evaluated and returned.
`Function[`*body*`] [` arg_1`, `arg_2`, ...]`	The result of evaluating arg_i is substituted for all occurrences of **#**i in *body* and the resulting expression is evaluated and returned.
`(`*body*`)&[`*arg*`]`	The result of evaluating *arg* is substituted for all occurrences of **#** in *body* and the resulting expression is evaluated and returned.
`(`*body*`)&[`arg_1`, `arg_2`, ...]`	The result of evaluating arg_i is substituted for all occurrences of **#**i in *body* and the resulting expression is evaluated and returned.

12.8 Exercises

This problem set is designed to give you experience with reading and writing anonymous functions.

12.1 Write named functions for doing the operations specified by the following anonymous functions.

    (a) `(#^3)&`

    (b) `(#^#)&`

    (c) `{#, #^2}&`

    (d) `If[# > 0, #, -#]&`

    (e) `(# /. x -> y)&`

12.2 Define an anonymous function to compute the cube of its argument.

12.3 Use `Select` and an anonymous function to obtain from a list of pairs those pairs in which the first item is greater than the second.

    Hint: In anonymous functions, the `#` symbol can refer to each pair in the list. The notation `p[[2]]` refers to the second element in the list `p`.

12.4 Define an anonymous function to set the option `PlotLabel` to the command that generated the plot. Map this function onto the plot-generating commands in *Mathematica*: `ContourPlot`, `DensityPlot`, `ParametricPlot`, `Plot`, `Plot3D`.

12.5 Write a function that determines the frequency of every element in a list. For example, `frequency[{c,a,b,b}]` should return `{{a,1},{b,2},{c,1}}`.

    Hint: The frequency of elements in a list can be determined by using the *Mathematica* functions `Union`, `Count`, and `Map`. The function `Union` returns a sorted list, in which all duplication of elements has been removed. The function `Count` gives the number of elements in a list that match a pattern. Here I use `Count` to find the number of 4's in a list.

    In[30] := `Count[{1,3,4,4,5,5,8}, 4]`
    Out[30] = 2

The `Map` function applies a function to each element of a list.

    In[31] := `Map[f, {1, 2, 3, 4, 5}]`
    Out[31] = `{f[1], f[2], f[3], f[4], f[5]}`

12.6 (a) Generate a list of 10 random points in three-space.

  (b) Generate 10 sets of three random values between 0 and 1. Use these values to represent the color of each of the data points.

  (c) Using Show and Graphics3D, plot the points.

12.7 *The Significant Other Problem. (Warning: You may find this problem more difficult than the others.)* This problem involves analyzing a particular strategy for finding a significant other. Suppose that there are n people you wish to consider. Each person has a distinct value, which is unknown to you until you meet the individual. You have only one opportunity to meet with each prospect. After each meeting, you must decide whether you want that individual as your significant other; otherwise you will never see him or her again. You are to analyze the following strategy: See n/e people, where e is the base of natural logarithms. Then select the first person who is more desirable than any of the people you have already seen. Run a simulation 50 times using the prescribed strategy with $n = 30$.

  (a) Calculate the percentage of times the simulation ends up with your first choice.

  (b) Calculate the percentage of times the simulation ends up without a significant other for you.

  (c) Calculate the percentage of times the simulation ends up with a person who is rated in the top 10%.

  Hint: For this problem, you might consider defining two subsidiary functions, randomize and selectSO. The function randomize shuffles the elements in the list so that they are randomly ordered. The function selectSO calls randomize on Range[n]. It then finds the value assigned to the most desirable individual in the first n/e people that you meet. Finally it returns the number of the first person after that who is more desirable, if there are any. Otherwise it returns the empty list.

  Disclaimer: I am not responsible for any undesirable outcomes of attempting to apply this strategy to real life, but I am willing to take credit if you are happy with the results.

13

Traps, Pitfalls, and Debugging

You have have now seen the essentials of programming in *Mathematica*. You should therefore be able to use *Mathematica* interactively and to program *Mathematica*. What do you do when *Mathematica* does not give you results that you expect? How do you figure out what went wrong? This chapter discusses some common traps and pitfalls that catch *Mathematica* users. It also describes tools for debugging.

13.1 Error Messages

Mathematica prints error messages when your input does not match its own internal rules. Error messages are of the form:

> *Symbol*::*error name*: *A brief message describing the error.*

For example, when I use the assignment statement, =, instead of the ==, for testing if $1 + 1$ is equal to 3, then *Mathematica* prints the following messages:

```
In[1] := 1 + 1 = 3
         Set::write: Tag Plus in 1 + 1 is Protected.
```

When *Mathematica* can interpret your input, it will do so even when your instructions do not do what you intended.

Wolfram Research Technical Report Number 9 describes all the error messages in *Mathematica*. This technical report can be ordered directly from Wolfram Research, Inc. See appendix H on page 347, for a list of other technical reports.

13.2 Syntax Errors

When you enter a command that does not obey *Mathematica*'s grammatical rules, *Mathematica* will tell you. It will put the cursor (or indicate with a caret, ^) the position where it became confused.

Version 1.2: In versions of *Mathematica* without the Notebook Front End, the user is asked to retype the line. Notice how *Mathematica* puts a caret (^) beneath the bracket that has no mate.

```
In[2] := 1 + )3 - 5
              ^ <retype line>
```

Notebook Front End, Version 1.2: When the user enters input with a syntax error, the computer beeps and positions the cursor where it got confused.

Notebook Front End, Version 2.0: As with version 1.2, when the user enters input with a syntax error, the computer beeps and positions the cursor where it got confused, and it also prints an error message.

```
In[2] := 1 + )3 - 5
         Syntax::bktx: "1 + " has extra ")" after it.
```

Notebook Front End: With *<command >*-B, you can check whether each bracket or brace has a mate.

13.3 Predefined Variables

A variable assigned a value retains the value until it is explicitly reassigned or cleared.

I assign the value 3 to t.

```
In[2] := t = 3
Out[2] = 3
```

When I integrate an expression with respect to t, *Mathematica* prints an error message because the variable t is replaced with its value. In essence I am asking *Mathematica* to integrate a number with respect to another number. This makes no sense.

```
In[3] := Integrate[t^2 + 5t + 6, t]
         General::bvar:
              3 is a number which cannot be used as a variable.
Out[3] = Integrate[30, 3]
```

To avoid using predefined values, clear the value you assign to a variable as soon as you finish with it or, whenever possible, declare variables to be local to a function by using `Block` (in version 1.2) or using `Module` (in version 2.0) or declare variables in a private context (see section 15.2 on page 247).

13.4 Missing or Incorrect Names or Arguments

There are several ways in which a function might not behave as you would expect. If the function is returned unevaluated, *Mathematica* either was unable to evaluate the function or does not know how to evaluate it. Make sure you call the function correctly by using the number and type of arguments expected. Be sure to spell the function name correctly. You can check the name of the function and number of arguments with the built-in help facility. For example, when integrating or differentiating, do not forget to specify the variable of integration.

In[4] := `D[x^2]`

```
       2
Out[4] = x
```

Why did *Mathematica* return x^2? The function `D` differentiates the first argument with respect to the second, third, ... arguments. For example, `D[x^2, y^3, x, y]` returns $\frac{d}{dy}\frac{d}{dx}x^2y^3$. The expression `D[x^2]` instructs *Mathematica* to differentiate x^2 zero times.

13.5 Missing or Incorrect Punctuation

Missing or incorrect punctuation can give you surprising results. Look at what happens when you omit a comma in an `If` statement. You might think that the function `f` would return the absolute value of its argument.

In[5] := `Clear[f]`
In[6] := `f[x_] := If[x > 0, x  -x]`

However, this function returns x − x or 0 if x > 0 and returns `Null` if x ≤ 0 because a comma is missing between the two arguments in the `If` statement.

In[7] := `f[3]`
Out[7] = 0

In[8] := `f[-3]`

Many users have made the mistake of using a symbol consisting of two characters to represent a product. The notation xy does not represent the product of x and y. It represents a symbol whose name consists of two characters.

13.6 Parentheses versus Brackets

Using parentheses, ( ), in place of brackets, [ ], can give substantially different results. The notation foo[0] calls the function foo with 0 as its argument. The notation foo(0) gives the product of 0 and the symbol foo.

> *In[9]* := foo[0]
> *Out[9]* = foo[0]

> *In[10]* := foo(0)
> *Out[10]* = 0

Let us look at how *Mathematica* represents the expression foo(a) to understand why foo(0) returns 0.

> *In[11]* := foo(a)
> *Out[11]* = a foo

The expression foo(a) is taken as the product of a and foo.

13.7 Row Vectors versus Column Vectors

Mathematica does not differentiate between row vectors and column vectors. In mathematics, when you multiply a 1-by-3 vector by a 3-by-1 vector you obtain a scalar and when you multiply a 3-by-1 vector by a 1-by-3 vector, you obtain a 3-by-3 matrix. When multiplying two vectors, *Mathematica* treats the first vector as a row vector and the second as a column vector. There is no way to override these assumptions. So the *dot* product of two vectors returns a single expression.

> *In[12]* := {a, b, c} . {d, e, f}
> *Out[12]* = a d + b e + c f

It is not possible to multiply a 1-by-3 vector, u, by a 3-by-1 vector, v, using Dot. But you can embed a vector in a matrix or use Table to instruct *Mathematica* to do so.

> *In[13]* := {{1}, {2}, {3}} . {{a, b, c}}
> *Out[13]* = {{a, b, c}, {2 a, 2 b, 2 c}, {3 a, 3 b, 3 c}}

> *In[14]* := Table[u[[i]] v[[j]], {i, Length[u]}, {j, Length[v]}]

13.8 Line Continuation (Notebook Front End)

If a command can be considered complete before a carriage return, *Mathematica* evaluates the line even if the expression continues on the next line. Notice that the following input returns 6, not 15 as you might expect.

```
In[15] := a = 4
             + 5
             + 6
Out[15] = 6
```

What is going on? In the first line, *Mathematica* assigns 4 to a. Next *Mathematica* returns a 5 and then returns a 6. Since the 6 is the last result calculated, it is printed. As you can see, a is assigned the value 4.

```
In[16] := a
Out[16] = 4
```

If *Mathematica* cannot parse the input after reading a line, it reads the next line of input. When a line ends with a plus sign, +, or some other character that indicates there is more input to be parsed, *Mathematica* reads the next input line.

```
In[17] := a = 4 +
             5 +
             6
Out[17] = 15
```

Now a is assigned the value 15.

```
In[18] := a
Out[18] = 15
```

13.9 Branch Cuts

There are two square roots of x^2, x and $-x$. Which is correct? It depends on the value of x.

Version 1.2: *Mathematica* picks one of the solutions to $\sqrt{x^2}$.

```
In[19] := Sqrt[x^2]
Out[19] = x
```

Where might you run into problems because of this simplification? Consider the definite integral:

$$\int_{\pi/6}^{3\pi/2} \sqrt{1 - \sin^2 x}\ dx$$

Notice that `Integrate` (version 1.2) and `NIntegrate` return different results when evaluating the integral.

In[20] := `Integrate[Sqrt[1 - Sin[x]^2], {x, Pi/6, 3Pi/2}]`

Out[20] = $-\left(\dfrac{3}{2}\right)$

In[21] := `NIntegrate[Sqrt[1 - Sin[x]^2], {x, Pi/6, 3Pi/2}]`
Out[21] = `2.5`

Why does `Integrate` get a negative result when the function is always non-negative? The expression $\sqrt{1 - \sin^2 x}$ is simplified to $\sqrt{\cos^2 x}$. Then *Mathematica* applies the rule `Sqrt[x_^2] :> x` to obtain incorrectly the expression $\cos x$. This is then integrated, and the result is evaluated at the limits, $\pi/6$ and $3\pi/2$. Thus `Integrate` obtains the incorrect value $-3/2$.

 Version 2.0: *Mathematica* does not attempt to guess the value of $\sqrt{x^2}$.

In[21] := `Sqrt[x^2]`
Out[21] = `Sqrt[x^2]`

 Version 2.0: For the definite integral

$$\int_{\pi/6}^{3\pi/2} \sqrt{1 - \sin^2 x}\ dx$$

`Integrate` returns the result `Indeterminate`.

Unfortunately, there is no mechanism in *Mathematica* to restrict a variable to a certain domain.

13.10 Order of Evaluation

Let us look at an example in which *Mathematica* evaluates functions in an order different from what you might expect. Let s be the fraction $2x/(10x + 5)$.

In[22] := `s = 2x/(10x + 5)`

Out[22] = $\dfrac{2\ x}{5 + 10\ x}$

Why is the plot of s (figure 13.1) identical to the plot of `Numerator[s]`?

In[23] := `Plot[s, {x, 0, 5}];`

In[24] := `Plot[Numerator[s], {x, 0, 5}];`

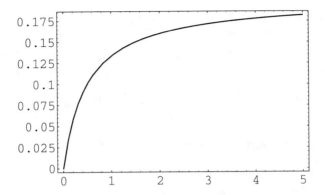

Figure 13.1: A plot of $2x/(10x + 5)$. Plotting `Numerator[2x/(10x + 5)]` produces the same graph.

In producing the plot of `Numerator[s]`, *Mathematica* evaluates s for various values of x, and then takes the numerator of the result. Since the result is a floating-point number, the numerator is the same as s. To get an accurate rendition, instruct *Mathematica* to evaluate `Numerator[s]` before `Plot` by using `Evaluate` or, in version 1.2, `Release`.

Version 1.2:

In[25] := `Plot[Release[Numerator[s]], {x, 0, 5}];`

Version 2.0:

In[26] := `Plot[Evaluate[Numerator[s]], {x, 0, 5}];`

13.11 Ordering Rules

When given a list of rules, *Mathematica* tries to apply the more specific rules first. Be aware that it is not always possible for *Mathematica* to determine how to order rules.

With the following definitions, the rule for `f[y_]` will never get invoked because it is overshadowed by the definition of `f[x_]`.

In[27] := `f[x_] := x^2`
In[28] := `f[y_] := y^3`

If, instead of specifying the argument as y_, the second rule was written in terms of the argument x_, the first rule would have been replaced by the second rule. However, because these assignments use different variables for the argument, *Mathematica* considers them two different rules.

Consider the following set of rules for oddness. If the argument is odd, oddness returns 1. If the argument is even, oddness returns a 0.

```
In[29] := oddness[x_?OddQ]  := (oddness[x] = 1)
In[30] := oddness[x_?EvenQ] := (oddness[x] = 0)
```

Call this function, oddness, on the first four integers.

```
In[31] := Table[oddness[x], {x, 4}]
Out[31] = {1, 0, 1, 0}
```

By using the ? operator, you see the order in which *Mathematica* tries to apply the rules.

Version 1.2: In the following list, notice that the most general rules are presented first and thus applied before the specific rules. This means that, if you ask for oddness[4], which *Mathematica* has already computed, it recalculates the result, ignoring the result it previously calculated.

```
In[32] := ?oddness
          oddness
          oddness/: oddness[(x_)?OddQ]  := oddness[x] = 1
          oddness/: oddness[(x_)?EvenQ] := oddness[x] = 0
          oddness/: oddness[1] = 1
          oddness/: oddness[2] = 0
          oddness/: oddness[3] = 1
          oddness/: oddness[4] = 0
```

You can reorder the rules by saving them in a file and rearranging the order of the rules, clearing the function, and then reading in the file.

13.12 Protected Functions

Most functions built into *Mathematica* are protected. *Mathematica* prints error messages if you try to specify your own rule for a protected function. For example, let us write a new rule for Integrate.

```
In[33] := Integrate[g[x_], x_] := G[x]
          SetDelayed::write:
              Tag Integrate in Integrate[g[x_], x_] is Protected.
```

By associating the rule with a user-defined symbol, you can add rules to built-in functions. Here I associate the rule Integrate[g[x_], x_] := G[x] with the symbol g.

In[34] := g/: Integrate[g[x_], x_] := G[x]

In[35] := Integrate[g[y], y]
Out[35] = G[y]

Mathematica is fragile. If you change the way the built-in functions work, other functions may break. To change a built-in symbol or function, remove protection with Unprotect and then add or modify the rules for the symbol.

In[36] := Unprotect[Pi]
Out[36] = {Pi}

In[37] := Pi = 3.1416
Out[37] = 3.1416

13.13 Undocumented Functions

In *Mathematica* there are functions that are not documented. For example in version 1.2, there are no usage statements for the built-in functions Inequality and Sequence. It is not advisable to use undocumented functions because Wolfram Research, Inc. does not support them and may change how they work or eliminate them completely.

13.14 Your Own Undocumented Functions

When you write code, it may be clear to you what you are doing. However, several hours, weeks, months, or years later, it may be difficult or time consuming to remember or figure out what you did. Comment your code and write usage statements for the functions you define.

```
In[38] := pascal[n_Integer] :=
          Table[                    (* Compute a list of the     *)
              Binomial[n, i],       (* values in a row of        *)
                  {i, 0, n}         (* Pascal's triangle.        *)
          ]
In[39] := pascal::usage="pascal[n] lists the nth row of
          Pascal's triangle."
```

13.15 Debugging

When your *Mathematica* code does not give the result you expect, asking the following questions might prove helpful in debugging your input.

- Did you type a lower-case letter where you should have typed an upper-case letter or vice versa?

- Does each bracket, parenthesis, and brace have a mate?

- Have any variables been assigned values inadvertently?

- Are your index variables distinct?

- Did you call the function you intended?

- Does each statement work as intended?

- Did you call functions with the correct number and type of arguments?

- Have you forgotten any punctuation?

- Are there semicolons or commas between statements or elements?

- Does the code work on test data?

- Have you loaded all relevant packages?

- Is the function defined in more than one context? (Contexts are described in section 15.2 on page 247.)

There are several functions that can be used for debugging *Mathematica* programs.

Command	Description	Added to 2.0
On, Off	Tracing	
Print	A primitive debugging tool	
Debug	Of little value (in version 1.2)	
Trace	Generate a list of intermediate expressions	yes
Input	In conjunction with ?	
Interrupt	To interrupt *Mathematica*	

Examples of each of these functions are provided.

13.15.1 Tracing

Let us define a couple of functions.

In[40] := f[x_] := x^2 + g[x]
In[41] := g[x_] := x + 9

Now let us turn tracing on.

In[42] := On[f, g]

You can see the steps *Mathematica* takes to arrive at a result for f[3].

In[43] := f[3]
$$
\text{f::trace: } f[3] \ \text{-->} \ 3 \ ^2 + g[3].
$$
           g::trace: g[3] --> 3 + 9.
Out[43] = 21

Turn tracing off with Off.

In[44] := Off[f, g]

13.15.2 Print

The Print function allows you to look at intermediate results.

```
In[45] := median[list_List] :=
          Block[{
                  sl,
                  len
                },
                len = Length[list];
                Print["Length of list: ", len];
                sl = Sort[list];
                Print["Sorted list: ", sl];
                If[
                    OddQ[
                        Length[sl]
                    ],
                    sl[[ (len + 1)/2 ]],
                    (sl[[len/2]] + sl[[len/2+1]])/2
                ]
          ]
In[46] := median[{43, 45, 23, 65}]
          Length of list: 4
          Sorted list: {23, 43, 45, 65}
Out[46] = 44
```

13.15.3 Debug (Version 1.2)

The Debug command rarely returns any useful debugging information. It works only on some control structures, such as For loops, and it does not work on the Macintosh. Let us look at an example showing the use of Debug. Do not try it on the Macintosh unless you are eager to reboot your computer.

```
In[47] := Debug[For[i = 1, i < 5, ++i, Print[i^2] ] ]
         action: n
         i: inspect current state
         s: step through execution
         n: continue to next expression (default)
         c: continue to end of block
         f: finish computation
         a: abort computation
         Print[i^2] action: n
         1
         Print[i^ 2] action: i
         >> i
         2
         >>
```

13.15.4 Trace (Version 2.0)

The function Debug has been replaced by Trace. Trace generates a list of the intermediate expressions computed when evaluating its argument. The output allows you to see the steps *Mathematica* takes to arrive at a result. Notice that *Mathematica* first evaluates the product of 2 and 3, then it evaluates the product of 5 and 7, and then it adds the two values to arrive at the result, 41.

```
In[48] := Trace[2 3 + 5 7]
Out[48] = {{2 3, 6}, {5 7, 35}, 6 + 35, 41}
```

If you do not want to see all intermediate steps, you can limit the intermediate steps recorded by specifying a second argument to Trace. The second argument can either be a symbol or a pattern or an option.

```
In[49] := Trace[2 3 + 5 7, Plus]
Out[49] = {6 + 35, 41}

In[50] := Trace[2 3 + 5 7, Times]
Out[50] = {{2 3, 6}, {5 7, 35}}

In[51] := Trace[2 3 + 5 7, x_ y_]
Out[51] = {{2 3}, {5 7}}
```

In[52] := Trace[2 3 + 5 7, TraceDepth -> 1]
Out[52] = {6 + 35, 41}

13.15.5 Input

When an Input statement is executed, the user can type ?var to obtain the value of the variable var.

```
In[53] := median[list_List] :=
            Block[{
                    sl,
                    len
                },
                len = Length[list];
                sl = Sort[list];
                Print[Input[ ]];
                If[
                    OddQ[
                        Length[sl]
                    ],
                    sl[[(len + 1)/2 ]],
                    (sl[[len/2]] + sl[[len/2+1]])/2
                ]
            ]
```

The variable len is local to the procedure. By inserting an Input statement in the middle of the procedure, *Mathematica* requests input from the user before calculating the median. At that time, you can ask *Mathematica* the value of a variable such as len. In the following example, len has the value 3.

```
In[54] := median[{4, 5, 6}]

        ?len
        3
```

Out[54] = 5

13.15.6 Interrupt

You can use Interrupt to generate a pause. This is particularly useful when you realize that some error has occurred and you want *Mathematica* to stop executing the function. As an example, suppose you have a function that computes some quantity and can proceed only if the result is positive. I define an error message to be associated with the function f.

```
In[55] := f::positive = "Junk was '1', must be
            positive"
```

This message is printed when `Message[f::positive, junk]` is invoked. The value of `junk` is given in place of '`1`'.

```
In[56] := Message[f::positive, 3]
        f::positive: Junk was 3, must be positive
        f[x_] := Block[{
                   ...
                   junk
                   ...
                   },

                       ...
                   junk = ...;
                   If[junk <= 0,
                           Message[f::positive, junk];
                           Interrupt[ ]
                   ];
                       ...
```

When *Mathematica* runs a long calculation, is there any way to check if it is actually processing the program or if it is simply stuck? The answer is essentially no. You can interrupt a calculation using *<command>*-. (on a Macintosh), *<control>*-c (on a Unix machine), or *<control><break>* (on an MS-DOS computer). Then you can turn on tracing so that you can see what *Mathematica* is doing. But you probably will not find the tracing information helpful.

13.15.7 Verify Results

It is advisable to verify your results. *Mathematica* makes it easy to obtain results. Take time to check the results you obtain. When possible, calculate results by alternative means.

Finding the inverse is often a good way to check results. For example, if you integrate an expression, try differentiating the result to see if you get back the original expression. If you find the inverse of a matrix, check that the product of the matrix and its inverse returns the identity matrix or something close to it.

13.15.8 Suggestions and Bug Reports

Wolfram Research, Inc. appreciates hearing suggestions and reports of suspected bugs in *Mathematica*. Send as much documentation as possible to bugs@wri.com, suggestions@wri.com, or send a fax to 217-398-0747.

13.15.9 Advice

Below are some words of advice from Andrew Koenig's book *C Traps and Pitfalls*, Addison–Wesley, 1989, Chapter 8, pp. 102 – 103. [Koenig] The suggestions below are valid whether you are using C, *Mathematica*, or any other programming language.

Make your intentions plain.

Andrew Koenig writes "When you write one thing that might be mistaken for another, use parentheses or other methods to make sure your intent is clear. Not only will this help you understand what you mean when you come back to the program, but it will also make things easier if someone else has to look at it later."

Look at trivial cases.

Test your code. Make sure it works on trivial cases.

Stick to well-used parts of the language.

Well-used parts of the language probably have been tested more extensively than other parts of the code.

Program defensively.

"Don't assume any more about your users or your implementation than you have to."

13.16 Summary

This section has provided a list of questions to ask when *Mathematica* does not give you what you expected. It also suggests some tools that can be used for debugging code.

13.17 Exercises

Though you will probably have plenty of opportunities to debug your own code,
I offer you a problem set anyway.

Debug the following examples.

13.1 `3 Plus 4`

13.2 `mean[x_] := Add[x]/Length[x]`

13.3 Why doesn't the following statement return a list of primes?

`Select[{2, 4, 7, 11, 15}, PrimeQ[x_]]`

13.4 Find the integral of $x\mathrm{Cos}(x)$ over the interval from 0 to $3pi$.

`Integral[xCos(x), (x, 0, 3pi)]`

13.5 The function `pickLotto` is intended to pick 5 numbers in the range from 0
to 99. Why does it print only a single number?

```
In[57] := pickLotto :=
            Block[{
                n = 1
                },
                While[n <= 5;
                    Print[
                        Random[Integer, {0, 99}]
                    ];
                    ++n
                ]
            ]
```

```
In[58] := pickLotto
          78
```

13.6 Below are definitions for the functions `aoi` and `eip`.

```
In[59] := aoi[f_[x_], min_, max_] := NIntegrate[f[x], {x, min, max}]
In[60] := eip[x_] := x^2 + 5 Exp[x]
```

Why doesn't `aoi` return a numerical value when given

```
In[61] := aoi[eip[t], 5, 10]

                    t    2
Out[61] = aoi[5 E  + t , 5, 10]
```

13.7 Find a more succinct way to write the function f shown below.

```
Clear[f];

f[g_, x_List] :=
    Block[{
        l = { },
        n = 1
    },
    Do[
        l = Join[l, {g[x[[i]]]}],
        {i, Length[x]}
    ];
    l
]
```

Input and Output

Not all data are generated by *Mathematica*. This chapter describes how to import data into *Mathematica*. It also discusses how to save expressions and data to a file and how to translate a *Mathematica* expression into C, FORTRAN, and TEX.

14.1 Input

There are several ways of obtaining data: (1) generating them, (2) requesting them from the user, or (3) importing them from a file. Until now, I have been showing you how you can generate data using *Mathematica*. This section focuses on the latter two techniques for acquiring data.

14.1.1 Getting Input from the User

The function Input and InputString are intended for requesting input from a user. Input treats the input as an expression while InputString treats the input as a string.

```
Input ["Prompt string"]
InputString ["Prompt string"]
```

These functions prompt the user for input using the string specified as the argument.

```
In[1] := userInput = Input["Type an integer between 1 and 10: "]
         Type an integer between 1 and 10:
```

If you put a call to Input in the middle of a function, *Mathematica* will prompt the user for input. The function convertToBinary converts a user-specified nonzero number into binary form. Notice that the definition includes a call to Input.

```
In[2] := convertToBinary :=
            Module[{
                    userInput
            },
            While[
                IntegerQ[
                    userInput = Input[
                        "Number to convert to binary? "]
                ],
                Print[userInput, " = ", BaseForm[userInput, 2]]
            ]
        ]

In[3] := convertToBinary
         Number to convert to binary?   3
         3 = 11
                2
```

Version 1.2: To be able to execute the definition `convertToBinary`, use `Block` in place of `Module`.

14.1.2 Importing Data

You may not want to prompt the user for data, particularly when your function requires a great deal of data or the data are already stored in a file. This section talks about how to import data from a file.

The `!!` operator displays the contents of a file.

```
In[4] := !!data.m

2.1   3.4   5   8.7   13.2   21
```

Macintosh, version 1.2: Be aware that in version 1.2, *Mathematica* fails to list the last digit if it is the last character in the file. The last number would be listed as 2 though the last number in the file is 21.

The operator `<<` reads a file. What do you think *Mathematica* returns when you read in the contents of the file `data.m` with the `<<` operator? Try it out.

```
In[5] := << data.m
Out[5] = 86095.5
```

This number is the product of the numbers in `data.m`, which is not what I wanted. I want the six numbers in the file. Fortunately, the function `ReadList` is specifically designed for reading data from a file (or a pipe on Unix-based systems) into *Mathematica*. It reads the data of a specified type and returns a list containing those items.

ReadList[*stream*, *type*]

When reading from a file, *stream* is the name of the file, a string. The second argument, *type*, can be any one of the following: Byte, Character, Number, String, Real, or Expression, and in version 2.0 Record or Word. The following table describes what ReadList returns for each of these types.

Type	Description	Added to 2.0
Number	Reads in exact or approximate numbers. Also supports FORTRAN scientific notation (%e format for C users)	
Real	Reads in all numbers as *Mathematica* floating-point numbers even if there is no explicit decimal point. Also supports FORTRAN scientific notation.	
Byte	Returns the bytes for each character in the file as integers.	
Character	Returns strings of length 1.	
String	Reads in strings which end with a newline character.	
Expression	Reads in a standard *Mathematica* expression.	
Record	Reads in a sequences of characters delimited by record separators.	yes
Word	Reads in a sequence of characters separated by spaces, tabs, or newlines.	yes

The file data.m contains numbers: two integers and four reals. Specifying the type as Real, ReadList converts the two integers to reals.

In[6] := ReadList["data.m", Real]
Out[6] = {2.1, 3.4, 5., 8.7, 13.2, 21.}

Specifying the type as Number, 5 and 21 are treated as integers.

In[7] := ReadList["data.m", Number]
Out[7] = {2.1, 3.4, 5, 8.7, 13.2, 21}

The second argument to ReadList can be one of the types listed above or it can be an expression or function involving one or more of these types. Notice that with the second argument as {Number, Number}, ReadList returns a list of pairs of numbers.

In[8] := ReadList["data.m", {Number, Number}]
Out[8] = {{2.1, 3.4}, {5, 8.7}, {13.2, 21}}

What if you ask *Mathematica* to read in groups of n numbers and the data consist of m numbers, where n does not evenly divide m? Let's try it out. Here I read in numbers in groups of four.

In[9] := ReadList["data.m", {Number, Number, Number, Number}]
Out[9] = {{2.1, 3.4, 5., 8.7}, {13.2, 21, EndOfFile, EndOfFile}}

Notice that *Mathematica* reads in all the numbers but adds the element EndOfFile to make the last group complete.

The second argument to ReadList can include a function.

ReadList [*stream*, *function[type]*]

Here ReadList computes the sin of each element in the list.

In[10] := ReadList["data.m", Sin[Number]]
Out[10] = {0.86321, -0.25554, Sin[5], 0.66297, 0.59207, Sin[21]}

With ReadList, you can read in files that contain numbers and strings. ReadList reads in strings which end with a newline character.

In[11] := !!products.m
          Mathematica Quick Reference Guides   14.95   3428
          Mathematica Help Stack   89.00   325

The command ReadList["products.m", {String, Number, Number }] causes *Mathematica* to interpret the first line as a string. It then looks for a number and instead finds a string. As you can see, it fails to read the entire contents of the file.

In[12] := ReadList["products.m", {String, Number, Number}]
Out[12] = {{Mathematica Quick Reference Guides   14.95   3428,
          EndOfFile, EndOfFile}}

When the second argument is simply String, ReadList imports each line as a string.

In[13] := ReadList["products.m", String]
Out[13] = {Mathematica Quick Reference Guides   14.95   3428,
          Mathematica Help Stack   89.00   325}

If I want to analyze the revenue for these two products, I'll need to parse these strings to extract the price and units sold. But instead of doing any string manipulation, I can simply reposition the string to the end of the line, as was done in the file cs50grades.m.

In[14] := !!cs50grades.m
          100   95   99   Gorsic, Bonnie
          89   98   100   Ireland, Blair
          92   95   98   Isaacs, Stan
          95   99   97   McGill, Paul

Now `ReadList` reads in the student's homework scores as numbers and the students names as strings.

```
In[15] := ReadList["cs50grades.m", {Number, Number, Number, String}]
Out[15] = {{100, 95, 99,  Gorsic, Bonnie },
           {89, 98, 100,  Ireland, Blair },
           {92, 95, 98,  Isaacs, Stan },
           {95, 99, 97,  McGill, Paul }}
```

I can now work with these numbers in *Mathematica*.

14.1.3 Reading Records and Words

This section discusses techniques for reading lines or records without needing to know how many fields are in each record. By default, a record is the information contained in a line of the file. Let's start by looking at the file `data.spreadsheet` created with a spreadsheet program such as Excel.

```
In[16] := !!data.spreadsheet
    1     345.4     43
    2     343.5     43
    3     323.6     54
    4     434.4     43
    5     323.6     42
    6     223.3     32
```

Using the technique described in the previous section, I instruct *Mathematica* to read in three numbers.

```
In[17] := ReadList["data.spreadsheet", {Number, Number, Number}]
Out[17] = {{1, 345.4, 43}, {2, 343.5, 43}, {3, 323.6, 54},
           {4, 434.4, 43}, {5, 323.6, 42}, {6, 223.3, 32}}
```

This technique is fine for a small file or for a file that contains the same number of items in each line. But what if you don't know how many columns are in your data, you are too lazy to count the number of columns, or different rows have different numbers of data?

 Version 2.0: To facilitate reading records and words, in version 2.0 the following options were added to `ReadList`.

Option Name	Default Value	Description
RecordLists	False	Make a separate list for objects in each record?
RecordSeparator	{"\n"}	Separator for records.
WordSeparators	{" ", "\t"}	Separators for words.
NullRecords	False	Keep zero-length records?
NullWords	False	Keep zero-length words?
TokenWords	{ }	Words to take as tokens.

Like the graphics functions, these options are specified after the arguments to ReadList.

> ReadList["*stream*", *type*, *options*]

How can you use these options to import the data from data.spreadsheet such that each line in the file is stored in a separate list?

```
In[18] := ReadList["data.spreadsheet", Word, RecordLists -> True]
Out[18] = {{1, 345.4, 43}, {2, 343.5, 43}, {3, 323.6, 54},
          {4, 434.4, 43}, {5, 323.6, 42}, {6, 223.3, 32}}
```

Notice that I did not have to count the number of columns in each line.

With these new options, you can read data strings that are not at the end of the line. In the file products.m, each field is tab-delimited (separated by tabs).

```
In[19] := ReadList["products.m", Word,
            WordSeparators -> {"\t"},
            RecordLists -> True]
Out[19] = {{Mathematica Quick Reference Guides, 14.95, 3276},
          {Mathematica Help Stack, 89.00, 347}}
```

The numbers are read in as strings, as you can see by looking at the FullForm of the result.

```
In[20] := FullForm[%]
Out[20] = List[List["Mathematica Quick Reference Guide", "14.95",
          "3276"], List["Mathematica Help Stack", "89.00",
          "347"]]
```

Specifying the second argument of ReadList to be {Word, Number, Number}, the price and quantity are read in as numbers.

```
In[21] := ReadList["products.m", {Word, Number, Number},
            WordSeparators -> {""},
            RecordLists -> True]
Out[21] = {{{Mathematica Quick Reference Guide, 14.95, 3276}},
          {{Mathematica Help Stack, 89., 347}}}
```

In[22] := FullForm[%]

Out[22] = List[List[List["Mathematica Quick Reference Guide", 14.95,
         3276]], List[List["Mathematica Help Stack", 89., 347]]]

Version 1.2: If you are not using version 2.0, then how can you instruct *Mathematica* to read in each line of data into a separate list? By writing your own function. The function tabSeparate takes a string of tab-separated fields and returns a list of the fields in each line.

This function reads in each line as a string, then converts the strings to characters, eliminates tabs, joins characters separated by tabs into a string, and converts each of these strings into an expression.

```
(* Given a string, str, of tab-separated fields,
 * return a list of the individual fields.
 *)
Clear[tabSeparate, tabSep];
tabSeparate[str_String] :=
        Apply[
                tabSep,
                Characters[str]
        ]


tabSep[x___String, "\t", y___String] :=
        Flatten[
                {
                        tabSep[x],
                        tabSep[y]
                },
                1
        ]


tabSep[x___String] :=
        ToExpression[
                StringJoin[x]
        ] /; FreeQ[{x}, "\t"]
```

Let us test this function on data in the file data.spreadsheet.

In[23] := ReadList["data.spreadsheet", tabSeparate[String]]

Out[23] = {{1, 345.4, 43}, {2, 343.5, 43}, {3, 323.6, 54},
       {4, 434.4, 43}, {5, 323.6, 42}, {6, 223.3, 32}}

Data can be parsed (read in and interpreted) much faster by using C, awk, or shell programming. Awk is a powerful, flexible language for manipulating data.

(Awk's name is derived from the first letters of the last names of its authors, Aho, Weinberger, and Kernighan.) Let us see how you can parse the data using awk.

```
#!/bin/sh
# Title:  reformatData
# Reformats tab-delimited data into a list.

awk '{
        printf "{"
        for (i = 1; i < NF; ++i)
                printf "%s, ", $i
        printf "%s}\n", $NF
}'
```

This *awk* script converts the data to the format that can be read in directly by *Mathematica*.

```
In[24] := !reformatData < data.spreadsheet
Out[24] = {1, 345.4, 43}
          {2, 343.5, 43}
          {3, 323.6, 54}
          {4, 434.4, 43}
          {5, 323.6, 42}
          {6, 223.3, 32}
```

 ### 14.1.4 External Commands

The first argument of ReadList can be an external command on all systems except the Macintosh.

> ReadList["!*command*", *type*]

By specifying !reformatData as the first argument, ReadList calls this awk program and reads the result into *Mathematica*.

```
In[25] := ReadList["!reformatData < data.spreadsheet", Expression]
Out[25] = {{1, 345.4, 43}, {2, 343.5, 43}, {3, 323.6, 54},
          {4, 434.4, 43},{5, 323.6, 42}, {6, 223.3, 32}}
```

Can *Mathematica* read binary files? Yes, that is what Byte is for, but it is very slow. I recommend that you write a program in another language, such as C, FORTRAN, or Pascal, to convert the binary data to ASCII and then read the converted data into *Mathematica*.

14.2 Exporting Data

If you want to export a matrix of data from *Mathematica* to Excel or another spreadsheet program, you need to insert tabs and carriage returns between data and write the result to a file.

```
In[26] := myData = Table[Random[Integer, {1,10}], {2}, {10}]
Out[26] = {{2, 3, 5, 3, 1, 6, 10, 6, 10, 5}, {5, 6, 9, 9, 6, 8,
    6, 5, 1, 1}}
```

The function writeMatrixToSpreadSheet, defined below, writes a matrix of data to a file, one row per line, with entries in each row separated by tabs. It takes a file name and a matrix as arguments. This function uses Scan, a function identical to Map except that it returns Null (i.e., it is used only for side effects). The function writeMatrixToSpreadSheet contains two nested calls to Scan. Both apply anonymous functions. The inner Scan applies the function

```
WriteString[file, "\t", #]&
```

to insert tabs between items in a row. The outer Scan applies an anonymous function to write out each row followed by a new line.

```
writeMatrixToSpreadSheet[filename_String, data_List] :=
    Block[{
            file = OpenWrite[filename]
        },
        Scan[
            (
                WriteString[file, First[#]];
                Scan[
                    WriteString[file, "\t", #]&,
                    Rest[#]
                ];
                WriteString[file, "\n"]
            )&,
            data
        ];
        Close[file]
    ]
```

Now I'll test this function by writing some data to the file someData.m.

```
In[27] := someData = Table[Random[Integer, {1, 10}], {2}, {6}]
Out[27] = {{4, 2, 3, 3, 1, 6}, {6, 8, 10, 4, 7, 9}}
```

In[28] := writeMatrixToSpreadSheet["someData.m", someData]
Out[28] = someData.m

As you can see, the file someData.m has tabs between each element and a newline after each row.

In[29] := !!someData.m

```
4    2    3    3    1    6
6    8    10   4    7    9
```

14.3 Saving Definitions

Besides saving data to a file, you might want to save definitions that you expect to use again. The function Save, as its name might suggest, saves the definition of symbols to a file. The second and subsequent arguments are the symbols whose definitions are to be appended to the file specified as the first argument.

Save["*file*", *symbol*₁, *symbol*₂, ...]

Here I save the definition pascal to the file pascal.m.

In[30] := pascal[n_] := Table[Binomial[n, i], {i, 0, n}]
In[31] := Save["pascal.m", pascal]

Now the file pascal.m contains the definition of pascal.

In[32] := !!pascal.m
```
pascal[n_] := Table[Binomial[n, i], {i, 0, n}]
```

Unfortunately, Save does not save the usage statements. You will need to add usage statements to the file manually.

14.4 Writing to a File

Mathematica adopted a Unix-like convention for writing to files. In Unix the command > writes to a file and >> appends to a file. Since the symbol > is used for greater than, *Mathematica* instead uses >> to write to a file and >>> to append to a file.

With the following command, you can save the first 100 primes in a file.

In[33] := Table[Prime[i], {i, 100}] >> primes.m

Notice that if I save a real number, the contents of the file might contain more precision than *Mathematica* displays on the screen.

In[34] := Sqrt[2.]
Out[34] = 1.41421

In[35] := Sqrt[2.] >> squareRoot2.m

In[36] := !!squareRoot2.m
          1.414213562373095049

Results shown on the screen are displayed in OutputForm while results saved to a file are stored in InputForm.

14.5 Manipulating Strings

Several functions require strings as arguments including: OpenAppend, OpenRead, Read, and ReadList. As you will see in the next chapter, context names are also strings.

Mathematica provides functions for creating, checking, and manipulating strings. Many of these functions, which are similar to the functions for manipulating lists, were added in version 2.0.

Function	Description	Added to 2.0
StringDrop	Returns a string without the first n characters.	yes
StringInsert	Inserts a string at any position in another string	yes
StringJoin	Joins two more more strings together.	
StringReplace	For replacing parts of strings.	yes
StringReverse	Reverses the order of the characters in a string.	yes
StringTake	Returns a string of the first n characters.	yes
StringLength	Gives the number of characters in a string.	
StringPosition	Gives a list of the positions of a substring.	yes
StringMatchQ	Tests if a string matches a pattern.	
StringQ	Tests if an expression is a string	yes
StringToStream	Opens an input stream for reading from a string.	yes
ToString	Converts an expression to a string	
WriteString	Converts an expression to a string and writes it to a file.	

Using StringJoin and ToString you can construct a list of strings or filenames of the form data.n, where n varies from 1 to 5.

In[37] := Table[StringJoin["data.", ToString[i]], {i, 5}]
Out[37] = {data.1, data.2, data.3, data.4, data.5}

14.6 Input and Output Form

Users enter expressions into *Mathematica* in ASCII in a one-dimensional form (i.e., a form that does not contain subscripts or superscripts). *Mathematica*'s response is printed in OutputForm, a form that supports both subscripts and superscripts and writes a fraction with a horizontal line.

```
In[38] := x^7 / 7 + y^z^3

             7    3
            x    z
Out[38] = -- + y
            7
```

The command InputForm returns an expression in a form suitable for entering into *Mathematica*.

```
In[39] := InputForm[%]
Out[39] = x^7/7 + y^z^3
```

OutputForm offers users a representation that more closely resembles mathematical representations. Because OutputForm writes results on multiple lines, it cannot be used as input to *Mathematica*. To enable results to be loaded from files, *Mathematica* writes expressions to a file in InputForm.

```
In[40] := x^7 / 7 + y^z^3 >> anExpression.m
```

```
In[41] := !!anExpression.m
          x^7 / 7 + y^z^3
```

14.6.1 Notebooks

A Notebook is a regular ASCII file with formatting information. After saving a Notebook, you can look at its contents with a text editor or word processor. Approximately the first 30 lines of the Notebook contain font information. Notice that this information is enclosed between (* and *). It is a *Mathematica* comment. This information will not be interpreted by the Kernel if you load the file.

```
(*^

::[paletteColors = 128; automaticGrouping; currentKernel;
    fontset = title, inactive, noPageBreakBelow, nohscroll,
        preserveAspect, groupLikeTitle, center, M7, bold,
        L1, e8, 24;
    fontset = subtitle, inactive, noPageBreakBelow, nohscroll,
        preserveAspect, groupLikeTitle, center, M7, bold,
        L1, e6, 18;
```

Because the Front End allows you to refer to or to execute any given result, it keeps a copy of the result in the Notebook even though it may not display it. In the Notebook shown below there are two copies of the result. The first version is in input form. The second result, which follows the line containing ;[o], is displayed on the screen. It is in OutputForm, the two-dimensional format used for making results look more like what people are accustomed to seeing when working with mathematical expressions. This result is for output purposes only.

```
:[font = input; preserveAspect; startGroup; ]
x^5 + x^4 + x^3 + x^2 + x + 1
:[font = output; output; inactive; preserveAspect; endGroup; ]
1 + x + x^2 + x^3 + x^4 + x^5
;[o]
            2    3    4    5
1 + x + x  + x  + x  + x


:[font = input; preserveAspect; startGroup; ]
N[Pi]
:[font = output; output; inactive; preserveAspect; endGroup; ]
3.141592653589793238
;[o]
3.14159
```

When a user requests that a previous result be re-executed, the Notebook Front End can pass the input form of the expression to the Kernel.

Macintosh: If you want to send a Notebook to someone who does not use a version of *Mathematica* that supports the Notebook Front End, you might want to strip off the font information. You can do this on a Macintosh by merging all the cells into one and making that cell an initialization cell.

The contents of all cells, except initialization cells, are commented out. If you want to load definitions from a Notebook into a non-Notebook Front End version, make all the cells containing those definitions initialization cells.

14.7 Translating Expressions

Mathematica allows you to translate an expression into three other languages: the C programming language (with CForm), FORTRAN (with FortranForm), and TEX, Knuth's language for typesetting (with TeXForm).

Forms	Description
CForm[*expr*]	Translates an expression to C.
FortranForm[*expr*]	Translates an expression to FORTRAN.
TeXForm[*expr*]	Translates an expression to TEX input notation.

Notice how *Mathematica* converts the expression $x^3/5$.

```
In[42] := x^3/5

            3
Out[42] = x
           --
            5


In[43] := CForm[%]
Out[43] = Power(x,3)/5


In[44] := FortranForm[%]
Out[44] = x**3/5
```

The TeXForm of the expression has more pairs of braces than necessary. Nevertheless, it works.

```
{{{x\caret 3}}\over5}
```

TEXing this result produces:

$$\frac{x^3}{5}$$

14.8 Splice

You might want to insert or "splice" output from *Mathematica* into a C or FORTRAN program or into a TEX document by using Splice.

Below is a sample C program. If you are familiar with C, you will be aware that the code between `<*` and `*>` is not valid C. It is *Mathematica* input.

```
In[45] := !!sample.mc
         #include <stdio.h>
         main()
         {
             double x;

             x = <* NSum[1/i^2, {i, 4, 10}] *>;
             . . .

         }
```

I splice the result returned when executing the expression between `<*` and `*>` in sample.mc to produce the file sample.c shown below.

```
In[46] := Splice["sample.mc"]
```

```
In[47] := !!sample.c
         #include <stdio.h>
         main( )
         {
             double x;

             x = 0.188657;
             . . .

         }
```

14.9 Format

You can write your own formatting instructions. Subscripted represents indices with subscripts.

```
In[48] := Subscripted[a[1]]
Out[48] = a
             1
```

Superscript is designed for printing an expression as a superscript, i.e., in the line above where it would normally be displayed. SequenceForm ensure that the terms are printed in the order they are specified.

```
In[49] := SequenceForm[a, Superscript[2]]

             2
Out[49] = a
```

Below I tell *Mathematica* to subscript elements of the array a.

In[50] := Format[a[n_, m_]] := Subscripted[a[n, m]]

In[51] := Array[a, {2, 2}] // MatrixForm
Out[51] = a   a
     1,1   1,2

    a   a
     2,1   2,2

Unfortunately *Mathematica* does not allow you to specify a format for an arbitrary array. *Mathematica* needs to be able to attach the format to a specific symbol. Above I attached the format to the symbol a.

14.10 Summary

With *Mathematica*, you can generate data or ask a user for data or read data from a file.

Function	Description
<< or Get	Read in a file, evaluate each expression in it, and return the last result.
>> or Put	Write an expression to a file.
Input ["*prompt*"]	Prompt the user for input and treat the result as an expression.
InputString ["*prompt*"]	Prompt the user for input and treat the result as a string.
ReadList [*stream*, *type*]	Read items from a file.
Save ["*file*", *symbol*]	Save definitions of *symbol* to a file.
Splice ["*file*"]	Splice *Mathematica* output into an external file.

Mathematica saves results to a file in InputForm so that they can be easily entered back into *Mathematica*. *Mathematica* can also generate expressions in C, FORTRAN, and TEX. You can also write your own formats.

Forms	Description
CForm [*expr*]	Translate an expression to C.
FortranForm [*expr*]	Translate an expression to FORTRAN.
InputForm [*expr*]	*Mathematica* input form.
OutputForm [*expr*]	Standard *Mathematica* output form.
TeXForm [*expr*]	Translate an expression into TEX input notation.

14.11 Exercises

This problem set is designed to give you practice with importing and exporting data, saving results into a file, and translating expressions into different formats.

14.1 **Version 1.2**: The package Mortgages.m uses the Input function.

(a) Determine the monthly payments for a house with a 20-year mortgage or for the car of your choice with a 3-year loan. It is in the Package directory in the Examples subdirectory.

    Needs["Examples`Mortgages`"]

(b) Look at Mortgages.m by using the !! operator.

14.2 Write a function that will test a user's knowledge of the multiplication tables for integers in the range [2,12] and, if the user gets the wrong answer, will give the correct answer.

14.3 Translate the outputs of the following expressions into C and FORTRAN.

(a) D[x Exp[x], x]

(b) a^b

(c) Sin[Pi/3]

14.4 Write a C program, a FORTRAN program, or a TEX document that includes a *Mathematica* expression enclosed in <* and *>. Convert the *Mathematica* expression into C, FORTRAN, or TEX by using Splice.

14.5 Write a format statement that, given b[c, d], displays c as a subscript and d as the exponent, i.e., b_c^d.

14.6 (a) Write a function that computes the nth Fibonacci number.

    fib[0] = 1
    fib[1] = 1
    fib[2] = fib[0] + fib[1]
     . . .
    fib[n] = fib[n-2] + fib[n-1]

(b) Instruct *Mathematica* to remember results calculated. Save your definition of Fibonacci in a file by using the Save command. When using the Front End, you need to make the cells containing definitions initialization cells to be able to load the definitions from a file.

15

Packages

Most functions in *Mathematica* are written in C. However, some functions, such as `Integrate` and `Laplace`, are written in *Mathematica* itself. Functions written in *Mathematica* are defined in files called *packages*. There are about 60 packages distributed with version 1.2 and about 130 packages distributed with version 2.0 covering areas such as algebra, calculus, discrete math, geometry, graphics, linear algebra, number theory, numerical mathematics, and statistics. This chapter describes the constructs used in packages, as well as guidelines for writing a package.

15.1 Why Write a Package?

A package is a file containing *Mathematica* definitions. Packages enable you to:

- Define a function or set of functions that you or others will use often

- Hide the implementation from the user

- Save a function or set of functions that you are developing

- Reload functions (automatically if you so choose) without having to type them in when you use them

By saving *Mathematica* definitions in a file, you can create a package. Then you can load this package when you need to use the functions in the package.

15.2 Contexts

Don't be surprised if you don't understand contexts completely the first time you read this chapter.

Contexts, like local-variable declarations, protect against symbols colliding with one another. A context is like a directory in Unix. It is a place where all symbol names in effect acquire the context name as extensions of their names, thus distinguishing them from the same names in any other context. Think of a context as a directory on a Unix-based system. There can be files named Faces in several different directories. Which file you access depends on where you are and in what order you search directories, as specified in $PATH. Like directories, contexts can be nested. Similarly, which function you access in *Mathematica* depends on the current context and the order in which you search contexts.

Context names are strings that terminate with a back quote. For example, "myContext`" is a valid context name.

15.2.1 The Current Context

The global variable $Context returns the current context. The function Context called with no arguments also returns the current context.

```
In[1] := $Context
Out[1] = Global`
```

```
In[2] := Context[ ]
Out[2] = Global`
```

The context Global` is like your home directory in Unix. If you do not change contexts, the current context is Global`.

15.2.2 The Context Path

Like $PATH in Unix, the global variable $ContextPath specifies the names of the contexts to search in trying to find the symbol entered if it is not defined in the current context. Let us look at $ContextPath, before loading any packages.

```
In[3] := $ContextPath
Out[3] = {Global`, System`}
```

The command Context[*symbol*] returns the context in which *symbol* is defined. Most objects built into *Mathematica* are put in the context System`.

```
In[4] := Context[Plot]
Out[4] = System`
```

15.2.3 Creating Symbols

When you ask *Mathematica* about a symbol, i.e., a variable or the name of a function, *Mathematica* checks if the symbol has been created in the current context. If the symbol is not defined in the current context or in any of the contexts in the context path, *Mathematica* creates the symbol in the current context.

```
In[5] := Context[flies]
Out[5] = Global`
```

Specifying the context of a symbol forces *Mathematica* to define the symbol in the specified context. There can be different definitions of a symbol in different contexts. For example, here I specify two definitions for the symbol flies.

```
In[6] := flies = 3 mph;
```

```
In[7] := Entomology`flies = "Flies are insects.";
```

If I ask about flies, *Mathematica* returns only one value of flies even though it has two definitions. *Mathematica* returns the value of flies in the current context.

```
In[8] := ?flies
        3 mph
```

The output of ?*`flies indicates that there is more than one symbol named flies, one in the current context and one in the context named Entomology`.

```
In[9] := ?*`flies
        flies    Entomology`flies
```

Note: *Mathematica* prints the context only for symbols not in the current context.

If the name of a symbol is preceded by a backquote or grave accent (`), *Mathematica* creates the symbol in a subcontext relative to the current context.

```
In[10] := `CSContext`bug = "A bug is a programming error.";
```

I can access the value of the symbol bug by specifying its context.

```
In[11] := Global`CSContext`bug
Out[11] = A bug is a programming error.
```

15.3 Changing Contexts

It is possible to change context simply by setting the environment variable $Context equal to the desired context.

```
In[12] := $Context = "Entomology`"
Out[12] = Entomology`
```

```
In[13] := $Context
Out[13] = Entomology`
```

Now let us restore the context to the default context Global`.

In[14] := $Context="Global`"
Out[14] = Global`

In[15] := $Context
Out[15] = Global`

However, users more often change context by using the built-in primitives Begin, BeginPackage, End, and EndPackage. The commands Begin and BeginPackage remember the context in which these functions were invoked so that it can be restored when End or EndPackage is subsequently called.

15.3.1 Begin

The command Begin changes the current context but does not affect the context path. Using Begin, I change the context to BakingContext`.

In[16] := $Context
Out[16] = Global`

In[17] := $ContextPath
Out[17] = {Global`, System`}

In[18] := Begin["BakingContext`"]
Out[18] = BakingContext`

In[19] := $Context
Out[19] = BakingContext`

In[20] := $ContextPath
Out[20] = {Global`, System`}

Now I'll create the symbol dough in the current context, BakingContext`.

In[21] := dough = "A mixture of flour and water.";

In[22] := Context[dough]
Out[22] = BakingContext`

When End is invoked, the current context reverts to what it was before Begin was invoked.

In[23] := End[ ]
Out[23] = BakingContext`

In[24] := $Context
Out[24] = Global'

The context path is not changed.

In[25] := $ContextPath
Out[25] = {Global', System'}

Notice that, when I now ask about dough, *Mathematica* does not access the symbol because BakingContext' is not in the context path.

In[26] := ?dough
        Information::notfound: Symbol dough not found.

However, I can access the definition of dough by specifying the context in which it is defined.

In[27] := ?BakingContext'dough
        BakingContext'dough

        BakingContext'dough = "A mixture of flour and water."

15.3.2 BeginPackage

In addition to changing and remembering the current context, BeginPackage changes the context path to consist of only the specified arguments of BeginPackage and System'.

In[28] := BeginPackage["SlangContext'"]
Out[28] = SlangContext'

In[29] := $Context
Out[29] = SlangContext'

In[30] := $ContextPath
Out[30] = {SlangContext', System'}

If I ask *Mathematica* about the symbols defined in the context named Global', *Mathematica* does not know about them because the context named Global' is not in the ContextPath. I set flies equal to 3 mph on page 249. Notice that *Mathematica* does not show me that definition unless I explicitly ask for it.

In[31] := ?flies
        Information::notfound: Symbol flies not found.

In[32] := ?Global`flies
          Global`flies

          Global`flies = 3*Global`mph

Let's get back to the context named SlangContext` and assign dough its meaning in slang.

In[33] := dough = money;

Calling EndPackage restores the context to what it was before the previous call to BeginPackage. The contexts specified as its arguments are prepended to the context path.

In[34] := EndPackage[ ]

In[35] := $Context
Out[35] = Global`

In[36] := $ContextPath
Out[36] = {SlangContext`, Global`, System`}

Notice that, if I now ask about dough, *Mathematica* finds the symbol since it is defined in a context that is included in $ContextPath.

In[37] := Context[dough]
Out[37] = SlangContext`

15.4 Loading Packages

Packages can be loaded with the << operator (Get) or with Needs. Once loaded, the functions, variables, and objects defined in the package can be used.

15.4.1 $Path

The global variable $Path is set to the list of directories *Mathematica* searches in attempting to find an external file. $Path typically contains the directories or folders that contain the packages distributed with *Mathematica*.

In[38] := $Path
Out[38] = {:Packages, :Packages:StartUp, :Packages:StartUp:Integrate}

The global variable $Path is set in the file init.m, which is read in every time that *Mathematica* starts up. You can modify the package Init.m by adding definitions and loading packages that you use or expect to use frequently. Thus you can customize *Mathematica* to suit your needs.

15.4.2 Get

You can load a file or package by using << or the Get command. Since the directory Packages is in $Path, I specify only the directory Graphics when loading the package Shapes.m.

In[39] := << Graphics/Shapes.m

Macintosh: Specify only the package name. A dialog box prompts you for the directory or folder.

In[39] := << Shapes.m

If the symbols in a package are protected (i.e., they have been assigned the attribute Protected), and you load the package more than once, then *Mathematica* prints a series of error messages when reloading the package.

In[40] := << Graphics/Shapes.m
       Set::write:
          Symbol Cylinder is write protected.
       Set::write:
          Symbol Cylinder is write protected.
       Set::write:
          Symbol Cone is write protected.
       General::stop: Further output of Set::write will be
          suppressed during this calculation.

15.4.3 Needs

Unlike <<, the Needs function does not load the package if it has already been loaded. The Needs function loads only packages whose corresponding contexts are not on the context path.

In[41] := $ContextPath
Out[41] = {Shapes`, Geometry`Rotations`, SlangContext`, Global`,
          System`}

Since the context Shapes` is already in $ContextPath, the package Shapes.m is not read in when I invoke the following statement.

In[42] := Needs["Graphics`Shapes`"]

If more than one argument is passed to BeginPackage, the context is changed to the first argument and packages corresponding to the other contexts are loaded if they haven't already been.

       BeginPackage["*context*`", "*needs1*`", "*needs2*`", ...]

Near the beginning of the package Shapes.m is the following call to BeginPackage:

Version 1.2:

    BeginPackage["Shapes`", "Geometry`Rotations`"]

Version 2.0:

    BeginPackage["Graphics`Shapes`", "Geometry`Rotations`"]

This statement first loads Geometry/Rotations.m, if is has not already been loaded. It then sets the context path to

Version 1.2:

    {Shapes`, Geometry`Rotations`, System`}

Version 2.0:

    {Graphics`Shapes`, Geometry`Rotations`, System`}

and the current context to Graphics`Shapes` (Shapes` in version 1.2).

15.5 Package Style

A package is just a file containing *Mathematica* definitions. See appendix D on page 323 for a complete list of the packages that are distributed with version 1.2 and version 2.0 of *Mathematica*.

If you look at these packages, you will see that a package typically starts with a comment describing the contents of the package. Then the package typically calls BeginPackage to change the context and load other relevant packages.

Some packages contain internal definitions that are not intended to be accessed by users. Such definitions tend to be specified in a context named *Pack-ageName*`Private`. Defining these functions in such a context makes it more difficult for users to access them accidentally. The following example is intended to show the structure of many of the packages that are distributed with *Mathematica*.

```
(* :Title:   PackageStructure.m *)
(* :Author:  T. Bufonidae  *)
(* :Summary:
  This package is intended to give you an idea of the
  structure of many of the packages distributed with
  Mathematica.
*)
```

```
(*
 * Change $Context to PackageStructure' and $ContextPath
 * to {PackageStructure', System'}
 *)
BeginPackage["PackageStructure'"]



(*
 * Usage statements for all functions that are intended to
 * be user-accessible. (Note, as a side effect, this creates
 * the symbol userAccessibleFunction in the PackagesStructure'
 * context (unless it already exists in that context or in
 * the System' context).)
 *)
userAccessibleFunction::usage = "userAccessibleFunction[x]
    is intended to be accessible by the user."

(*
 * Change $Context to PackageStructure'Private'.
 *)
Begin["'Private'"]

(*
 * Function definitions.
 * (Note, as a side effect, this creates the symbols
 * helperFunction1 and helperFunction2 in the context
 * PackageStructure'Private (unless they already exist
 * in that context, PackageStructure' or System').)
 *)
userAccessibleFunction[x_] := helperFunction1[x] +
    helperFunction2[x]

(*
 * Definitions of functions that are not intended to
 * be accessed directly by those using the package.
 *)
helperFunction1[x_] := x
helperFunction2[x_] := x
```

```
(*
 * The following End[ ] balances the Begin["Private'"] above.
 * It changes $Context back to what it was before Begin was
 * invoke,  i.e., $Context becomes PackageStructure'.
 *)
End[ ]


(*
 * Protect user-accessible functions.
 *)
Protect[userAccessibleFunction]



(*
 * The following EndPackages[ ] balances the
 * BeginPackage["PackageStructure'"] above.  It changes
 * $Context  back to what it when BeginPackage was invoked.
 * $ContextPath is also restored to its previous value,
 * except PackageStructure' is added to it (if it wasn't
 * already there).
 *)
EndPackage[ ]

(*
 * Since loading a file returns the result of evaluating
 * the last expression in the file, packages typically
 * end with Null so that no result is printed.
 *)
Null
```

Loading this package sets up a definition for userAccessibleFunction in the context PackageStructure' and helperFunction1 and helperFunction2 in the context PackageStructure'Private'. So after loading this package, you should be able to call userAccessibleFunction. As you will see in the next section, you might have problems accessing a function defined in a package.

15.6 Conflicting Names

Packages in which definitions are specified in a context other than the current context can cause naïve users confusion.

If you call a function before loading the package in which it is defined, *Mathematica* returns the input unevaluated. Suppose I call Laplace (version 1.2) or LaplaceTransform (version 2.0) before loading the package Calculus/Laplace.m (version 1.2) or Calculus/LaplaceTransform.m (version 2.0).

```
In[43] := Laplace[(1 + 4t + 5t^2) Exp[ -3t], t, s]
```
$$Out[43] = Laplace\left[\frac{1 + 4\ t + 5\ t^2}{E^{3\ t}},\ t,\ s\right]$$

Mathematica does not evaluate Laplace[(1 + 4t + 5t^2) Exp[-3t], t, s] because I did not load the package Laplace.m (or LaplaceTransform.m in version 2.0). Since *Mathematica* did not know about the function Laplace, it created the symbol Laplace in our current context (Global'). When I ask about Laplace, *Mathematica* does not return a usage statement, but it does indicate that it knows about a symbol named Laplace.

```
In[44] := ?Laplace
          Laplace
```

Now I load the package Laplace.m.

```
In[45] := Needs["Calculus'Laplace'"]
```

Even though I loaded the package, when I ask for information on Laplace, I am not shown the usage statement specified in the package. Instead of accessing the symbol defined in the package, I am assessing the symbol Laplace in our current context that was created when I first called Laplace. The function Laplace is defined in the context Calculus'Laplace', but I don't access that definition because *Mathematica* checks the current context before checking contexts in the context path.

```
In[46] := ?Laplace
          Laplace
```

After removing the symbol Laplace in the current context, I am able to access the definition from the package. This command doesn't affect the package; it only removes the symbol in the global context.

```
In[47] := Remove[Laplace]
```

Now I can see the usage statement for Laplace and obtain the Laplace transform.

In[48] := ?Laplace

   Laplace[expr, t, s] gives the Laplace transform of expr.

In[49] := Laplace[(1 + 4t + 5t^2) Exp[-3t], t, s]

```
              10            4          1
Out[49] =  -------- + -------- + -----
              3            2      3 + s
           (3 + s)     (3 + s)
```

Version 2.0: When you load a package, if any definitions in the package will be overshadowed by a symbol with the same name, *Mathematica* prints a warning message.

In[50] := LaplaceTransform[(1 + t) Exp[-3t], t, s]

```
                          1 + t
Out[50] = LaplaceTransform[-----, t, s]
                           3 t
                          E
```

In[51] := << Calculus'LaplaceTransform'

   LaplaceTransform::shdw:
      Warning: Symbol LaplaceTransform
       appears in multiple contexts
       {Calculus'LaplaceTransform', Global'}
       ; definitions in context Calculus'LaplaceTransform'
       may shadow other definitions.

Being unable to access the definitions in a package that has been loaded confuses many *Mathematica* users. Why are packages written in this style? One reason is that you can access all definitions in a particular context with the notation ?*context*'*. Here I load the package Algebra/Trigonometry.m and then ask for all the accessible definitions that I loaded.

In[52] := Needs["Algebra'Trigonometry'"]

In[53] := ?Algebra'Trigonometry'*

   ComplexToTrig TrigCanonical TrigFactor   TrigReduce
   TrigToComplex

The next section describes a package style specifically designed to help naïve users and allow sophisticated users the flexibility of loading definitions into whatever contexts they choose.

15.6.1 The Recommended Package Style

This package style is endorsed by Henry Cejtin, one of the original developers of *Mathematica*, and by Theo Gray, the primary architect and developer of the Notebook Front End.

Theo Gray wrote about this style in a document call `ProtoNotebook.m`. The following example is from this document.

Start your package with a comment describing what the package does.

```
(*
 * ProtoNotebook.m
 *
 * Adapted from a Notebook by Theo Gray.
 *
 * This package demonstrates the recommended package style.
 *)
```

Prepend a context to `$ContextPath` with a call to `BeginPackage` followed immediately by a call to `EndPackage`. Because the context for the package is prepended to the context path, `Needs` will be able to determine when the package has been loaded.

```
(*
 * Prepend the context ProtoNotebook` to $ContextPath.
 *)
BeginPackage["ProtoNotebook`"]
EndPackage[ ]
```

Write a usage statement for each function in the package. The usage statement should specify the arguments.

```
ExamplePlot::usage = "ExamplePlot[n, m] draws \
        n starbursts and m spirals. \
        ExamplePlot[n] draws n starbursts and \
        no spirals.";

SamplePlot::usage = "SamplePlot  is Vaporware.  It \
        does nothing.";
```

Declare all global objects.

```
(*
 * Global objects.
 *)
ExamplePlot;
SamplePlot;
```

Change to a private context. Declare all local objects not intended to be accessed by users. If a definition is preceded by a backquote ', the context of the object is specified relative to the current context.

```
Begin["ProtoNotebook`Private`"];

(*
 * Local object.
 *)
'starBurst;
'spiral;
```

Specify the functions. Indent to show the structure of the program.

Be clear. Make your code straightforward and understandable. (Though APL is a powerful programming language, it has not been widely adopted because it is difficult to browse through APL programs and figure out what they do.)

```
(*
 * Define starBurst and spiral.
 *)
starBurst[center_, radius_, n_] :=
    Block[
        {
            'r
        },
        Table[
            Line[{
                center,
                center + radius {Cos[r], Sin[r]}
            }],
            {r, 0, 2Pi - 2Pi/n, 2Pi/n}
        ]
    ]
```

```
spiral[center_, radius_, loops_] :=
    Block[
        {
            `t
        },
        Line[
            Table[
                center +
                radius t {Cos[t], Sin[t]} / (2Pi loops),
                {t, 0, 2 Pi loops, 2Pi/30}
            ]
        ]
    ]


ExamplePlot[stars_] :=
    Show[
        Graphics[
            Table[
                starBurst[
                    4 {Random[ ], Random[ ]},
                    0.3 + Random[ ],
                    20
                ],
                {stars}
            ]
        ],
        AspectRatio->Automatic
    ]
```

```
ExamplePlot[stars_, spins_] :=
    Show[
        Graphics[{
            Table[
                starBurst[
                    4 {Random[ ], Random[ ]},
                    0.3 + Random[ ],
                    20
                ],
                {stars}
            ],
            Table[
                spiral[
                    4 {Random[ ], Random[ ]},
                    0.3 + Random[ ],
                    Random[Integer, {2, 5}]
                ],
                {spins}
            ]
        }],
        AspectRatio->Automatic
    ]
```

Protect the functions to prevent users from inadvertently modifying them. Lock private functions to prevent modification.

```
(*
 * Protect the function and lock the private
 * functions.
 *)
Protect[ExamplePlot, SamplePlot];
Append[Attributes[ExamplePlot], Locked]
Append[Attributes[SamplePlot], Locked]
```

```
End[ ];
```

Now I load the package and try ExamplePlot (see figure 15.1).

```
In[54] := Needs["ProtoNotebook`"]
In[55] := ExamplotPlot[4, 3]
```

Figure 15.1: A plot produced with the function `ExamplePlot`.

What if you want `ExamplePlot` to be defined in a context other than the current context? No problem. You can easily load the package into a context of
your choice by changing the context, then loading the package. Here I load
`ExamplePlot` in to the context `PlottingExamples‘"`.

```
Begin["PlottingExamples‘"];
    Needs["ProtoNotebook‘"];
End[ ]
```

With packages specified in this style, naïve users do not have have to know
when to remove symbols, but users who understand contexts can still load definitions into the context of their choice.

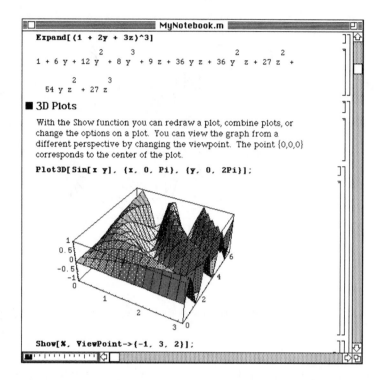

Figure 15.2: A Notebook produced using the Notebook Front End.

15.7 Notebooks

Notebooks are *Mathematica* documents that contain a mixture of text, graphics, and *Mathematica* definitions (see figure 15.2).

When writing a Notebook, make sure to put context-manipulation commands on separate lines and in separate cells. Let me show you what can happen if you don't. Let us set the symbol Global`doe equal to the string "Department of Energy".

In[56] := doe = "Department of Energy";

In[57] := Context[doe]
Out[57] = Global`

Let us change the context by using BeginPackage and set doe equal to the string "Female deer" in the same line.

In[58] := BeginPackage["ZoologyContext`"]; doe = "Female deer";

Now let us ask about doe.

In[59] := doe
Out[59] = doe

Why does doe not have a value? The two expressions in *In[58]* are parsed before they are evaluated. When *Mathematica* finds the declaration of doe, it looks to see if it knows anything about doe. It finds doe in the current context. Then *Mathematica* evaluates the compound expression in *In[58]*, changing the context to ZoologyContext` and setting Global`doe equal to the string "Female deer". In *In[59]*, when I ask about doe, the context Global` is not in the context path and so *Mathematica* does not access Global`doe. Unable to find the symbol doe, *Mathematica* creates the symbol ZoologyContext`doe.

In[60] := Context[doe]
Out[60] = ZoologyContext`

The symbol ZoologyContext`doe was not set. Instead Global`doe was set to the string "Female deer".

In[61] := Global`doe
Out[61] = Female deer

An expression that changes the context should be placed on a line or in a cell (Notebook Front End users) by itself. Never put other declarations in the same line or cell.

15.8 Summary

Packages are useful for grouping together definitions of related functions that you or others expect to use frequently.

Function	Description
Begin[*context*`]	Changes the current context.
End[ ]	Reverts to the previous context.
BeginPackage[*context*`]	Changes active contexts.
EndPackage[ ]	Prepends current context to $ContextPath.
	Reverts to previous context.
Context[*symbol*]	Gives the current context or the context of a symbol.
$Context	The current context
$ContextPath	The list of contexts to search for a symbol.
$Path	A list of directories to search in attempting to find an external file.

15.9 Exercises

15.1 Load the package Colors.m found in the Graphics directory. List all the colors that are specified in the package.

15.2 Write a package for computing the mean and median of a list of numbers. (See section 15.6.1 on page 259 for style recommendations.)

Part III:
Appendices

Appendix	Description
Answers	Answers to most of the odd numbered problems in this book.
Bibliography	Bibliography and other references on *Mathematica*.
Commands	Commands built into *Mathematica*, version 2.0.
Directory	Directory of packages distributed with versions 1.2 and 2.0.
Electronic	Electronic sources of information on *Mathematica*.
Front End	The Notebook Front End, pointers and cell brackets.
Glossary	Glossary of terms used in this book.
Help	Where to get help on *Mathematica*.
Index	Index.
Just	Just what more should I say?

A

a **A** α a A

Answers to the Exercises

This appendix contains solutions to most of the odd numbered problems in this book.

A.1 Getting Started with *Mathematica*

1.1 (a) Find all the commands whose names begin with the letter O.

```
In[1] := ?O*
    O               OpenRead        Options      Outer
    OddQ            OpenTemporary   Or           OutputForm
    Off             OpenWrite       Order        OutputStream
    On              Operate         OrderedQ     Overflow
    OneIdentity     Optional        Orderless    Overlaps
    OpenAppend      OptionQ         Out          OwnValues
```

(b) Find all commands that have the word List in their names.

```
In[2] := ?*List*
    CoefficientList        List              $MessageList
    ComposeList            Listable          MessageList
    FactorList             ListContourPlot   NestList
    FactorSquareFreeList   ListDensityPlot   ReadList
    FactorTermsList        ListPlay          RecordLists
    FindList               ListPlot          SampledSoundList
    FixedPointList         ListPlot3D        ValueList
    FoldList               ListQ
```

1.3 Use `Alias[ ]` to generate a list of the aliases built into *Mathematica*.

```
In[3] := Alias[ ]
Out[3] = ! :> Not
         " :> String
         # :> Slot

             .
             .
             .

         === :> SameQ
         ::= :> Alias
```

The output of `Alias[ ]` was used in generating the list of special forms on the inside back cover of this book.

1.5 After loading the package `Graphics.m`, make a bar chart showing *Mathematica* users by job title. See figure A.1.

Macintosh: With version 1.2 of Macintosh *Mathematica*, the titles are clipped.

```
In[4] := Needs["Graphics`Graphics`"];
In[5] := BarChart[{{31, "Research"},
         {26, "Prof"},
         {15, "Eng"},
         {8, "Student"},
         {13, "CS"},
         {7, "Other"}}];
```

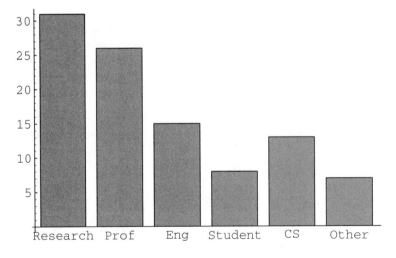

Figure A.1: A bar chart of *Mathematica* users classified by job title.

A.2 Numerical Problem Set

2.1 Compute the number of minutes in a 365-day year.

In[1] := 365 Day (24 Hour/Day) (60 Minutes/Hour)
Out[1] = 525600 Minutes

2.3 Use NumberForm to separate the digits of the number 123456789 into blocks of 3 digits.

In[2] := NumberForm[
            123456789,
            DigitBlock -> 3
        ]
Out[2] = 123,456,789

2.5 Find what *Mathematica* returns in response to the following expressions and determine whether the last inequality is true or false.

In[3] := Sqrt[3] + 3
Out[3] = 3 + Sqrt[3]

Notice *Mathematica* changes the order of the terms.

In[4] := Exp[2 Pi I]
Out[4] = 1

In[5] := 5 > 3
Out[5] = True

In[6] := Pi^E > E^Pi

                E   Pi
Out[6] = Pi   > E

Mathematica does not indicate if the statement is true or false. *Mathematica* treats the Pi and E as symbols unless instructed to compute their values. Only after using N to compute numerical approximations for the symbols can *Mathematica* determine if the expression is true or false.

In[7] := N[Pi^E > E^Pi]
Out[7] = False

2.7 Compute the inverse of the 3-by-3 Hilbert matrix, the matrix whose i, jth element is $1/(i + j - 1)$ for $1 \leq i, j \leq 3$.

```
In[8] := MatrixForm[Inverse[Table[1/(i + j - 1), {i, 3}, {j, 3}]]]
```
```
Out[8] = 9      -36    30

        -36    192    -180

        30     -180   180
```

2.9 Find five roots of the following equations:

(a) $x^5 + 5x^4 + 4x^3 + 3x^2 + 2x + 1 = 0$

```
In[9] := NRoots[x^5 + 5x^4 + 4x^3 + 3x^2 + 2x + 1 == 0, x]
Out[9] = x == -4.19273 || x == -0.564099 - 0.390903 I ||
         x == -0.564099 + 0.390903 I ||
         x == 0.160462 - 0.693272 I ||
         x == 0.160462 + 0.693272 I
```

(c) $x \tan x = 1$

Since $x \tan x = 1$ is not a polynomial equation, NRoots cannot be used to find the roots. Instead I use FindRoot.

```
In[10] := Table[FindRoot[x Tan[x] == 1, {x, x0}], {x0, 11}]
Out[10] = {{x -> 0.860334}, {x -> 3.42562}, {x -> 3.42562},
          {x -> 3.42562}, {x -> 6.4373}, {x -> 6.4373},
          {x -> 6.4373}, {x -> 9.52933}, {x -> 9.52933},
          {x -> 9.52933}, {x -> 12.6453}}
```

Though there are eleven solutions, if you look closely, you will notice that five are distinct.

A.3 Symbolic Problem Set

3.1 Have *Mathematica* solve the following equations.

In[1] := Solve[x^2 + 2x + 1 == 0]
Out[1] = {{x -> -1}, {x -> -1}}

Notice Solve lists a double root twice.

In[2] := Solve[ax^2 + bx + c == 0, x]
Out[2] = {{}}

In *Mathematica*, the equation ax^2 + bx + c == 0 does not contain the variable x. It contains variables named ax, bx, and c.

In[3] := Solve[{x + y == 5, 2x + 6y == 23}]

$$Out[3] = \{\{x \to \frac{7}{4}, y \to \frac{13}{4}\}\}$$

3.3 Use Apart to find partial fractions.

In[4] := Apart[x/(x^2 + 5x + 6)]

$$Out[4] = \frac{-2}{2 + x} + \frac{3}{3 + x}$$

In[5] := Apart[(2x + 7)/(x^3 + 3x^2 + 3x + 1)]

$$Out[5] = \frac{5}{(1 + x)^3} + \frac{2}{(1 + x)^2}$$

3.5 (a) Using `Array`, generate the 2-by-2 matrix m with elements `b[i, j]`.

In[6] := m = Array[b, {2, 2}]
Out[6] = {{b[1, 1], b[1, 2]}, {b[2, 1], b[2, 2]}}

(c) Create the 2-by-2 matrix n with elements `c[i, j]`.

In[7] := n = Array[c, {2, 2}];
In[8] := MatrixForm[n]
Out[8] = c[1, 1]   c[1, 2]

        c[2, 1]   c[2, 2]

(d) Calculate the values of m n and m . n. Examine the results and describe how they differ.

In[9] := m n
Out[9] = {{b[1, 1] c[1, 1], b[1, 2] c[1, 2]},
          {b[2, 1] c[2, 1], b[2, 2] c[2, 2]}}

In[10] := m . n
Out[10] = {{b[1, 1] c[1, 1] + b[1, 2] c[2, 1],
            b[1, 1] c[1, 2] + b[1, 2] c[2, 2]},
           {b[2, 1] c[1, 1] + b[2, 2] c[2, 1],
            b[2, 1] c[1, 2] + b[2, 2] c[2, 2]}}

The so-called dot product, m . n, is how matrices are conventionally multiplied.

3.7 Use *Mathematica* to compute the exact values of these integrals.

(a) $\int_0^1 \int_0^{\sqrt{1-x}} xy^2 \, dy \, dx$

In[11] := Integrate[x y^2, {x, 0, 1}, {y, 0, Sqrt[1-x]}]

           4
Out[11] = ---
          105

(b) $\int_0^1 \int_0^{\sqrt{x}} ye^{x^2} \, dy \, dx$

In[12] := Integrate[y Exp[x^2], {x, 0, 1}, {y, 0, Sqrt[x]}]

            1   E
Out[12] = -(-) + -
            4   4

3.9 See if you can experimentally discover rational expressions having the following power-series expansions.

(a) $1 - x + x^2 - x^3 + x^4 - x^5 + \dots$

In[13] := `Series[1/(1 + x), {x, 0, 7}]`

```
            2   3   4   5   6   7      8
Out[13] = 1 - x + x - x + x - x + x - x + O[x]
```

(c) $1 + 2x + 3x^2 + x^3 + 2x^4 + 3x^5 + x^6 + 2x^7 + 3x^8 + \dots$

In[14] := `(1 + 2x + 3x^2) Series[1/(1 - x^3), {x, 0, 8}]`

```
            2     3     4     5     6     7     8      9
Out[14] = 1 + 2 x + 3 x + x + 2 x + 3 x + x + 2 x + 3 x + O[x]
```

3.11 Use the function `DSolve`, available in version 1.2 and later releases of *Mathematica*, to solve each of the following differential equations:

(a) $y'(x) - y(x) \tan x = x$

In[15] := `DSolve[y'[x] - y[x] Tan[x] == x, y[x], x]`

```
                 C[1]     -1 + Cos[x] + x Sin[x]
Out[15] = {{y[x] -> ------ + ----------------------}}
                 Cos[x]          Cos[x]
```

(c) $y'(x) = y(x)$ with the boundary condition $y'(0) = 1$

Note: The first argument of `DSolve` can be an equation or a list of equations.

In[16] := `DSolve[{y'[x] == y[x], y'[0] == 1}, y[x], x]`

```
                  x
Out[16] = {{y[x] -> E }}
```

(e) $y'(x)y(x) + x^2 = x$

Version 1.2: DSolve cannot solve this particular equation as it is stated here.

In[17] := DSolve[y'[x] y[x] + x^2 == x, y[x], x]
```
    DSolve::NotYet: Built-in procedures cannot solve this
        differential equation.
```

```
                        2
Out[17] = DSolve[x  + y(x) y'(x) == x, y[x], x]
```

Version 2.0: The differential-equation-solving capabilities have been enhanced in version 2.0.

In[17] := DSolve[y'[x] y[x] + x^2 == x, y[x], x]

```
                        2      3
               Sqrt[3 x  - 2 x  + 6 C[1]]
Out[17] = {{y[x] -> -------------------------},
                        Sqrt[3]


                           2      3
                  Sqrt[3 x  - 2 x  + 6 C[1]]
       {y[x] -> -(-------------------------)}}
                        Sqrt[3]
```

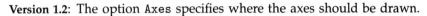

A.4 Graphics Problem Set

4.1 Plot the function $\sin x$ for x in the range $[0, 6\pi]$ (see figure A.2).

Version 1.2: The option `Axes` specifies where the axes should be drawn.

```
In[1] := Plot[Sin[x], {x, 0, 6 Pi},
          AspectRatio -> 1/2,
          PlotLabel -> "Sin[x]",
          AxesLabel -> {"x", "y"},
          Axes -> {2 Pi, 1/2}
        ];
```

Version 2.0: The option `AxesOrigin` specifies where the axes should cross.

```
In[1] := Plot[Sin[x], {x, 0, 6 Pi},
          AspectRatio -> 1/2,
          PlotLabel -> "Sin[x]",
          AxesLabel -> {"x", "y"},
          AxesOrigin -> {2 Pi, 1/2}
        ];
```

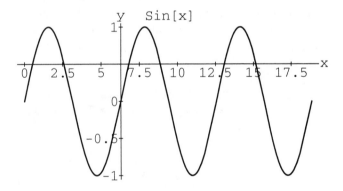

Figure A.2: Using options, you can label the plot and change the origin of the axes.

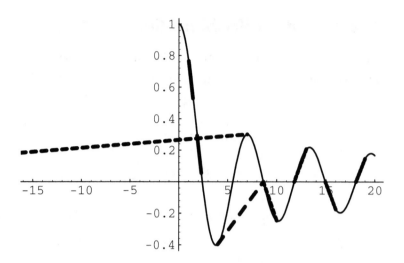

Figure A.3: This plot shows the roots found by **FindRoot** for each of seven distinct starting values.

4.3 Produce a plot that contains the curve $y = J_0(x)$ (BesselJ[0, x]) for x from 0 to 20 together with seven line segments. Each of those line segments should have endpoints $\{x, J_0(x)\}$ and $\{r, 0\}$ where r is the root returned by FindRoot when given the starting value x.

The following code generates such as plot (see figure A.3).

```
In[2] := Show[
            Plot[BesselJ[0, x], {x, 0, 20},
                DisplayFunction -> Identity],
            Table[
                Graphics[{
                    Dashing[{1/(10t)}],
                    Thickness[0.01],
                    Line[{
                        {t, BesselJ[0, t]},
                        {x /. FindRoot[BesselJ[0, x]==0, {x, t}], 0}
                    }]
                }],
                {t, 1, 20, 3}
            ],
            DisplayFunction :> $DisplayFunction
        ];
```

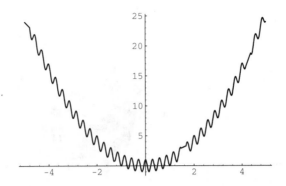

Figure A.4: *Mathematica* does not, by default, sample frequently enough to render this curve accurately.

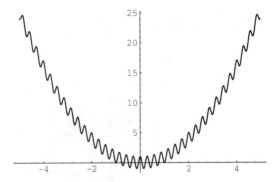

Figure A.5: Setting the option `PlotPoints` equal to 70 ensures that *Mathematica* samples at least 70 points along the curve.

4.5 (a) Plot the function $x^2 + \cos 22x$ for x in the range $[-5, 5]$ (see figure A.4).

In[3] := `Plot[x^2 + Cos[22x], {x, -5, 5}];`

(b) Make the same graph with the option `PlotPoints` set to 70.
Setting the option `PlotPoints` equal to 70 ensures that *Mathematica* samples at least 70 points on the graph. Because of *Mathematica*'s adaptive-sampling algorithm, *Mathematica* samples more frequently in regions where the function varies significantly (see figure A.5).

In[4] := `Plot[x^2 + Cos[22x], {x, -5, 5}, PlotPoints -> 70];`

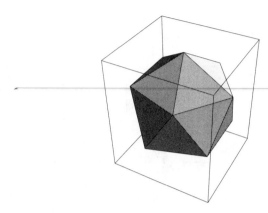

Figure A.6: An icosahedron, a 20-faced polyhedron.

Figure A.7: A stellated icosahedron.

4.7 Load the package `Polyhedra.m`, which contains the definitions of various polyhedra. Then plot a regular icosahedron (a 20-faced polyhedron) and a stellated icosahedron (an icosahedron with a tetrahedron on each of its faces). With the stellation ratio of 3, you get the "great stellated dodecahedron," which has 12 star-shaped intersecting faces. See figures A.6 and A.7.

```
In[5] := Needs["Graphics'Polyhedra'"];
In[6] := Show[Graphics3D[Icosahedron[ ]]];
In[7] := Show[Graphics3D[Stellate[Icosahedron[ ],3]], Boxed->False];
```

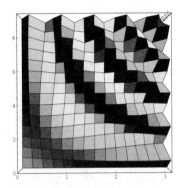

Figure A.8: A simulation of a color density plot by viewing a color plot from directly overhead.

4.9 (a) Simulate a color density plot of Sin[x y] by producing a graph with the command Plot3D and viewing it from directly overhead (see figure A.8).

In[8] := Plot3D[Sin[x y], {x, 0, Pi}, {y, 0, 3 Pi},
        Lighting -> True, ViewPoint -> {0, 0, 3}];

(b) Change the view point to simulate viewing the graph from father away. What sad effect does this have on the colors in the graph? See figure A.9.

In[9] := Plot3D[Sin[x y], {x, 0, Pi}, {y, 0, 3 Pi},
        Lighting -> True, ViewPoint -> {0, 0, 10}];

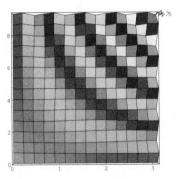

Figure A.9: A simulation of a color density plot by viewing a color plot from far away.

Just as in real life, the farther you stand from an object, the less well you can distinguish the colors in the object.

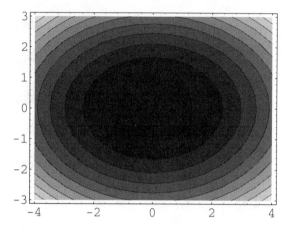

Figure A.10: ContourPlot can plot the set of ellipses $x^2 + 2y^2 = n$.

4.11 Plot a set of concentric ellipses $x^2 + 2y^2 = n$ using ContourPlot (see figure A.10).

In[10] := ContourPlot[x^2 + 2 y^2, {x, 0, 4}, {y, 0, 4},
        AspectRatio -> Automatic];

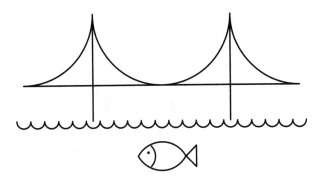

Figure A.11: A fish swimming under the Golden Gate Bridge drawn using *Mathematica*.

4.13 Use graphics primitives such as Point, Disk, Line, and Circle to draw a
fish (see figure A.11) or a face (see figure A.12).

```
In[11] := Show[
            Graphics[{  (* Golden Gate Bridge *)
                Circle[{-2, 1}, 1, {3 Pi/2, 2 Pi}],
                Circle[{0, 1}, 1, {Pi, 2 Pi}],
                Circle[{2, 1}, 1, {Pi, 3 Pi/2}],
                Line[{{-2, 0}, {2, 0}}],
                Line[{{-1, -0.5}, {-1, 1}}],
                Line[{{1, -0.5}, {1, 1}}]
            }],
            Graphics[  (* Water *)
                Table[Circle[{x, -0.5}, 0.1, {Pi, 2 Pi}],
                    {x, -2, 2, 0.2}
                ]
            ],
            Graphics[{  (* Fish *)
                Circle[{0, -1.2}, 0.4, {Pi/6, 5 Pi/6}],
                Circle[{0, -0.8}, 0.4, {7 Pi/6, 11 Pi/6}],
                Point[{-0.2, -.95}],
                Circle[{-0.3, -1}, 0.2, {-Pi/4, Pi/4}],
                Line[{{0.35, -1}, {0.5, -0.85},
                    {0.5, -1.15}, {0.35, -1}}]
            }],
            AspectRatio -> Automatic,
            PlotRange -> All
        ];
```

Figure A.12: A face made by using the *Mathematica* graphics primitives.

```
In[12] := Show[
    Graphics[{
        (* eyes  *) PointSize[0.04],
                    Point[{-.3, .1}], Point[{.3, .1}],
        (* nose  *) Disk[{0, 0}, .35, {23 Pi/16, 25 Pi/16}],
        (* mouth *) Line[{{-.3, -.5},{0, -.6}}],
                    Line[{{0, -.6}, {.3, -.5}}],
        (* head  *) Circle[{0,0}, 1]
    }],
    AspectRatio -> Automatic, PlotRange -> All
];
```

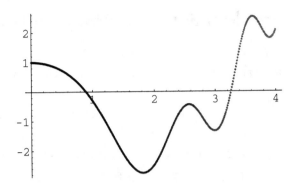

Figure A.13: A line that varies in color.

4.15 Draw colored dots along the curve $\cos x^2 - x \sin x$ so that it appears to vary in color from blue to green (see figure A.13).

```
In[13] := Show[
           Graphics[
             Table[{
               RGBColor[0, x/4., 1. - x/4.],
               Point[{x, Cos[x^2] - x Sin[x]}]},
               {x, 0, 4, .01}
             ]
           ],
           Axes -> Automatic
         ];
```

A.5 Problem Set on Getting Around

5.1 List the input lines in your current session by using ??In.

Note: The ?? must be the first two characters on the line.

In[14] := ??In

> In[n] is a global object that is assigned to have a delayed
> value of the nth input line.
>
> Attributes[In] = {Listable, Protected}
>
> In[1] := (Plot[Sin[x], {x, 0, 6*Pi}, AspectRatio -> 1/2,
>   PlotLabel -> "Sin[x]", AxesLabel -> {"x", "y"},
>   Axes -> {2*Pi, 1/2}]; Null)
>
> In[2] := (Plot[2*x^3 - 7*x^2 - 17*x + 10, {x, -6, 6}]; Null)
>
> In[3] := Solve[2*x^3 - 7*x^2 - 17*x + 10 == 0, x]
>
> In[4] := (Plot[BesselJ[0, x], {x, 8, 12}]; Null)
>
> In[5] := (Plot[BesselJ[0, x], {x, 11.7, 11.9}]; Null)
>
> In[6] := (Plot[BesselJ[0, x], {x, 8.5, 8.7}]; Null)
>
> .
> .
> .

5.3 Find how much CPU time it takes to invert a 3 x 3 matrix on the computer
you are using. Use postfix notation (i.e., specify the timing function to the
right of its argument).

In[15] := m = Table[Random[ ], {3}, {3}]
Out[15] = {{0.707385, 0.620549, 0.264483}, {0.366174, 0.0188787,
    0.161556}, {0.137272, 0.937395, 0.41958}}

In[16] := m // Inverse // MatrixForm // Timing

$$\begin{matrix} 1.54315 & 0.133816 & -1.02425 \\ 1.41349 & -2.80091 & 0.187472 \end{matrix}$$

Out[16] = {0.05 Second, $\begin{matrix} -3.66279 & 6.2138 & 2.2996 \end{matrix}$ }

Find how much CPU time it takes to invert a 10 x 10 matrix.

In[17] := Table[Random[ ], {10}, {10}] // Inverse; // Timing
Out[17] = {1.65 Second, Null}

A.6 List Manipulation Problem Set

6.1 Create a list of the first 10 odd positive numbers (i.e., 1, 3, 5, ..., 19) by using Range and by using Table.

In[1] := Range[1, 20, 2]
Out[1] = {1, 3, 5, 7, 9, 11, 13, 15, 17, 19}

In[2] := oddList = Table[2i - 1, {i, 10}]
Out[2] = {1, 3, 5, 7, 9, 11, 13, 15, 17, 19}

6.3 Call the functions Dimensions and Length on the matrices m and n.

In[3] := m = {{2, 4, 6}, {5, 7, 9}}; n = {{1, 2, 3}, {4, 5}};

In[4] := Dimensions[m]
Out[4] = {2, 3}

In[5] := Dimensions[n]
Out[5] = {2}

In[6] := Length[m]
Out[6] = 2

In[7] := Length[n]
Out[7] = 2

The matrix m is a nested rectangular list with 2 rows and 3 columns. Length returns the number of rows in the matrix (the number of elements in m). Dimensions returns both the number of rows and the number of columns (the number of elements in each row) for a nested rectangular list. The nested list n is not rectangular, and so Dimensions returns the number of sublists in the list.

6.5 Given a list named myList, how would you check whether all the elements in the list are the same by using only list-oriented primitives?

If all the elements are the same, Length[Union[myList]] will be 1.

```
In[8] := myList = {{-1,-1,2}, {-1,-1,2}, {-1,-1,2}, {-1,-1,2}};
In[9] := Length[Union[myList]]
Out[9] = 1
```

Though the expressions $x^2 - 1$ and $(x-1)(x+1)$ are equivalent in value, they are not considered the same by *Mathematica*.

```
In[10] := myList = {{x^2-1, x^2-1, x^2-1, x^2-1, (x-1)(x+1)}};
In[11] := Length[Union[myList]]
Out[11] = 2
```

6.7 Use the Select command to pick out integers that exceed 50 from the list of random integers you generated in the previous problem.

Here are the data I created in the previous problem.

```
In[12] := data
Out[12] = {76, 21, 49, 27, 13, 42, 21, 54, 16, 1, 68, 41, 51, 83,
           79, 37}


In[13] := greater50[x_] := x > 50


In[14] := Select[data, greater50]
Out[14] = {76, 54, 68, 51, 83, 79}
```

6.9 In a town there are three stores selling 5 popular toys. Store A sells the toys for $15, $17, $18, $32, and $29. Store B sells the same 5 toys for $14, $18, $22, $29, and $26. The policy of store C is to match the most competitive price in town. Write a *Mathematica* expression to determine store C's selling prices for the 5 toys.

```
In[15] := Map[Min, Transpose[{{15,17,18,32,29}, {14,18,22,29,26}}]]
Out[15] = {14, 17, 18, 29, 26}
```

A.7 Problem Set on Assignments and Rules

7.1 Find the value of f[3 + a] and g[3 + a] given the following definitions:

```
In[1] := f[x_] = x /. a -> 7
Out[1] = x
```

```
In[2] := g[x_] := x /. a -> 7
```

```
In[3] := f[3 + a]
Out[3] = 3 + a
```

```
In[4] := g[3 + a]
Out[4] = 10
```

```
In[5] := f[x_] = Expand[2x]
Out[5] = 2 x
In[6] := g[x_] := Expand[2x]
```

```
In[7] := f[3 + a]
Out[7] = 2 (3 + a)
```

```
In[8] := g[3 + a]
Out[8] = 6 + 2 a
```

Notice that the definitions for f and g are different.

```
In[9] := ?f
        f
        f/: f[x_] = 2 x
In[10] := ?g
        g
        g/: g[x_] := Expand[2 x]
```

7.3 (a) Given the pairs of data, double the second element in each pair.

In[11] := {{1, 1}, {2, 2}, {3, 3}} /. {x_, y_} :> {x, 2y}
Out[11] = {{1, 2}, {2, 4}, {3, 6}}

(b) Given the pairs of data, why doesn't the rule {x_, y_} :> {x, 2y} double the second element in each pair? What does this rule do?

In[12] := {{1, 1}, {2, 2}} /. {x_, y_} :> {x, 2y}
Out[12] = {{1, 1}, {4, 4}}

The quantity {{1, 1}, {2, 2}} is a pair where the first element is the pair {1, 1} and the second element is the pair {2, 2}.

7.5 Write a rule that takes a list of pairs, $\{x_i, y_i\}$ and a list of values z_i for $i = 1$ to 4 and transforms the two lists into a single list of triplets $\{x_i, y_i, z_i\}$.

In[13] := pairs = Table[{x[i], y[i]}, {i, 4}]
Out[13] = {{x[1], y[1]}, {x[2], y[2]}, {x[3], y[3]}, {x[4], y[4]}}

In[14] := zValues = Table[z[i], {i, 4}]
Out[14] = {z[1], z[2], z[3], z[4]}

In[15] := {pairs, zValues} /.
              {xyList_List, zList_List} :>
                  Transpose[Append[Transpose[xyList], zList]]
Out[15] = {{x[1], y[1], z[1]}, {x[2], y[2], z[2]},
            {x[3], y[3], z[3]}, {x[4], y[4], z[4]}}

7.7 In the package Trigonometry.m distributed with version 1.2, TrigFactor contains the following rule.

    a_. Cos[x_] Cos[y_] + a_. Sin[x_] Sin[y_] :> a Cos[x - y]

Why doesn't it also contain the rule

    a_. Cos[x_ - y_] :> a Cos[x] Cos[y] + a Sin[x] Sin[y]?

If TrigFactor contained both rules, *Mathematica* would go into an infinite loop when it encountered any expression that matches the left-hand side of either of the rules above.

A.8 Problem Set on Data Types

8.1 Determine how *Mathematica* internally represents the following expressions.

In[1] := FullForm[35a]
Out[1] = Times[35, a]

In[2] := FullForm[a35]
Out[2] = a35

In[3] := FullForm[-x]
Out[3] = Times[-1, x]

In[4] := FullForm[-3]
Out[4] = -3

In[5] := FullForm[x - 3]
Out[5] = Plus[x, -3]

In[6] := FullForm[3 - x]
Out[6] = Plus[3, Times[-1, x]]

In[7] := FullForm[Sqrt[5]]
Out[7] = Power[5, Rational[1, 2]]

In[8] := Series[Tan[x], {x, 0, 9}]

$$Out[8] = x + \frac{x^3}{3} + \frac{2 x^5}{15} + \frac{17 x^7}{315} + \frac{62 x^9}{2835} + O[x]^{10}$$

In[9] := FullForm[Series[Tan[x], {x, 0, 9}]]
Out[9] = SeriesData[x, 0, List[1, 0, Rational[1, 3], 0,
          Rational[2, 15], 0, Rational[17, 315], 0,
          Rational[62, 2835]], 1, 10, 1]

In[10] := FullForm[Normal[Series[Tan[x], {x, 0, 9}]]]
Out[10] = Plus[x, Times[Rational[1, 3], Power[x, 3]],
          Times[Rational[2, 15], Power[x, 5]],
          Times[Rational[17, 315], Power[x, 7]],
          Times[Rational[62, 2835], Power[x, 9]]]

8.3 The function `MemoryInUse` gives the number of bytes of memory used to store data in the current session of *Mathematica*. See how much memory *Mathematica* uses storing a list of 1000 random integers that are between 100 and 200, 1000 integers that are between 300 and 400, 1000 floating-point numbers with the default level of precision, and 1000 floating-point numbers with 30 places of precision. Can you draw any conclusions from your study?

```
In[11] := firstCall = MemoryInUse[ ];
In[12] := smallInt = Table[Random[Integer, {100, 200}], {1000}];

In[13] := secondCall = MemoryInUse[ ];
In[14] := secondCall - firstCall
Out[14] = 5280

In[15] := largeInt = Table[Random[Integer, {300, 400}], {1000}];

In[16] := thirdCall = MemoryInUse[ ];
In[17] := thirdCall - secondCall
Out[17] = 26196
```

In this simulation it took nearly five times as much memory to store numbers that are between 300 and 400 as numbers between 100 and 200. Because users tend to use integers less than 200 often, *Mathematica* was designed to store those numbers efficiently.

```
In[18] := defaultReal = Table[Random[ ], {1000}];

In[19] := fourthCall = MemoryInUse[ ];
In[20] := fourthCall - thirdCall
Out[20] = 37896

In[21] := preciseReal = Table[Random[Real, {0, 1}, 30], {1000}];

In[22] := fifthCall = MemoryInUse[ ];
In[23] := fifthCall - fourthCall
Out[23] = 58016
```

Obviously more memory is needed to store real numbers with more precision than the default machine precision. Moreover, real numbers require more memory than integers.

A.9 Problem Set on Writing Functions

9.1 After specifying the following assignments and rules,

```
In[1] := f[2] = 3;
In[2] := f[u] := 2u^2
In[3] := f[v_] := 1/v
In[4] := u = 2;
```

What is f[u]?

```
In[5] := f[u]
Out[5] = 3
```

The symbol u is immediately replaced by the value 2; so *Mathematica* returns the value of f[2] even though *In[2]* specifies f[u] := 2 u^2 (which, since u = 2, would be equal to 8).

9.3 Write a function that takes a pair, {x, y}, and returns {x, 2y}. Map this function onto the list of data {{1, 1}, {2, 2}}.

```
In[6] := Clear[doubleY]
In[7] := doubleY[{x_, y_}] := {x, 2y}

In[8] := Map[doubleY, {{1, 1}, {2, 2}}]
Out[8] = {{1, 2}, {2, 4}}
```

Cf. Problem 3a on page 152. The result here is different because Map applies doubleY to each pair in the list, first to {1, 1} and then to {2, 2}.

9.5 Write the signum function, sgn[x], which is equal to 1 if x is positive and is equal to −1 if x is negative (see page 178). Plot your sgn function. Specify sgn[0.] = 0 by convention, as 0 is neither positive nor negative.

```
In[9]  := sgn[0.] = 0.
In[10] := sgn[x_] := 1 /; x > 0
In[11] := sgn[x_] := -1 /; x < 0
In[12] := sgn::usage="sgn[x] is equal to 1 if  x is positive, \
          -1 if x is negative and 0 if x is equal to 0."

In[13] := Plot[sgn[x], {x, -2, 2},
              PlotStyle -> {{
                  Thickness[0.01],
                  GrayLevel[0.5]
              }}
          ];
```

9.7 Notice that the rule `s[- x_] :> - s[x]` transforms `s[-a]` to `-s[a]` but it does not transform `s[-3]`. What do you think this rule will do to `s[1 - x]` and why?

```
In[14] := sRule = s[- x_] :> - s[x]
Out[14] = s[-(x_)] :> -s[x]
```

```
In[15] := s[-a] /. sRule
Out[15] = -s[a]
```

```
In[16] := s[-3] /. sRule
Out[16] = s[-3]
```

Look at how *Mathematica* interprets -a and -3.

```
In[17] := FullForm[-a]
Out[17] = Times[-1, a]
```

```
In[18] := FullForm[-3]
Out[18] = -3
```

The expression -a matches the pattern $-(x\_)$ while -3 does not.

The expression 1 - x does not match the pattern $-(x\_)$.

```
In[19] := FullForm[1 - x]
Out[19] = Plus[1, Times[-1, x]]
```

So the rule `s[- x_] :> - s[x]` will not transform the expression `s[1 - x]`.

```
In[20] := s[1 - x] /. sRule
Out[20] = s[1 - x]
```

9.9 Determine the functions whose names begin with the letters A – E that have the attribute `Listable`.

```
In[21] := listableQ[symbol_String] :=
              MemberQ[Attributes[symbol], Listable]
In[22] := Select[Names["A* B* C* D* E*"], listableQ]
```

A.10 Problem Set on Procedural Programming

10.1 Determine the number of steps required to get an approximation to $\sqrt{2}$ to 30 decimal places by using Newton's method. Start with the value 2, and compute $\sqrt{2}$ by using the formula $x_{i+1} = (x_i + 2/x_i)/2$.

```
In[1] := newtonsMethod[x_] :=
        Module[{
            count = 1,
            two = N[2, 30],
            approx = N[x, 40]
        },
        While[approx^2 != two,
            Print[count, ":  ", N[approx, 30]];
            approx = (approx + 2/approx)/2;
            ++count;
        ];
        Print[count, ":  ", N[approx, 30]];
        ]

In[2] := newtonsMethod[2]
        1: 2.
        2: 1.5
        3: 1.41666666666666666666666666667
        4: 1.41421568627450980392156862745
        5: 1.41421356237468991062629557889
        6: 1.41421356237309504488016896235
        7: 1.41421356237309504880168872421

In[3] := N[Sqrt[2], 30]
Out[3] = 1.41421356237309504880168872421
```

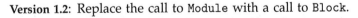

Version 1.2: Replace the call to Module with a call to Block.

10.3 Suppose families have children until they have a boy. Run a simulation
with 1000 families and determine how many children a family will have on
average. On average, how many daughters and how many sons will there
be in a family?

```
In[4] := makeFamily[ ] :=
        Module[{
              children = { }
        },
        While[Random[Integer] == 0,
           AppendTo[children, "girl"]
        ];
        Append[children, "boy"]
        ]
In[5] := makeFamily::usage="makefamily[ ] returns a list of children."

In[6] := numChildren[n_integer] :=
        Module[{
              allChildren
        },
        allChildren = Flatten[Table[makeFamily[ ], {n}]];
        {
           avgChildren -> Length[allChildren]/n,
           avgBoys -> Count[allChildren, "boy"]/n,
           avgGirls -> Count[allChildren, "girl"]/n
        }
        ]
In[7] := numChildren::usage="numChildren[n] returns statistics on
        the number of children from n families."

In[8] := numChildren[1000]
```

$$Out[8] = \{avgChildren \rightarrow \frac{403}{200}, avgBoys \rightarrow 1, avgGirls \rightarrow \frac{203}{200}\}$$

Version 1.2: Replace the call to Module with a call to Block.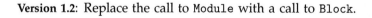

10.5 Look at the following examples. They are identical except the first uses Block while the second uses Module. Explain why *Mathematica* returns different results.

The global variable a is replaced by i. Inside the Block, i is declared local. So no i inside the Block gets replaced by the value of the global variable i. The expression Table[i, {i, 2}] evaluates to {1, 2}.

```
In[9] := a = i;
In[10] := i = 3;
In[11] := Block[{i},
              Table[a, {i, 2}]
          ]
Out[11] = {1, 2}
```

Version 2.0: Each occurrence of the variable i inside the Module is replaced by a variable with a name of the form i$1 The variable a is replaced by i. This i refers to the value 3. So the variable a gets replaced by 3. *Mathematica* evaluates the expression Table[3, {i, 2}], which returns the list {3, 3}.

```
In[12] := a = i;
In[13] := i = 3;
In[14] := Module[{i},
              Table[a, {i, 2}]
          ]
Out[14] = {3, 3}
```

A.11 Problem Set on Pattern Matching

11.1 Write a function, geometricMean, that returns the geometric mean of a list of numbers.

```
In[1] := Clear[geometricMean]
In[2] := geometricMean[{x__}] := Times[x]^(1/Length[{x}])

In[3] := geometricMean[{a, b, c, e, d}]

          1/5   1/5   1/5   1/5   1/5
Out[3] = a     b     c     d     e
```

11.3 (a) Implement the function fold as described here.

```
In[4] := Clear[fold]
In[5] := fold::usage = "fold[f, base, list] gives
         f[...[f[f[base, x1], x2], ..., xn]
         where list is {x1, x2, ... xn}"
In[6] := fold[f_, base_, {}] := base
In[7] := fold[f_, base_, {x1_, xrest___}] :=
         fold[f, f[base, x1], {xrest}]
```

The function Fold is included in version 2.0 of *Mathematica*.

(b) Describe what fold[Plus, 0, list] returns.

```
In[8] := fold[Plus, 0, {a, b, c}]
Out[8] = {a + b + c}
```

It returns the sum of the elements in the list.

(c) Describe what fold[Max, -Infinity, list] returns.

```
In[9] := fold[Max, -Infinity, {a, b, c}]
Out[9] = Max[a, b, c]
```

It returns the maximum value in the list.

11.5 You can use the pattern x___List to specify a function that takes a variable number of lists for its argument. How can you find the length of each list?

```
In[10] := Clear[processLists]
In[11] := processLists[x___List] := Map[Length, {x}];

In[12] := processLists[{1, 3, 7}, {3, 3}, {4, 6, 7}]
Out[12] = {3, 2, 3}
```

11.7 Rework problem 9 on page 135 by defining a function with the attribute Listable.

In a town there are three stores selling 5 popular toys. Store A sells the toys for $15, $17, $18, $32, and $29 and store B sells the same 5 toys for $14, $18, $22, $29, and $26. The policy of store C is to match the most competitive price in town. Write a *Mathematica* expression to determine store C's selling prices for the 5 toys.

```
In[13] := ClearAll[calculateCompetitivePrice]
In[14] := SetAttributes[calculateCompetitivePrice, Listable]
In[15] := calculateCompetitivePrice[p___] := Min[p]

In[16] := calculateCompetitivePrice[
            {15, 17, 18, 32, 29}, {14, 18, 22, 29, 26}
          ]
Out[16] = {14, 17, 18, 29, 26}
```

A.12 Problem Set on Anonymous (Pure) Functions

12.1 Write named functions for doing the operations specified by the following anonymous functions.

(a) `(#^3)&`

```
f[x_] := x^3
```

(c) `{#, #^2}&`

```
f[x_] := {x, x^2}
```

(e) `(# /. x->y)&`

```
f[z_] := (z /. x -> y)
```

12.3 Use `Select` and an anonymous function to obtain from a list of pairs those pairs in which the first item is greater than the second.

```
In[1] := Select[{{1, 3}, {13, 4}}, (#[[1]] > #[[2]])&]
Out[1] = {{13, 4}}
```

12.5 Write a function that determines the frequency of every element in a list. For example, `frequency[{c,a,b,b}]` should return `{{a,1},{b,2},{c,1}}`.

This function counts the number of occurrences of each distinct element in the list.

```
In[2] := frequency[x_List] :=
           Module[{
                    elements = Union[x]
                   },
                   Map[
                     {#, Count[x, #]}&,
                     elements
                   ]
                 ]
In[3] := frequency::usage="frequency[list] returns a list of \
           the distinct elements in list together with the  \
           frequencies with which they occur."
```

Now I'll run frequency on some test data.

```
In[4] := testList = Table[Random[Integer, {1, 10}], {15}]
Out[4] = {5, 1, 3, 8, 1, 3, 10, 3, 4, 1, 4, 2, 4, 5, 1}

In[5] := frequency[testList]
Out[5] = {{1, 4}, {2, 1}, {3, 3}, {4, 3}, {5, 2}, {8, 1}, {10, 1}}
```

By sorting `testList`, you can easily verify the results above.

```
In[6] := Sort[testList]
Out[6] = {1, 1, 1, 1, 2, 3, 3, 3, 4, 4, 4, 5, 5, 8, 10}
```

12.7 *The Significant Other Problem.* This problem involves analyzing a particular strategy for finding a significant other. Suppose that there are n people you wish to consider. Each person has a distinct value, which is unknown to you until you meet the individual. You have only one opportunity to meet with each prospect. After each meeting, you must decide whether you want that individual as your significant other; otherwise you will never see him or her again. You are to analyze the following strategy: See n/e people, where e is the base of natural logarithms. Then select the first person who is more desirable than any of the people you have already seen.

Run a simulation 50 times using the prescribed strategy with $n = 30$.

(a) Calculate the percentage of times the simulation ends up with your first choice.

First, I define the function `randomize`, which takes a list of people and returns the list in a random order. There are several ways to define this function.

```
In[7] := randomize1[{}] := {}
In[8] := randomize1[people_List] :=
        Block[{
                n = Random[Integer, {1, Length[people]}]
            },
            Prepend[
                randomize1[
                    Drop[people, {n}]
                ],
                people[[n]]
            ]
        ]
```

Alternatively, `randomize` can be defined using `RotateLeft`.

```
In[9] := randomize2[{}] := {}
In[10] := randomize2[people_List] :=
       Block[{
               n = Random[Integer, {0, Length[people] - 1}],
               shifted
           },
           shifted = RotateLeft[people, n];
           Prepend[randomize2[Drop[shifted, 1]],
               shifted[[1]]
           ]
       ]
```

A third approach is to use Sort with an ordering function. The following definition creates pairs, $\{r, p\}$, where r is a random number and p is the value assigned to a person. These pairs are then sorted on r.

```
In[11] := randomize[people_List] :=
       Map[
           Last,
           Sort[
               Map[{Random[ ], #}&, people],
               (#1[[1]] > #2[[1]])&
           ]
       ]
In[12] := randomize::usage="randomize[list] returns a random \
       permutation of the elements in list."
```

I give the people rank-order names from 1 (the most preferred) to n (the least preferred). The function selectSO, takes n people, puts them in a random order. It looks at the first n/e people (rounded to the nearest integer value) and sets the variable mmin to the most desirable person in that set. Then selected is set to the people who are more desirable than the most desirable person in the first n/e people. If selected contains more than 0 people, selectSO returns the first more desirable person, otherwise it returns the empty set.

```
In[13] := selectSO[n_Integer] :=
            Module[{
                people = randomize[Range[n]],
                m = Round[N[n/E]],
                mmin,
                selected
            },
            mmin = Min[Take[people, m]];
            selected = Select[people, (# < mmin)&];
            If[ Length[selected] > 0,
                First[selected],
                { }
            ]
        ]
In[14] := results = Table[selectSO[30], {50}];
```

The percentage of times this simulation pairs you with your first choice
is computed by counting the number of times that you end with number 1.

```
In[15] := N[Count[results, 1]/50]
Out[15] = 0.38
```

Notice that this is close to $1/e$.

```
In[16] := N[1/E]
Out[16] = 0.367879
```

(b) The percentage of times this simulation ends without identifying a significant other can be computed as follows:

```
In[17] := N[Count[results, { }]/50]
Out[17] = 0.26
```

(c) The percentage of times the simulation ends up with a person who
is rated within the top 10% is the number of times you end up with
someone whose value is 3 or less.

```
In[18] := N[Length[Select[results, (# <= 3)&]]/50]
Out[18] = 0.72
```

A.13 Problem Set on Debugging

Debug the following examples.

13.1 3 Plus 4

The function Plus computes the sum of its arguments. Plus was not used as a function.

In[1] := 3 + 4
Out[1] = 7

In[2] := Plus[3, 4]
Out[2] = 7

13.3 Why doesn't the following statement return a list of primes?

Select[{2, 4, 7, 11, 15}, PrimeQ[x_]]

The second argument of Select is the criterion to be applied to each member of the list. Do not list the argument of the criterion unless you are using an anonymous function.

In[3] := Select[{2, 4, 7, 11, 15}, PrimeQ]
Out[3] = {2, 7, 11}

13.5 The function pickLotto is intended to pick 5 numbers in the range from 0 to 99. Why does it print only a single number?

The While statement should contain a comma, not a semicolon.

```
In[4] := pickLotto :=
        Block[{
            n = 1
            },
            While[n <= 5,
                Print[
                    Random[Integer, {0, 99}]
                ];
                ++n
            ]
        ]
```

```
In[5] := pickLotto
        89 6 22 55 50
```

Below is a much better way to implement pickLotto.

```
In[6] := pickLotto :=
        Do[
            Print[
                Random[Integer, {0, 99}]
            ],
            {5}
        ]
```

13.7 Find a more succinct way to write the function f shown below.

```
In[7] := Clear[f];
In[8] := f[g_, x_List] :=
        Block[{
            l = { },
            n = 1
        },
        Do[
            l = Join[l, {g[x[[i]]]}],
            {i, Length[x]}
        ];
        l
    ]
```

```
In[9] := f[g, {a, b, c}]
Out[9] = {g[a], g[b], g[c]}
```

The function f is equivalent to mapping the function g onto x.

```
In[10] := Clear[fNew];
In[11] := fNew[g_, x_List] := Map[g, x]
```

```
In[12] := fNew[g, {a, b, c}]
Out[12] = {g[a], g[b], g[c]}
```

A.14 Problem Set on Input/Output

14.1 **Version 1.2:** The package Examples/Mortgages.m uses the Input function. Determine the monthly payments for a house with a 20-year mortgage or for the car of your choice with a 3-year loan.

```
In[1] := Needs["Examples'Mortgages'"]
        Term of the loan in year: 3
        Number of payments per year: 12
        Annual interest rate (percent): 7
        Principal amount: 15000

        Each payment is $463.156
        The total amount paid over the life of
            the loan is $16673.6
        After 1 year the principal remaining is 10344.6
        After 2 years the principal remaining is 5352.75
        After 3 years the principal remaining is 0
```

14.3 Translate the outputs of the following expressions into C and FORTRAN.

(a) D[x Exp[x], x]

(b) a^b

(c) Sin[Pi/3]

```
In[2] := Map[{CForm[#], FortranForm[#]}&,
          {D[x Exp[x], x], a^b, Sin[Pi/3]}]
Out[2] = {{Power(E,x) + Power(E,x)*x, E**x + E**x*x},
            {Power(a,b), a**b}, {Sqrt(3)/2, Sqrt(3)/2}}
```

14.5 Write a format statement that, given b[c, d], will display c as a subscript and d as the exponent, i.e., b_c^d.

```
In[3] := Format[b[c_, d_] ] :=
            SequenceForm[Subscripted[b[c]], Superscript[d] ]
In[4] := b[2, 3]

             3
Out[4] = b
          2
```

A.15 Problem Set on Writing Packages

15.1 Load the package Colors.m found in the Graphics directory. List all the colors that are specified in the package.

In[1] := Needs["Graphics'Colors'"]

In[2] := ?Graphics'Colors'*

Aquamarine	Firebrick	Maroon	SeaGreen
Black	ForestGreen	MidnightBlue	Sienna
Blue	Gold	Navy	SkyBlue
BlueViolet	Goldenrod	NavyBlue	SlateBlue
Brown	Gray	Orange	SpringGreen
CMYColor	Green	OrangeRed	SteelBlue
CadetBlue	GreenYellow	Orchid	Thistle
Coral	HLSColor	PaleGreen	Turquoise
CornflowerBlue	HSBColor	Peach	Violet
Cyan	IndianRed	Pink	VioletRed
DarkGreen	Khaki	Plum	Wheat
DarkOliveGreen	LightBlue	PrussianBlue	White
DarkOrchid	LightGray	Purple	YIQColor
DarkSlateBlue	LightSteelBlue	Red	Yellow
DarkSlateGray	LimeGreen	Salmon	YellowBrown
DarkTurquoise	Magenta	SandyBrown	YellowGreen
DimGray			

CMYColor, HLSColor, HSBColor, and YIQColor are not colors. They are functions for specifying colors.

B

Bibliography

[**Abelson**] Abelson, Harold and Gerald Jay Sussman. *Structure and Interpretation of Computer Programs*, MIT Press and McGraw-Hill, 1987. (ISBN 07-000422-6)

[**Churchhouse**] Churchhouse, R.F., B. Cornu, A.G. Howson, J.-P. Kahane, J.H. van Lint, F. Pluvinage, A. Ralston, M. Yamaguti, *The Influence of Computers and Informatics on Mathematics and its Teaching*, Cambridge University Press, 1986. (ISBN 0-521-31189-6)

[**Gray**] Gray, Theodore, and Jerry Glynn. *Exploring Mathematics with Mathematica.* © 1991 by Addison-Wesley Publishing Company, Inc., The Advanced Book Program. Reprinted material from page 17 with permission of the publisher. (ISBN 0-201-52818-5 paperback, ISBN 0-201-52809-6 hardback)

[**MmaQuickRef**] Blachman, Nancy. *The Mathematica Quick Reference Guide*, Variable Symbols, Inc.[1], 1990. This reference guide provides a complete summary of *Mathematica*'s commands.

[**MmaHelpStack**] Campbell, Robert. *The Mathematica Help Stack*, Variable Symbols, Inc., 1990. This stack makes it easy to find information about functions and commands by categorizing and cross-referencing all of *Mathematica*'s commands and by providing visual icons.

[**Koenig**] Koenig, Andrew. *C Traps and Pit Falls*, © 1989 by Addison–Wesley Publishing Company, Inc. Reprinted excerpts from pages 102-103 with permission of the publisher. (ISBN 0-201-17928-8)

[**Wolfram**] Wolfram, Stephen. *Mathematica: A System for Doing Mathematics by Computer*. Reading, MA: Addison-Wesley, 992 pp., 1991 (2nd edition). (ISBN 0-201-51507-5 paperback, ISBN 0-201-51502-4 hardback) This book is the reference manual for *Mathematica*.

[1]Variable Symbols, Inc., 2161 Shattuck Ave., Suite 202, Berkeley, CA 94704-1313, 415-843-8701 (changing to 510-843-8701), Fax 415-843-8702 (changing to 510-843-8702)

Reference Material

Because of the popularity of *Mathematica*, the amount of reference material on the program is growing. This section lists books, video tapes, and other references of interest to *Mathematica* users.

Crandall, Richard E. *Scientific Applications of Mathematica*. Reading, MA: Addison-Wesley. (ISBN-0-201-51001-4)

W. Ellis and Ed Lodi. *A Tutorial Introduction to Mathematica*, Brooks/Cole, 92 pp., 1990. (ISBN 0-534-15588-X)

Maeder, Roman. *Programming in Mathematica*, Reading, MA: Addison-Wesley, 288 pp., 1990. (ISBN 0-201-51002-2) This book is intended for experienced *Mathematica* users.

Pinsky, Mark A. (Appendix by Alfred Gray) *Partial Differential Equations with Boundary Value Problems and Applications*, Second Edition, McGraw–Hill.

Riddle, Alfred, *Nodal: The Symbolic & Numerical Circuit Analysis Package*, Macallan Consulting, 1583 Pinewood Way, Milpitas, CA 95035.

Skiena, Stephen. *Implementing Discrete Mathematics: Combinatorics and Graph Theory with Mathematica*. Reading, MA: Addison-Wesley, 1990. (ISBN 0-201-50943-1)

Smith, Cameron. *The Mathematica Graphics Guidebook*. Reading, MA: Addison-Wesley, 1991.

Uhl, Jerry, J., H. Porta, and Don P. Brown. *Calculus & Mathematica*, Reading, MA: Addison-Wesley. This book is being used in teaching first-year calculus.

Vardi, Ilan. *Computational Recreations in Mathematica*, Reading, MA: Addison-Wesley, 208 pp., 1991. (ISBN 0-201-52989-0)

Wagon, Stan. *Doing Mathematics with Mathematica*. W. H. Freeman, 352 pp., 1991. (ISBN 0-7167-2202-X paperback, 0-7167-2229-1 hardback)

Journals and Newsletters

The Mathematica Journal, Addison-Wesley, P. O. Box 67, Belmont, CA 94002. To order, call 415-594-4423.

Mathematica in Education, Paul Wellin, editor, Department of Mathematics, Sonoma State University, 1801 E. Cotati Avenue, Rohnert Park, CA 94928, email wellin@sonoma.edu, telephone 707-664-2368, fax 707-664-2505. The first issue of this quarterly newsletter is planned for fall of 1991. Subscriptions cost $15 per year.

NeXT on Campus, David Spitzler, managing editor, NeXT Computer, Inc., 900 Chesapeake Drive, Redwood City, CA 94063, telephone 800-848-NeXT. This newsletter, intended for the higher-education community, often contains articles on *Mathematica*.

Video Tapes

Four video tapes give introductions to *Mathematica*.

Mathematica: A Practical Approach, a 10-hour video series taught by Nancy Blachman and Cameron Smith, sponsored by the National Technological University (NTU) and Stanford University's Instructional Television Network (SITN). This 1991 course will be available by SITN, 401 Durand, Stanford University, Stanford, CA 94305, telephone 415-725-3001.

Working with Mathematica, an eight-part video series taught by Nancy Blachman with a guest lectures from Henry Cejtin and David Jacobson, produced in 1990 by Stanford University's Instructional Television Network, 401 Durand, Stanford University, Stanford, CA 94305, telephone 415-725-3001.

Mathematica for Engineers, a video tape by F. S. Hill, Jr., and Lawrence Seiford, produced in 1990 by the Video Instructional Program at the University of Massachusetts at Amherst, 113 Marcus Hall, University of Massachusetts, Amherst, MA 01003, telephone 413-545-0063.

Introducing Mathematica, a video tape produced in 1989 by Science Television, P.O. Box 2498, Times Square Station, New York, NY 10108.

Other References

This section lists other references on computer algebra.

Hearn, Anthony C., workshop chairman , *Future Directions for Research in Symbolic Computation*, Society for Industrial and Applied Mathematics, Philadelphia, 1990, 86 pp.

Small, Donald B. and John M. Hosack. *Explorations in Calculus with a Computer Algebra System*, McGraw–Hill, Inc., 1991, 226 pp.

Davenport, J. H., Y. Siret and E. Tournier. *Computer Algebra — Systems and Algorithms for Algebraic Computation*, Academic Press, London, 1988.

Pavelle, Richard. *Applications of Computer Algebra*, Kluwer Academic Publishers, Boston, 1985.

C

Show

End

Add

N

Polygon

Limit

Commands

Commands that are in version 1.2 but are not in version 2.0 appear in italics.
Commands that have been added to version 2.0 appear in bold face.
File names and external commands appear in Courier.
All other commands appear in Palatino.

C.1 Graphics

C.1.1 Two-Dimensional Graphics

AbsoluteDashing, **AbsolutePointSize**, **AbsoluteThickness**, Circle, Dashing, Disk, Display, FontForm, FrameLabel, FrameStyle, FrameTicks, **FullAxes**, **FullGraphics**, Graphics, **GraphicsArray**, Line, ListPlot, ParametricPlot, Plot, Point, PointSize, Polygon, PostScript, **Raster**, **RasterArray**, Rectangle, Show, Text, Thickness

C.1.2 Three-Dimensional Graphics

AbsoluteDashing, **AbsolutePointSize**, **AbsoluteThickness**, ContourGraphics, ContourPlot, **Cuboid**, Dashing, DensityGraphics, DensityPlot, Display, EdgeForm, FaceForm, **FaceGrids**, FontForm, **FullGraphics**, Graphics3D, **GraphicsArray**, Line, ListContourPlot, ListDensityPlot, ListPlot3D, **ParametricPlot3D**, Plot3D, Point, **PointForm**, PointSize, Polygon, PostScript, Show, **SurfaceColor**, SurfaceGraphics, Text, Thickness, **ViewCenter**, **ViewVertical**

C.1.3 Graphics Primitives

AbsoluteDashing, **AbsolutePointSize**, **AbsoluteThickness**, **CMYKColor**, CellArray, Circle, **Cuboid**, Dashing, Disk, EdgeForm, FaceForm, FontForm, **GraphicsArray**, GrayLevel, **Hue**, Line, Point, **PointForm**, PointSize, Polygon, PostScript, RGBColor, **Raster**, **RasterArray**, Rectangle, Scaled, Text, Thickness, **ToColor**

C.1.4 Graphics Options

All, AmbientLight, AspectRatio, Axes, AxesEdge, AxesLabel, **AxesOrigin**, AxesStyle, Background, BoxRatios, BoxStyle, Boxed, ClipFill, **ColorFunction**, **ColorOutput**, *ContourLevels* **ContourLines**, **ContourShading**, **ContourSmoothing**, *ContourSpacing*, **ContourStyle**, Contours, DefaultColor, **DefaultFont**, DisplayFunction, Epilog, **FaceGrids**, Frame, FrameLabel, FrameStyle, FrameTicks, *Framed*, **FullGraphics**, **FullOptions**, **GraphicsSpacing**, **GridLines**, HiddenSurface, LightSources, Lighting, MaxBend, Mesh, MeshRange, MeshStyle, Plot3Matrix, *PlotColor*, PlotDivision, PlotJoined, PlotLabel, PlotPoints, PlotRange, **PlotRegion**, PlotStyle, **PolygonIntersections**, Prolog, RenderAll, **RotateLabel**, Shading, **SphericalRegion**, **SurfaceColor**, Ticks, **ViewCenter**, ViewPoint, **ViewVertical**

C.1.5 Output Functions

$Display, $DisplayFunction

C.1.6 Sound

ListPlay, **Play**, **PlayRange**, **SampleDepth**, **SampleRate**, **SampledSoundFunction**, **SampledSoundList**, **Sound**

C.1.7 Utilities

Display, **Hardcopy**, `psfix`

C.2 Mathematics

C.2.1 Algebraic Manipulation

Expression Manipulation

Apart, **ApartList**, Cancel, Collect, **ComplexExpand**, Decompose, Denominator, Distribute, Expand, ExpandAll, ExpandDenominator, ExpandDenominator, ExpandNumerator, Factor, FactorList, FactorSquareFree, FactorSquareFreeList, FactorTerms, FactorTermsList, **GaussianIntegers**, Numerator, **OldExpand**, **PowerExpand**, Simplify, **TargetFunctions**, Together, *TrigExpand*

Extracting Parts of Expressions

Coefficient, CoefficientList, Exponent, Variables

Manipulating Polynomials

PolynomialDivision, PolynomialGCD, **PolynomialLCM**, **PolynomialMod**, PolynomialQuotient, *PolynomialQuotientRemainder*, PolynomialRemainder, Resultant, Resultant2, **SparseCoefficientList**

C.2.2 Basic
Complex Numbers
Abs, Arg, Complex, ComplexInfinity, Conjugate, I, Im, Re

Elementary Functions
Abs, Ceiling, Divide, Floor, Max, Min, Minus, NonCommutativeMultiply, Plus, Power, **RealInterval**, Round, Sqrt, Subtract, Times

Exp, Log, and Hyperbolic Functions
ArcCosh, ArcCoth, ArcCsch, ArcSech, ArcSinh, ArcTanh, Cosh, Coth, Csch, Exp, Log, Sech, Sinh, Tanh

Trigonometry
ArcCos, ArcCot, ArcCsc, ArcSec, ArcSin, ArcTan, Cos, Cot, Csc, Sec, Sin, Tan

C.2.3 Calculus
Integrate, Product, Residue, Series, Sum

Differential Equations
C, DSolve, **DSolveConstants**

Differentiation
Constant, Constants, D, Derivative, Dt, NonConstants

Series and Limits
Direction, Limit, SequenceLimit

C.2.4 Constants
ComplexInfinity, Degree, DirectedInfinity, GoldenRatio, I, Indeterminate, Infinity

Transcendental
Catalan, E, EulerGamma, Pi

C.2.5 Linear Algebra
Array, **CharacteristicPolynomial**, Det, DiagonalMatrix, Dimensions, Dot, Eigensystem, Eigenvalues, Eigenvectors, IdentityMatrix, Inner, Inverse, **JordanForm**, LinearSolve, MatrixExp, MatrixPower, MatrixQ, Minors, NullSpace, Outer, **Pivoting**, PseudoInverse, **QRDecomposition**, Range, RowReduce, **SchurDecomposition**, SingularValues, Table, TensorRank, Tolerance, Transpose, VectorQ, ZeroTest

C.2.6 Number Theory

DivisorSigma, Divisors, EulerPhi, ExtendedGCD, FactorComplete, FactorInteger, Factorial, Factorial2, GCD, **GaussianIntegers**, JacobiSymbol, LCM, LatticeReduce, Mod, MoebiusMu, Multinomial, PartitionsP, PartitionsQ, PowerMod, Prime, **PrimePi**, PrimeQ, *ProbablePrimeQ*, Quotient, StirlingS1, StirlingS2

C.2.7 Numerical
Numerical Functions
ArithmeticGeometricMean, *ExtraFactors*, *ExtraTerms*, *Factors*, FindMinimum, FindRoot, Fit, Fourier, Gradient, **InterpolatingFunction**, **InterpolatingFunction**, InterpolatingPolynomial, **Interpolation**, InverseFourier, Jacobian, N, NBernoulliB, NBernoulliB, **NDSolve**, NIntegrate, NProduct, **NSolve**, NSum, *Terms*

Numerical Options

AccuracyGoal, DampingFactor, DoubleExponential, DoublyInfinite, **GaussKronrod**, **GaussPoints**, *GaussianQuadrature*, **InterpolationOrder**, LerchPhi, MaxIterations, MaxRecursion, **MaxSteps**, Method, MinRecursion, **MultiDimensional**, **NProductExtraFactors**, **NProductFactors**, **NSumExtraTerms**, **NSumTerms**, NValues, *Points*, **PrecisionGoal**, SingularityDepth, **StartingStepSize**, **Trapezoidal**, **VerifyConvergence**, WorkingPrecision, WynnDegree

Related Functions
Accuracy, Chop, **MachineNumberQ**, Precision, Rationalize, SetAccuracy, SetPrecision

C.2.8 Solving Equations
Eliminate, FindRoot, GroebnerBasis, MainSolve, NRoots, Reduce, Solve, SolveAlways, **VerifySolutions**

Minimization Functions

ConstrainedMax, ConstrainedMin, LinearProgramming

Options
Cubics, Generic, InverseFunctions, MakeRules, Mode, Modular, Modulus, Rational, Real, Sort

Other Functions
AlgebraicRules, Auxiliary, **EquatedTo**, FixedPoint, **FixedPointList**, InverseFunction, LinearSolve, Multiplicity, Quartics, Roots, **SameTest**, ToRules

C.2.9 Special Functions
AiryAi, **AiryAiPrime**, **AiryBi**, **AiryBiPrime**, BernoulliB, BesselI, BesselJ, BesselK, BesselY, Beta, BetaRegularized, CosIntegral, **CoshIntegral**, Erf, **Erfc**, **Erfi**, ExpIntegralE, ExpIntegralEi, **FresnelC**, **FresnelS**, Gamma, GammaRegularized, Hypergeometric0F1, Hypergeometric0F1Regularized, Hypergeometric1F1, Hypergeometric1F1Regularized, Hypergeometric2F1, Hypergeometric2F1Regularized, **HypergeometricPFQ**, **HypergeometricPFQRegularized**, HypergeometricU, **IncludeSingularTerm**, LegendreQ, LegendreType, **LogGamma**, LogIntegral, NBernoulliB, Pochhammer, PolyGamma, PolyLog, **RiemannSiegelTheta**, **RiemannSiegelZ**, **SinhIntegral**, SinIntegral, **StieltjesGamma**, Zeta

Polynomials
BernoulliB, ChebyshevT, ChebyshevU, **ClebschGordan**, Cyclotomic, EulerE, GegenbauerC, HermiteH, JacobiP, LaguerreL, LegendreP, NBernoulliB, **SixJSymbol**, **SixJSymbol**, SphericalHarmonicY, **ThreeJSymbol**

C.2.10 Statistics
Erf, **Erfc**, **Erfi**

C.3 Programming
C.3.1 Attributes
Attributes, ClearAttributes, Constant, Flat, HoldAll, HoldFirst, HoldRest, Listable, **Lock**, Locked, OneIdentity, **OptionQ**, Orderless, Protect, Protected, ReadProtected, SetAttributes, **Stub**, **Temporary**, Unprotect

C.3.2 Input/Output
RawPrint, RecordSeparators, SetStreamPosition, Skip, StreamPosition, Streams, StringToStream, StringTurnedIntoStream, WordSeparators

File Manipulation
!!file, !cmd, Close, ContextToFilename, Delimiters, Encode, Environment, Get, MachineID, MachineName, *Medium*, OpenAppend, OpenRead, OpenTemporary, OpenWrite, Put, PutAppend, RawMedium, ResetMedium, Run, RunThrough, Splice

Formatting Expressions
AccountingForm, BaseForm, CForm, DigitBlock, *Digits*, EngineeringForm, **ExponentFunction**, *ExponentStep*, FormatValues, FortranForm, FullForm, InputForm, **IntegerDigits**, **MantissaExponent**, NumberForm, **NumberFormat**, **NumberPadding**, NumberPoint, NumberSeparator, **NumberSigns**, OutputForm, **PaddedForm**, **RealDigits**, ScientificForm, **SignPadding**, TeXForm, TreeForm

Functions for Formatting

Above, Below, Bottom, Center, ColonForm, ColumnForm, Continuation, Format, *Hide*, HoldForm, HorizontalForm, Indent, Infix, Left, MatrixForm, NonAssociative, None, Postfix, PrecedenceForm, Prefix, **PrintExpr**, PrintForm, Right, SequenceForm, **Shallow**, Short, SpaceForm, StringBreak, StringForm, Subscript, Subscripted, Superscript, **TableAlignments**, **TableDepth**, **TableDirections**, TableForm, **TableHeadings**, **TableSpacing**, TextForm, ValueForm, VerticalForm

Input Commands

$Echo, $IgnoreEOF, Byte, Character, EndOfFile, Expression, Input, **InputStream**, InputString, **NullRecords**, **NullWords**, Number, **OutputStream**, PromptForm, Read, ReadList, Real, **Record**, **RecordLists**, String, **TokenWords**, **Word**

MathLink

CallPacket, CallProcess, EndProcess, **EvaluatePacket**, **ExternalCall**, **Install**, **LinkPatterns**, StartProcess, **ThisLink**, **Uninstall**

Messages

General, Message, **MessageList**, MessageName, Messages, Off, On

Options

FormatType, *GraphicsFont*, *GraphicsLeading*, LineBreak, PageHeight, PageWidth, Plain, PostScript, Skeleton, StringSkeleton, *TextFont*, *TextLeading*, TextRendering, TotalHeight, TotalWidth

Output

Definition, FullDefinition

Output Commands

$Messages, Headers, Null, Print, Save, Write, WriteString

C.3.3 Logic

Logical Operations

And, False, Implies, LogicalExpand, Not, Or, True, Xor

Predicates

AtomQ, **DigitQ**, EvenQ, FreeQ, Greater, GreaterEqual, IntegerQ, Less, LessEqual, **LetterQ**, **ListQ**, **LowerCaseQ**, **MachineNumberQ**, **MatchLocalNameQ**, MatrixQ, NameQ, Negative, NonNegative, NumberQ, OddQ, **OptionQ**, OrderedQ, PolynomialQ, Positive, PrimeQ, *ProbablePrimeQ*, Sign, **StringQ**, **SyntaxQ**, TrueQ, ValueQ, VectorQ

Relations
Equal, Inequality, MatchQ, MemberQ, SameQ, StringMatchQ, Unequal,
UnsameQ

C.3.4 Patterns
Alternatives, Blank, BlankNullSequence, BlankSequence, Condition, Default,
DefaultValues, *Fail*, NValues, Optional, OwnValues, Pattern, PatternTest,
Repeated, RepeatedNull, **SubValues**,

C.3.5 Procedural
Compile, Compiled, CompiledFunction,

Flow Control
Block, Break, Catch, Check, CompoundExpression, Continue, Do, For, Goto, If,
Label, **Module**, **Pause**, Return, Scan, Switch, Throw, Which, While, **With**

Variables
AddTo, Decrement, DivideBy, DownValues, FormatValues, Increment, NValues,
OwnValues, PreDecrement, PreIncrement, *SubValue*, **SubValues**, SubtractFrom,
TimesBy, ValueList

C.3.6 Rules
Dispatch, **Evaluate**, **HeldPart**, Hold, Literal, Release, **ReleaseHold**, Replace,
ReplaceAll, **ReplaceHeldPart**, **ReplacePart**, ReplaceRepeated, Rule, **RuleCondition**,
RuleDelayed, RuleTable, Set, SetDelayed, TagSet, TagSetDelayed, TagUnset,
Unevaluated, Unset, UpSet, UpSetDelayed, **UpValues**, Update

C.3.7 Sets
Complement, Intersection, MemberQ, Union

C.3.8 String Manipulation
Characters, *FromASCII*, **FromCharacterCode**, *ToASCII*, **ToCharacterCode**,
ToExpression

C.3.9 Strings
AnchoredSearch, **DigitQ**, Find, **FindList**, **IgnoreCase**, **LetterQ**, **LowerCaseQ**,
MetaCharacters, **RecordSeparators**, Space, **SpellingCorrection**, **StringByteCount**,
StringConversion, **StringDifference**, **StringDrop**, **StringInsert**, StringJoin,
StringLength, **StringPosition**, **StringQ**, **StringReplace**, **StringReverse**, **StringTake**,
StringToStream, **StringTurnedIntoStream**, Syntax, SyntaxLength, SyntaxQ, Tab,
ToLowerCase, ToString, **ToUpperCase**, WordSearch, **WordSeparators**

C.3.10 Structure

Extracting Parts Of Expressions

Cases, Count, **Delete**, **DeleteCases**, Depth, Drop, First, Head, **HeldPart**, Last, Length, Level, Part, Position, Rest, Select, Take

Generating Lists

Accumulate, Append, AppendTo, Array, Insert, Join, Partition, Permutations, Prepend, PrependTo, Range, Table

Others

Flatten, **FlattenAt**, Inner, List, Outer, Reverse, RotateLeft, RotateRight, Sequence Sort, Transpose

Pure Functions

Apply, *Compose*, **ComposeList**, **Composition**, FixedPoint, **FixedPointList**, **Fold**, **FoldList**, Function, HeadCompose, **Heads**, Identity, Map, MapAll, MapAt, **MapIndexed**, **MapThread**, Nest, NestList, Operate, **SameTest**, Slot, SlotSequence, Thread, Through

C.3.11 Types

Complex, Integer, List, Rational, Raw, Real, String, Symbol

C.4 System

Environment, Overflow, RepeatedString, RuleForm, Second, **TimeZone**, **ToDate**, TooBig, Top, Underflow

C.4.1 Context Manipulation

Begin, BeginPackage, **DeclarePackage**, End, EndAdd, EndPackage, Needs, **Stub**

C.4.2 Contexts

Context, ContextToFilename, **Contexts**, **GetContext**

C.4.3 Resource Management

Clear, ClearAll, Remove, Removed

C.4.4 System Variables

$Aborted, $BatchInput, $BatchOutput, $CommandLine, $ConditionHold, $Context, $ContextPath, $CreationDate, $Credits, $DefaultFont, $Display, $DisplayFunction, $DumpDates, $DumpSupported, $Echo, $Epilog, $Failed, *$GenericForm*, $IgnoreEOF, $Input, $Inspector, *$Interrupted*, $IterationLimit, $Language, $Letters, $Line, $LinkSupported, $Linked, $MachineEpsilon, $MachineID, $MachineName, $MachinePrecision, $MachineType, $MaxMachineNumber, $MaxNumber, $MessageList, $MessagePrePrint, $Messages

C.4.5 Utilities

BlankForm, **Date**, **FromDate**, Information, MatchBox, Using, `end.m`, `init.m`, `psfix`

Debugging

Debug, Definition, FullDefinition, **MatchLocalNameQ**, **MatchLocalNames**, Off, On, **Stack**, **StackBegin**, **StackComplete**, **StackInhibit**, **Trace**, **TraceAbove**, **TraceAction**, **TraceBackward**, **TraceDepth**, **TraceDialog**, **TraceForward**, **TraceLevel**, **TraceOff**, **TraceOn**, **TraceOriginal**, **TracePrint**, **TraceScan**

File Management

CopyDirectory, **CopyFile**, **CreateDirectory**, **DeleteDirectory**, **DeleteFile**, **Directory**, **DirectoryStack**, **File**, **FileByteCount**, **FileDate**, **FileInformation**, **FileNames**, **FileType**, **HomeDirectory**, **ParentDirectory**, **RenameDirectory**, **RenameFile**, **ResetDirectory**, **SetDirectory**, **SetFileDate**

Names

Alias, NameQ, Names, *UnAlias*, Unique

Other Utilities

Abort, **AbortProtect**, **CheckAbort**, **Dialog**, **DialogIndent**, **DialogProlog**, **DialogSymbols**, Dispatch, Dump, Edit, EditDef, EditIn, Exit, Hash, HashTable, In, **InString**, Interrupt, Out, Quit, *Recall*

Resource Management

AbsoluteTime, ByteCount, LeafCount, MaxMemoryUsed, MemoryConstrained, MemoryInUse, **SessionTime**, Share, **Temporary**, *TimeConstrained*, **TimeUsed**, Timing

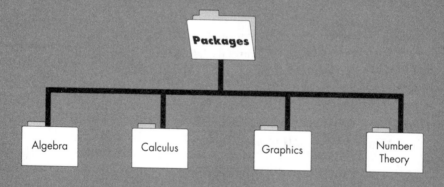

Directories of the Mathematica Packages

Packages Distributed with Version 1.2

Full Name		MS-DOS	
Directory	Package	Directory	Package
Algebra	CountRoots.m	algebra	countroot.m
	GosperSum.m		gospersu.m
	ReIm.m		reim.m
	Trigonometry.m		trigonom.m
Calculus	DefiniteIntegrate.m	calculus	*
	InverseLaplace.m		inversel.m
	Laplace.m		laplace.m
	VectorAnalysis.m		vectoran.m
DataAnalysis	ConfidenceIntervals.m	dataanal	confiden.m
	ContinuousDistributions.m		continuo.m
	DataManipulations.m		datamani.m
	DescriptiveFunctions.m		descripf.m
	DescriptiveStatistics.m		descrips.m
	DiscreteDistributions.m		discrete.m
DiscreteMath	ClebschGordan.m	discrete	clebschg.m
	CombinatorialFunctions.m		combinaf.m
	CombinatorialSimplification.m		combinas.m
	Permutations.m		permutat.m
	Tree.m		Tree.m

* The package DefiniteIntegrate.m was not distributed with MS-DOS *Mathematica*, version 1.2.

Packages Distributed with Version 1.2 – Continued

Full Name		MS-DOS	
Directory	Package	Directory	Package
Examples	CellularAutomata.m	examples	cellular.m
	CollatzProblem.m		collatzp.m
	CrystalStructure.m		crystals.m
	EllipticCurves.m		elliptic.m
	Factor.m		factor.m
	FunctionalProgramming.m		function.m
	ModularArithmetic.m		modulara.m
	Mortgages.m		mortgage.m
	RingTheory.m		ringtheo.m
	RungeKutta.m		rungekut.m
Geometry	Polytopes.m	geometry	polytope.m
	Rotations.m		rotation.m
Graphics	Colors.m	graphics	colors.m
	Animation.m		animatio.m
	Graphics.m		graphics.m
	ParametricPlot3D.m		parametr.m
	Polyhedra.m		polyhedr.m
	Shapes.m		shapes.m
	ThreeScript.m		threescr.m
LinearAlgebra	Cross.m	linearal.m	cross.m
	Vectors.m		vectors.m
Miscellaneous	PhysicalConstants.m	miscella	physical.m
	Units.m		units.m
NumberTheory	ContinuedFractions.m	numberth	continue.m
	IntegerRoots.m		integerr.m
	Recognize.m		recogniz.m
NumericalMath	Approximations.m	numerica	approxim.m
	InverseStatisticalFunctions.m		inverses.m
	ListIntegrate.m		listinte.m
	RungeKutta.m		rungekut.m
Utilities	Record.m	Utilitie	record.m
	ShowTime.m		showtime.m

Packages Distributed with Version 1.2 – Continued

Full Name		MS-DOS	
Directory	Package	Directory	Package
StartUp	Attributes.m		
	Digits.m		
(preloaded on	Edit.m		
MS-DOS and	Elliptic.m		
workstation	Formats.m		
versions of	GroebnerBasis.m		
Mathematica)	Info.m		
	IntegralTables.m		
	InverseFunctions.m		
	LinearProgramming.m		
	RunThrough.m		
	Series.m		
	ValueQ.m		

Packages Distributed with Version 2.0

	Full Name		MS-DOS	
Directory	Package		Directory	Package
Algebra	CountRoots.m		algebra	countroo.m
	Master.m			master.m
	ReIm.m			reim.m
	SymbolicSum.m			symbolic.m
	Trigonometry.m			trigonom.m
Calculus	Common/Support.m		calculus	common/support.m
	FourierTransform.m			fouriert.m
	LaplaceTransform.m			laplacet.m
	Master.m			master.m
	Pade.m			pade.m
	VectorAnalysis.m			vectoran.m
DiscreteMath	CombinatorialFunctions.m		discrete	combinaf.m
	CombinatorialSimplification.m			combinas.m
	Combinatorica.m			combinat.m
	ComputationalGeometry.m			computat.m
	FiniteAutomata.m			finiteau.m
	Master.m			master.m
	Permutations.m			permutat.m
	RSolve.m			rsolve.m
	Tree.m			tree.m
Examples	CellularAutomata.m		examples	cellular.m
	Collatz.m			collatz.m
	Class.m			class.m
	FileBrowse.m			filebrow.m
	Life.m			life.m
	OneLiners.m			oneliner.m
	OptionUtilities.m			optionut.m
	RiemannSiegel.m			riemanns.m
Geometry	Master.m		geometry	master.m
	Polytopes.m			polytope.m
	Rotations.m			rotation.m

Packages Distributed with Version 2.0 – Continued

Full Name		MS-DOS	
Directory	Package	Directory	Package
Graphics	Animation.m	graphics	animatio.m
	ArgColors.m		argcolor.m
	Colors.m		colors.m
	ComplexMap.m		complexm.m
	FilledPlot.m		filledpl.m
	Graphics.m		graphics.m
	Graphics3D.m		graphic3.m
	ImplicitPlot.m		implicit.m
	Legend.m		legend.m
	Master.m		master.m
	MultipleListPlot.m		multiple.m
	ParametricPlot3D.m		parametr.m
	PlotField3D.m		plotfie3.m
	PlotField.m		plotfiel.m
	Polyhedra.m		polyhedr.m
	Shapes.m		shapes.m
	Spline.m		spline.m
	SurfaceOfRevolution.m		surfaceo.m
	ThreeScript.m		threescr.m
LinearAlgebra	Cholesky.m	linearal	cholesky.m
	CrossProduct.m		crosspro.m
	GaussianElimination.m		gaussian.m
	Master.m		master.m
	MatrixManipulation.m		matrixma.m
	Orthogonalization.m		orthogon.m
	Tridiagonal.m		tridiago.m
Miscellaneous	Calendar.m	miscella	calendar.m
	ChemicalElements.m		chemical.m
	Geodesy.m		geodesy.m
	Master.m		master.m
	PhysicalConstants.m		physical.m
	SIUnits.m		siunits.m
	Units.m		units.m
	WorldData.m		worlddat.m
	WorldNames.m		worldnam.m
	WorldPlot.m		worldplo.m

Packages Distributed with Version 2.0 – Continued

Full Name		MS-DOS	
Directory	Package	Directory	Package
NumberTheory	ContinuedFractions.m	numberth	continue.m
	FactorIntegerECM.m		factorin.m
	IntegerRoots.m		integerr.m
	Master.m		master.m
	NumberTheoryFunctions.m		numberth.m
	PrimeQ.m		primeq.m
	Ramanujan.m		ramanuja.m
	Rationalize.m		rational.m
	Recognize.m		recogniz.m
NumericalMath	Approximations.m	numerica	approxim.m
	Butcher.m		butcher.m
	CauchyPrincipalValue.m		cauchypr.m
	ComputerArithmetic.m		computer.m
	GaussianQuadrature.m		gaussian.m
	IntervalArithmetic.m		interval.m
	ListIntegrate.m		listinte.m
	Master.m		master.m
	NewtonColtes.m		newtonco.m
	NLimit.m		nlimit.m
	PolynomialFit.m		polynomi.m
ProgrammingExamples	AlgExp.m	programm	algexp.m
	ArgColors.m		argcolor.m
	Atoms.m		atoms.m
	BookPictures.m		bookpict.m
	Collatz.m		collatz.m
	ComplexMap.m		complexm.m
	ComplexTest.m		complext.m
	Contants.m		constant.m
	ExpandBoth.m		expandbo.m
	Fibonacci1.m		fibonacc.m
	FilterOptions.m		filterop.m
	GetNumber.m		getnumbe.m
	MakeFunctions.m		makefunc.m
	MyReadList.m		myreadli.m
	Newton.m		newton.m
	Numerical.m		numerica.m
	OddEvenRules.m		oddevenr.m
	OptionUse.m		optionus.m

Packages Distributed with Version 2.0 – Continued

Full Name		MS-DOS	
Directory	Package	Directory	Package
	ParametricPlot3D.m		parametr.m
	PrimePi.m		primepi.m
	PrintTime.m		printti.m
	RandomWalk.m		randomwa.m
	ReadLoop1.m		readloop.m
	RungeKutta.m		rungekut.m
	SessionLog.m		sessionl.m
	ShowTime.m		showtime.m
	Skeleton.m		skeleton.m
	SphericalCurve.m		spherica.m
	Struve.m		struve.m
	SwinnertonDyer.m		swinnert.m
	Tensors.m		tensors.m
	Transcript.m		transcri.m
	TrigDefine.m		trigdefi.m
	TrigSimplification.m		trigsimp.m
	Until.m		until.m
	VectorCalculus.m		vectorca.m
	WrapHold.m		wraphold.m
Statistics	DataManipulations.m	statisti	datamani.m
	Common/DistributionsCommon.m		common/distribu.m
	Common/HypothesisCommon.m		common/hypothes.m
	ConfidenceIntervals.m		confiden.m
	ContinuousDistributions.m		continuo.m
	DescriptiveStatistics.m		descript.m
	DiscreteDistributions.m		discrete.m
	HypothesisTests.m		hypothes.m
	InverseStatisticalFunctions.m		inverses.m
	LinearRegression.m		linearre.m
	Master.m		master.m
	MovingAverage.m		movingav.m
	NormalDistribution.m		normaldi.m
Utilities	FilterOptions.m	utilitie	filterop.m
	Language.m		language.m
	Master.m		master.m
	ShowTime.m		showtime.m

E

Electronic Information

A great wealth of information on *Mathematica* is available electronically. Some information you can access by using a modem hooked up to a computer. Other information is available to those with accounts on Internet or Bitnet.

E.1 News Group

The Usenet electronic bulletin board can be a great source of information. The news group `sci.math.symbolic` often contains discussions of *Mathematica*. The programs `rn` and `readnews` are intended for reading postings on Usenet. These programs typically can be found on systems that have access to Usenet. A subscription to Usenet can be obtained through UUNET Technologies.

> UUNET Technologies, Inc.
> 3110 Fairview Park Drive, Suite 570
> Falls Church, VA 22042
> Email: `info@uunet.uu.net`
> Fax: 703-876-5059
> Tel. 703-876-5050

E.2 *Mathematica* Mailing List

Steve Christensen maintains an electronic mailing list catering to *Mathematica* users. Send email to `MathGroup@yoda.physics.unc.edu` or `MathGroup@wri.com` asking to be added to this mailing list.

E.3 Electronic Archives

Archives of *Mathematica* notebooks and packages are maintained at the National Center for Supercomputing Applications (NCSA) and at Stanford University.

Sha Xin Wei, a doctoral student in Mathematics at Stanford University, is maintaining an archive of *Mathematica* packages and Notebooks, which are accessible to users by the Internet File-Transfer Protocol (FTP) from `otter.stanford.edu` (36.21.0.104). The archive can be found in the directory `mma`.

The archive at NCSA can be accessed from `zaphod.ncsa.uiuc.edu` (141.142.20.50).

E.3.1 Using FTP

This section describes some of the commands useful when using FTP.

Start an FTP session by logging in to a computer having access to Internet and then typing `ftp` *hostname*. For example, to get access to files on `otter.stanford.edu`, type:

```
ftp otter.stanford.edu
```

If your machine does not know the name of the host (`otter.stanford.edu`), specify the host's numerical address (36.21.0.104).

```
ftp 36.21.0.104
```

When you connect, the remote host will prompt you for a name and password. Log in as either `ftp` or anonymous with your name as the password.

```
Name:  anonymous
```

After starting an ftp session, the following commands are available to you.

Command	Description
dir or ls	List the names of files and directories
cd *dir*	Change directory to *dir*
cd ..	Change to the parent directory
get *file*	Transfer *file* to your local host
mget *files*	Transfer multiple files
quit or bye	Terminate an ftp session
?	Print a list of the available commands
Help *command*	Print information on *command*

E.3.2 A Sample Session

Below is a sample ftp session showing how to log in, list files, change directories, get files, and exit from ftp.

```
Sunburn> ftp otter.stanford.edu
```

```
Connected to otter.stanford.edu.
220 otter FTP server (Version 5.18 (NeXT 1.0) Aug 23 '89) ready.
Name (otter.stanford.edu:nb): anonymous
331 Guest login ok, send ident as password.
Password:
230 Guest login ok, access restrictions apply.
ftp> cd mma
250 CWD command successful.
ftp> ls
200 PORT command successful.
150 Opening ASCII mode data connection for file list.
.places       Numerics    Statistics   misc         Number_Theory
RMaeder       Algebra     Analysis     Geometry     Graphics
Graph_Theory  Topology    Symbolic     Utilities    Calculus
Economics     Physics     Logic
226 Transfer complete.
164 bytes received in 0.03 seconds (5.3 Kbytes/s)
ftp> cd Symbolic
250 CWD command successful.
ftp> ls
200 PORT command successful.
150 Opening ASCII mode data connection for file list.
.places
ExprEditor.m
226 Transfer complete.
21 bytes received in 5e-06 seconds (4.1e+03 Kbytes/s)
ftp> get ExprEditor.m
200 PORT command successful.
150 Opening ASCII mode data connection for ExprEditor.m (9030 bytes).
226 Transfer complete.
local: ExprEditor.m remote: ExprEditor.m
9349 bytes received in 0.06 seconds (1.5e+02 Kbytes/s)
ftp> bye
221 Goodbye.
```

E.4 CompuServe

Wolfram Research set up a discussion group or forum on CompuServe. For more information contact Wolfram Research, Inc. at 217-398-0700 or call CompuServe at 800-848-8199 and ask for Representative 207 (outside the U.S. and Canada, call 614-457-0802).

If you are already a CompuServe member, enter GO WOLFRAM to reach the Wolfram Research Forum.

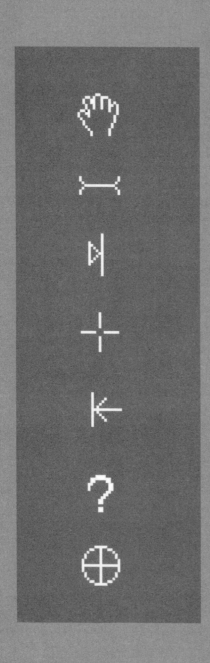

The Front End

The user interface to *Mathematica* is called the Front End. There are essentially two different Front Ends to *Mathematica*: a command-line interface, and the Notebook interface, which is currently available on Macintoshes and NeXT computers. Notebook Front Ends are being developed for MS-DOS and X-Windows.

When you move your mouse around while using the Notebook Front End, the pointer on the screen changes shape. After you enter a calculation, the Notebook Front End draws cell brackets in the right margin. This section describes the different types of pointers and markings for cell brackets and when they are used.

F.1 Pointers

The shape of the pointer indicates the kind of action possible. I recommend that you try using each of the pointers while reading this section.

The Vertical I-bar

The vertical I-bar appears when pointing to text (or input) that can be edited. Click the mouse button anywhere in the text. The pointer will then change to a blinking vertical I-bar.

The Horizontal I-bar

The horizontal I-bar appears when pointing to the space between two cells, or before the first and after the last cell. When you click the mouse button, a horizontal line is drawn. Then, when you type some characters, a new cell is created.

The Cell-Bracket Pointer

The cell-bracket pointer appears when pointing to a cell bracket. Click the mouse to select the cell or group of cells enclosed by the bracket. Then you can copy the cell, paste something else in the cell, or re-execute the cell. Double-click to open or close a group of cells. The contents of closed cells are not shown. Instead a small rectangle is drawn near the base of the cell to indicate that the cell is closed.

The Formatted-Cell Pointer

The formatted-cell pointer appears when pointing to cells that are formatted. The cells containing *Mathematica* output and graphics are formatted. Click anywhere in the graphics cell to select the graphic. A bounding box enclosing the graphic is drawn when the graphics cell is selected. In a selected graphics cell, the formatted-cell pointer appears only when the pointer is outside the bounding box enclosing the graphic. The formatted-cell pointer indicates that the cell is formatted, and more importantly, that you cannot enter input at that position.

The Graphics Pointer

The graphics pointer appears when pointing inside the bounding box of a selected graphic. Drag the graphic on the screen by depressing the mouse button and then moving the mouse.

The Coordinates Pointer

The coordinates of the pointer appear when you hold down the *<command>* key while pointing inside the bounding box of a selected graphic. The coordinates of the pointer are displayed in the status line at the bottom left of the Notebook window. Click the mouse to place dots on top of the image or drag the mouse with the button depressed to draw a series of dots. Obtain a list of the coordinates for the dots by by typing *<command>*-c or by selecting *Copy* from the *Edit* menu. Paste the coordinates by selecting *Paste* from the *Edit* menu or by typing *<command>*-v.

The Sizing Pointers

The sizing pointers appear when pointing to handles of a graphic's bounding box. Click and drag the mouse to rescale the graphic in the direction indicated by the pointer. Hold down the *<command>* key together with the tilde (˜) key or the *<option>* and *<command>* keys while dragging the mouse to crop a graphic or increase the white space without changing the size of the actual graphic.

The Hand Pointer

The hand pointer appears when you hold down the *<option>* key while pointing in the Notebook window. Instead of using scroll bars, with the hand you can drag or move the contents of the window right, left, up, or down.

The Wristwatch Pointer

The wristwatch pointer appears when *Mathematica* is starting up or when the Front End is busy. No commands can be entered while the wristwatch is on the screen. You can only move the mouse and wait for another pointer to appear. If the wristwatch pointer stays on your screen for an inordinate amount of time, you might consider rebooting your machine.

The Question Mark Pointer

The pointer changes to a question mark when you press *<command>* and the question mark key ? or the Help key on an Apple Extended keyboard. The question mark pointer is for obtaining information about the Notebook Front End. Move the question mark to anything in the Notebook window you want to know about. When you depress the mouse button, a dialog box with information pops up.

F.2 Cell Brackets

What is a cell? It is the basic unit of organization in a Notebook. A cell contains text, *Mathematica* input, *Mathematica* output, or other cells. *Mathematica* differentiates text from input by looking at the attributes of a cell. The style or markings on the brackets in the right margin indicate the attributes of a cell, and the size of the brackets indicates its extent.

Unformatted Cells

An unformatted cell contains ordinary text that can be edited by using standard editing techniques. Unformatted cells contain *Mathematica* input (in `InputForm`) or text. Unformatted cells containing *Mathematica* input typically have the attribute *Active*. An *Active* cell can be evaluated by *Mathematica*.

Inactive Cell

The contents of an inactive cell cannot be executed. Notice that cells containing *Mathematica* output (expressions in `OutputForm` or graphics) are inactive. Inactive cells typically have the attribute *Formatted*. The formatted-cell pointer appears when pointing to cells that are formatted. You can identify an inactive cell by a horizontal tick mark below the top of its bracket.

Initialization Cell

The contents of an initialization cell are evaluated when the Notebook is read with either << (Get) or Needs. When you open a Notebook, the Front End asks you if you want to evaluate the initialization cells. If you wish, you can instruct the Front End to evaluate the initialization cells automatically when opening a Notebook. All definitions in packages are contained in initialization cells. You can identify an initialization cell by an I-shaped tick mark below the top of its bracket.

Locked Cell

The contents of a locked cell cannot be changed in any way unless you remove the *Locked* attribute. However, unlike a formatted cell, you can select and copy text in a locked cell. You can identify a locked cell by an X below the top of its bracket.

PICT Cell

Graphics in *Mathematica* are represented in PostScript. You can convert any graphic to PICT to save disk space. However, PICT graphics do not scale as nicely as PostScript graphics. So, if you envision changing the size or printing a graphic, it is best left in PostScript. You can identify a PICT cell by the thick top of its bracket together with a horizontal tick mark just below the top of its bracket.

Fixed-Height Cell

Fixed-height cell can be adjusted to any height. You can change the size of a graphic in a fixed-height cell. However, if the graphic is enlarged outside the boundary of the cell, only the portion in the cell is displayed. You can identify a fixed-height cell by the filled rectangle at the bottom bracket. With this rectangle, you can resize the height of the cell.

Closed Group

You can close a group of nested cells so that only the first cell in the group is visible. By closing or collapsing groups of cells, you can create an outline form of the Notebook. When a cell is closed, the contents of the closed cells are not displayed on the screen. Instead, a rectangle is drawn. The width of the rectangle indicates the number of the cells that are collapsed. Double-click on the rectangle or the outermost cell to open the group. Double-click on the outermost cell of an open group to close the group. You can identify a closed group by a solid (filled) triangle at the bottom of the grouping bracket and by a rectangle at the bottom and to the left of the head-cell bracket. When the closed group is selected, the rightmost cell is highlighted and the rectangle is filled or highlighted.

Evaluation Group

A group of cells can be designated as an *evaluation group*. All the cells in the group are automatically evaluated whenever one of the cells is evaluated. You can identify an evaluation group by a small open triangle at the top of the grouping bracket.

Running or Evaluating

When the kernel is computing a result, the Front End inserts the word **Running** followed by three dots (...) in the title bar of the window, and an outline encloses the cell bracket containing the *Mathematica* input being evaluated. Once the result is computed, the name of the Notebook is returned to the title bar, and the outline enclosing the cell bracket is erased.

Changing the Attributes

There are menu items to change the attributes of a cell. If you unformat a cell containing *Mathematica* output, the input form of the contents of the cell is displayed. If you unformat a cell containing graphics, you will see the PostScript used to render the graphic.

F.2.1 Cell Styles

This section lists the various cell styles available to Notebook Front End users.

Cell Style	Description	Default Value
Input	*Mathematica* input in InputForm	12 point, `Courier Bold`
Output	*Mathematica* output in OutputForm	12 point, `Courier`
Message	Messages printed by the kernel	12 point, `Courier`
Print	Output generated by `Print`	12 point, `Courier`
Information	Information obtained from the kernel	12 point, `Courier`
Graphics	PostScript or PICT graphics	12 point, `Courier`
Name	Cell names (numbered Input/Output)	10 point, *Geneva*

The following table lists styles for text cells.

Cell Style	Description	Default Value
Title	The title of the Notebook	24 point, **bold**
Subtitle	The subtitle of the Notebook	18 point, **bold**
Subsubtitle	The subsubtitle of the Notebook	14 point, *italic*
Section	Section headings	18 point, **bold**
Subsection	Subsection headings	14 point, **bold**
Subsubsection	Subsubsection headings	12 point, **bold**
Text	Text which appears in the Notebook	12 point
Small text	Small text	10 point

G

APL
ASCII
C
Cell
Compiler
CPU
Excel
Fixed-width font
FORTRAN
Front End
FTP
Function template
Icon
Kernel
MS-DOS
MS Windows
Notebook
Postfix notation
PostScript
RAM
Session
T$_E$X
Unix
Variable-width font
Version 1.2
Version 2.0
Workstation
WYSIWYG

Glossary

APL A Programming Language was invented by Kenneth E. Iverson. APL is one of the most concise computer languages. Because it uses a special character set, APL is not understandable to those not familiar with the language.

ASCII American Standard Code for Information Interchange is code used to represent 128 characters on most computers. Extended ASCII represents 256 characters.

C A general purpose programming language that was developed by Dennis Ritchie at Bell Laboratories. The C programming language runs on UNIX-based computers.

Cell The basic unit of organization for a Notebook. The information in a Notebook is contained in cells whose type can be: text, input, output, or graphics. The cell bracket in the right margin indicates the extent of a cell (see section F.2 on page 337). The shape and marking on the cell indicate the attributes of the cell.

Compiler A program that translates another program into machine language so that the program can be executed. Languages such as C, FORTRAN, and Pascal are compiled.

CPU The Central Processing Unit is the part of a computer that performs computations.

Excel A spreadsheet program developed by Microsoft in which data or input and results are displayed as a two-dimensional array. When an Excel file is saved as text, elements in each row are separated by tabs and rows are separated with carriage returns.

Fixed-width font A font in which all characters have the same width. Courier is a fixed-width font.

FORTRAN A programming language developed by IBM in the 1950's that has been used for doing scientific computations.

Front End The user interface to *Mathematica* is called the Front End. There are essentially two different Front Ends to *Mathematica*: a command-line interface, and the Notebook interface, which is currently available on Macintoshes and NeXT computers. Notebook Front Ends are being developed for MS-DOS and X-Windows.

FTP The File Transfer Protocol, abbreviated FTP, is a program available on Internet for transferring files. Appendix E on page 332 describes how to transfer a file by using FTP.

Function template The template for a command indicates the number and type of arguments with which to call the function. For example, the template Abs[z], indicates that this function takes a complex number as its argument.

GNU Emacs Emacs is a widely used text editor. It is available from the Free Software Foundation, 675 Massachusetts Avenue, Cambridge, MA 02139. It is available by ftp from prep.ai.mit.edu in /u2/emacs/GETTING.GNU.SOFTWARE.

  Icon A little picture on a computer screen representing an item. The Macintosh and NeXT computers use icons to represent programs, files, disks, and other items.

Kernel The computational software engine of *Mathematica* is called the Kernel.

 MS-DOS An operating system developed by Microsoft for 80286- and 80386-based computers.

MS Windows Microsoft Windows is a program that offers a mouse-based interface for MS-DOS computers. Wolfram Research, Inc. is currently working on a Notebook Front End for MS DOS-based computers using MS Windows.

 Notebook A document that contains a mixture of text, *Mathematica* input, *Mathematica* results, and graphics. A Notebook Front End is available on the Macintosh and NeXT computers.

Postfix notation In postfix notation, the expression to the left of // is taken as the argument of the function to its right, e.g., Pi // N.

PostScript A page-description language, developed by Adobe. It has become a graphics standard for laser printers.

RAM An acronym for **R**andom **A**ccess **M**emory. RAM is used by a computer when processing inputs and computing results. The access time for this type of memory is shorter than that of a hard disk. Hard disks are used for storing data and programs, while RAM is typically used for executing programs.

Session When using *Mathematica*, the user has a dialog with the computer. The user specifies input, and the computer gives a response. Each "interchange" is assigned a number in sequence starting with the number 1. Whenever you restart *Mathematica*, you are starting a new session. You can access input and output only from the current session.

TEX A system for typesetting. It is particularly good at representing mathematical expressions. This book was typeset by using TEX.

Unix An operating system that runs on many workstations.

Variable-width font A font in which characters have various widths. In a variable-width font, an **i** is narrower than an **m**.

Version 1.2 A version of *Mathematica* first released at the end of 1988.

Version 2.0 A version of *Mathematica* first released in the summer of 1991.

Workstation A computer larger than a personal computer, such as a Macintosh or PC, but smaller than a mainframe.

WYSIWYG This acronym stands for What You See Is What You Get. It describes programs whose interfaces are visual. The Macintosh programs Milo and Theorist are WYSIWYG programs. The user manipulates symbols on the screen as opposed to entering words that represent symbols.

H

? ? ? ¿ ?

Help

If you have difficulties with *Mathematica*, where can you turn for help?

H.1 User Groups

Local *Mathematica* User Groups are forming all over the world. Here is a list of just a few.

Berkeley Mathematical Software User Group
Contact: Nancy Blachman
Variable Symbols, Inc.
2161 Shattuck Ave., Suite 202
Berkeley, CA 94704-1313
Email: nb@cs.stanford.edu
Fax: 510-843-8702
Telephone: 510-843-8701

Stanford University Mathematical Software User Group
Contact: Sha Xin Wei
Sweet Hall, 3rd floor
Stanford University
Stanford, CA 94305-3090
Email: xinwei@jessica.stanford.edu
NeXTMail: xinwei@otter.stanford.edu
Fax: 415-725-8240
Telephone: 415-725-3152

U.K. *Mathematica* Users Group
Contact: Dr. Allan Hayes
Dept. of Mathematics
University of Leicester
Leicester, U.K.
Email: Hay@Leicester.ac.uk
Fax: 0533-522200
Telephone: 0533-523883
Telephone: 0533-714198 (home)

Club Ritme des Utilisateurs *Mathematica*
Contact: Laurence Benoist
Ritme Informatique
86 Grande Rue
92310 Sèvres, FRANCE
Email: Ritme@prodix.fr
Fax: 33-1-45-34-02-51
Telephone: 33-1-45-34-74-74

Lawrence Livermore *Mathematica*
User Group
Contact: Al Kaufman
Lawrence Livermore Laboratories
Mail Stop L85, P.O. Box 808
Livermore, CA 94550
Email: kaufman@icdc.llnl.gov
Telephone: 415-422-1599

High School *Mathematica*
User Group
Contact: Sandra Dawson
Glenbrook South High School
4000 West Lake Ave.
Glenview, IL 60025
Telephone: 708-729-2000

REL-MIT
Contact: Amaury Fonseca Jr.
Room 1-008
MIT
Cambridge, MA 02139
Email: amaury@rel.mit.edu
Telephone: 617-253-2318

MATHPRUSER
Contact: Dr. Ernesto Esteban
P.O. Box 10100
CUH Station
Humacao, Puerto Rico 00661
Email: E-Estaban@upr1.upr.clu.edu
Telephone: 809-852-7810

If you are interested in forming a *Mathematica* User Group, Wolfram Research would like to help you. Contact Brad Horn for more information.

Brad Horn
Wolfram Research, Inc.
100 Trade Center Drive
Champaign, IL 61820-7237
Email: brad@wri.com
Telephone: 217-398-0700

H.2 Math-Mode

Math-mode is a customization package for GNU Emacs users that facilitates interacting with *Mathematica*. This package was developed by David Jacobson of Hewlett-Packard Laboratories.

GNU Emacs is an advanced, widely used text editor. It is available from the Free Software Foundation, 675 Massachusetts Avenue, Cambridge, MA 02139. It is available by ftp from prep.ai.mit.edu in /u2/emacs/GETTING.GNU.SOFTWARE. GNU Emacs runs on most Unix[1] platforms. GNU Emacs is customizable by writing code in a dialect of Lisp.

For those with access to the Internet, math-mode is available through anonymous ftp from otter.stanford.edu (36.21.0.104). Look in the directory mma or its subdirectories for a file named math.el. You can copy math-mode from anybody else who has it. If none of these works, you can send electronic mail to David Jacobson, jacobson@hplabs.hp.com and ask for a copy.

---

[1]Unix is a registered trademark of AT&T in the U.S.A. and other countries.

TEX/*Mathematica* is a set of tools that provide facilities of *Mathematica* Notebooks in a UNIX environment, under GNU Emacs. It also supports the use of TEX/LATEX. These tools are available by anonymous ftp from `chem.bu.edu` (128.197.30.18) in the directory `/pub/tex-mathematica`.

H.3 Wolfram Research Technical Reports

Wolfram Research has developed a set of technical reports describing different aspects of *Mathematica*. The following table lists the titles of some of the technical reports.

No.	Title	Pages	Price
1	The MathTalk Communication Protocol	6	no charge
2	The 3-Script File Format	6	no charge
3	Information about Contexts and Packages (for Version 1.2)	17	no charge
5	Tips for TCP (MacTCP Network Installation Tips)	5	
6	MathLink External Communication in *Mathematica*	45	$10.00
7	PostScript Generated by *Mathematica*	30	$10.00
8	The *Mathematica* Compiler, 5 pages		no charge
9	*Mathematica* Warning Messages	147	$10.00
10	Guide to Standard *Mathematica* Packages	200	$10.00
11	Upgrading packages to *Mathematica* Version 2.0	5	no charge
12	Major New Features in Version 2.0	22	no charge
13	Enhancements to the Macintosh Front End		

H.4 *Mathematica* Training

Many studies have shown that people learn best by doing. That is why I have included examples and exercises at the end of each chapter. Sometimes, however, you might appreciate guidance from someone who has used *Mathematica* extensively. I founded Variable Symbols, Inc. for just that purpose. We offer workshops in *Mathematica* for novices as well as experienced users. Our hands-on training goes hand-in-hand with my book. Because we customize our workshops to meet the specific needs of the participants, even those who have previously worked with *Mathematica* will benefit from a seminar. If you are interested in scheduling training for your department or company or if you simply want more information about our workshops, please contact us directly.

> Variable Symbols, Inc.
> 2161 Shattuck Ave., Suite 202
> Berkeley, CA 94704-1313
> Fax: 510-843-8702
> Telephone: 510-843-8701

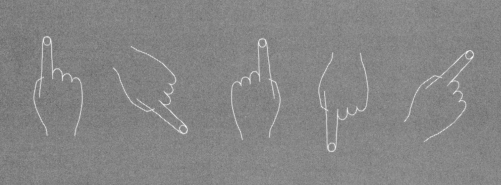

Index

M

J

Just What More?

Just what more should I say?

I sincerely hope my practical approach has helped you to become (more) proficient in *Mathematica*. I have tried to anticipate your questions and problems. Please let me know if I have missed something. I welcome all comments. I look forward to hearing from you.

Nancy R. Blachman
Variable Symbols, Inc.
2161 Shattuck Ave., Suite 202
Berkeley, CA 94704-1313
Email: nb@cs.stanford.edu
Fax: 510-843-8702
Telephone: 510-843-8701

Mathematica® Help from Variable Symbols

Dedicated to giving you the tools to experience the power of Mathematica, call us when you want to be a more proficient Mathematica user—510-843-8701.

Mathematica Help Stack

HyperCard-based help system makes it easy to find information about functions and commands by categorizing and cross-referencing all of Mathematica's commands. Easy-to-follow icons, detailed explanations, and clear examples make the Help Stack the perfect work aid for anyone who uses Mathematica on a Macintosh. Version 2.0, $99.00

Mathematica Quick Reference

The ideal reference to have alongside the computer while working with Mathematica. Neatly bound and logically organized, the Quick Reference Guide contains all the basic information about commands and functions that the Mathematica user needs for daily reference. Version 2.0, $18.95

Mathematica Training

Hands-on workshops for 5–20 people at introductory, intermediate, and advanced levels. Our clients include Boeing, Boston University, Chevron, Genentech, Howard University, MITRE, Shell Development, Stanford University, Xerox, and Wolfram Research, Inc.

Variable Symbols, Inc.
2161 Shattuck Avenue, Suite 202; Berkeley, CA 94704-1313
Telephone: 510-843-8701; Fax: 510-843-8702

VARIABLE SYMBOLS

Mathematica is a registered trademark of Wolfram Research, Inc.
HyperCard is a registered trademark of Apple Computer, Inc.

Send me more information on the following

☐ On-site training
☐ Off-site training
☐ On-line tutorials
☐ Training video tapes
☐ Macintosh demo of the Mathematica Help Stack
☐ MS Windows-based Mathematica on-line help
☐ Unix-based Mathematica on-line help

I would like to order the following products from Variable Symbols

Mathematica Quick Reference Guide for version 2.0: qty. _____ @ $18.95 ea. = $_____

Mathematica Help Stack (for the Macintosh), version 2.0: qty. _____ @ $99.00 ea. = $_____

California residents only, add 8.25% sales tax + $_____

Shipping and Handling: North America, $5.00; Pacific Rim, $15.00; All Others $10.00 + $_____

(For large orders, additional postage will be charged.)

Total $_____

☐ Check enclosed, in U.S. Dollars, payable to Variable Symbols, Inc.

☐ Bill my credit card (check one): ☐ VISA ☐ MasterCard ☐ American Express

Card number: _____ Exp. Date: _____

Signature: _____

Name on card: _____

Contact information (please print)

Name: _____

Title: _____

Organization/affiliation: _____

Computer system on which Mathematica is used: _____

Number of people in my department or organization using Mathematica: ☐ 0 ☐ 1 ☐ 2-5 ☐ 6-10 ☐ 11-20 ☐ Over 20

Shipping address: _____ ☐ Home ☐ Office

City: _____ State: _____ Zip: _____

Country: _____ Telephone: ( )

Fax: ( ) Electronic mail: _____

Variable Symbols, Inc.
2161 Shattuck Avenue, Suite 202
Berkeley, CA 94704-1313